GENDER AND THE SOUTHERN BODY POLITIC

Gender and the Southern Body Politic

Essays and Comments by
PETER BARDAGLIO
KATHLEEN M. BROWN
LAURA F. EDWARDS
JACQUELYN DOWD HALL
TERA W. HUNTER
WINTHROP D. JORDAN
CHANA KAI LEE
NANCY MacLEAN
STEPHANIE McCURRY
LOUISE M. NEWMAN
BRYANT SIMON

Edited by
NANCY BERCAW

UNIVERSITY PRESS OF MISSISSIPPI
Jackson

www.upress.state.ms.us

Copyright © 2000 by University Press of Mississippi
All rights reserved
Manufactured in the United States of America

08 07 06 05 04 03 02 01 00   4 3 2 1
∞

Library of Congress Cataloging-in-Publication Data

Gender and the southern body politic : essays and comments / by Peter
Bardaglio . . . [et al.]; edited by Nancy Bercaw.
    p.   cm.—(Chancellor's symposium series)
    Includes bibliographical references and index.
    ISBN 1-57806-257-8 (cloth : alk. paper)
    1. Sex role—Southern States—History.   2. Sex role—Political
aspects—Southern States—History.   3. Southern States—Social
conditions.   4. Southern States—Politics and government.   I.
Bercaw, Nancy. II. Series.
HQ18.U5G46 2000
305.3′0975—dc21   99-051779

British Library Cataloging-in-Publication Data available

This volume is dedicated to
the memory of

JOANNE VARNER HAWKS

Founding Director of the Sarah Isom Center for
Women's Studies at the University of Mississippi

Contents

Acknowledgments

The Porter L. Fortune Chancellor's Symposium in Southern History is held annually in honor of former Chancellor Fortune's longstanding commitment to excellence in higher education. I would like to thank Mrs. Elizabeth Fortune for maintaining the symposium and Dean of Liberal Arts, Dale Abadie, for his support.

In organizing and editing the symposium, I received valuable assistance from many people. Foremost among them are Debra Rae Cohen, who helped edit and proofread each essay, and Robert Haws, Betty Harness, and Rona Skinner who provided last minute departmental support to complete the volume. In addition, Robert Haws and Ted Ownby provided helpful advice at each stage of the process. Much is also owed to the panel moderators, Professors Joanne Hawks, Libby Nybakken, Charles Ross, Sheila Skemp, Marjorie Wheeler, and Charles Wilson.

I also received important support in editing the volume from Leigh McWhite and Ben Wynne. I could not have organized the conference without the help of Steve Budney, Katherine Clark, Charles Eagles, Chiarella Esposito, Jim Foley, Dan Fountain, Caroline Herring, Richard Howorth, Alice Hull, David King, Anthony James, Michael and Carole Landon, Karl Rohr, Fara Shook, Ted Smith, Douglass Sullivan-Gonzales, Tonya Thames, Minoa Uffleman-Evans, Jeff and Isabella Watt, and Joanna Williams.

My greatest debt is to the conference participants. The success of the symposium can be attributed to their professionalism.

Thank you all.

Introduction

In May 1865 headlines screamed that Jefferson Davis was captured in women's clothing. Cartoonists depicted Jefferson Davis running in a hoop skirt, tripping over a sword suggestively caught between his legs. Others cried foul play and claimed that Davis simply grabbed his wife's shawl for warmth as he went out into the cool night air. Though facts of the case may appear trivial, the Davis incident embodied an important struggle over social memory. As historian Nina Silber has eloquently argued, the controversy centered on who had the right to tell the nation's story. Would the Confederacy be forever emasculated in the public memory, or could the South redeem its manhood and claim the right to self-governance? It all hinged on Davis's gender identity.[1]

The work of feminist historians demonstrates that gender is a constitutive element of social power. Gender "naturalizes" power relations, providing a structure and a metaphor for contesting or upholding social order. Until recently, most historians overlooked gender narratives such as the Davis incident. These stories reeked of gossip, rumor, and slander—distracting tangents to serious political history. Yet, as French historian Lynn Hunt suggests, all politics has a family model and every revolution its family romance.[2]

Southern historians are at the forefront in revising political history. Proving that gender is a "useful category of analysis," feminist historians significantly challenge our understanding of the most hallowed subjects in southern history—the origins of slavery, Bacon's Rebellion, the Nullification crisis, the origins of the Civil War, Reconstruction, the Lost Cause, Populism, and Jim Crow.[3] By and large, the historical profession listens to these voices, granting many of these authors the top prizes awarded by the discipline. Individually each of these authors has been lauded for opening up new conceptual ground in how we define politics. Their combined efforts, however, have never been represented in a single volume. The purpose of the 1997 Porter Fortune Southern History Symposium was to bring many of these individuals together in order to recognize this important new direction in southern history.

Gender and the Southern Body Politic introduces most of these scholars' new research projects. The topics and the analytical issues they address suggest future directions in the field. As a whole, their work complicates our definition of politics. Using the lens of gender, these historians convincingly argue that politics is not limited to the machinations of parties, candidates, and voters. Instead they suggest that the "private" sphere of domestic relations is integral to the construction of "public" power. Public rights often rest on private obligations. Southerners, through custom or by law, legitimized the right to vote, to unionize, to lynch, and the right of legal protection by speaking of their obligations to family, home, and womenfolk. The "public," therefore, can only be understood in relation to the "private," and the study of politics becomes the study of the entire body politic.

This expanded definition of politics broadens our subjects and our analytical tools. These essays use gender to explore the politics of memory, masculinity, domestic violence, political obligation, the male body, and affirmative action. While each of these authors uses gender as a springboard for the analysis of power, their arguments rest on different conceptual foundations.

The household is one of the most significant frameworks used by southern gender historians. In fact, one can measure the impact gender historians have made in southern history by the ubiquity of the term "household" in recent studies. Originally historians of class adopted the household as a marker of pre-bourgeois social relations. As such, the household was a place of production where the family and community worked for the common welfare first before risking any contact with the market.[4] Gender historians, still clearly interested in issues of class hegemony, questioned the removal of the household from the class and race relations in which it was embedded. By opening up the household and examining gender relations, they demonstrated its critical role in southern class formation.[5]

Kathleen Brown's "Nathaniel Bacon and the Dilemma of Colonial Masculinity" is an excellent example of this work. In her essay reexamining Bacon's Rebellion, Brown succinctly summarizes the role of the household in bridging domestic and political authority. Brown states that "the householder's domestic authority reinforced his claim to be admitted to public life and became the defining feature of his civil manhood." A man's political authority, indeed his very masculinity, rested upon his property in land and people—his wife, children, servants, and slaves. Domestic inequalities, therefore, upheld a loose civic equality between men. This tension between hierarchy and equality runs throughout southern history. By developing the social relations of household, feminist historians provide an excellent means of understanding the South's peculiar claims to tradition and rebellion, independence and obedience, courtesy and violence. As such, the household has been used to explain almost every major political event from the origins of slavery to the rise of the second Ku Klux Klan.

The sheer explanatory power of the household leaves it open to criticism. In its ability to explain so much, does it explain anything at all? Does the household simply replace patriarchy and become a universal "truth," a constant throughout time? Brown addresses this issue in her essay by demonstrating that the household is historically constructed. Bacon's Rebellion, she argues, was a struggle over political rights articulated in the relations of the household. During the rebellion, Anglo-Virginians reconfigured the basis of colonial masculinity. As householders and Englishmen, they demanded the right to bear arms to protect their dependents against Indians. Violence became a constitutive element of their definition of masculinity and household. As important, household, in their minds, was integrally related to a new form of identity defined in terms of masculinity, race, and ethnicity. As Brown states, "The duty to protect one's household and provide for one's dependents had become not just the mark of manhood, but the mark of Englishness, defined by an identity that coursed in the 'bloud'." Household remained the basis of political rights but it was now understood (and written into law) as a special preserve of whiteness. Brown demonstrates that household structures ordered society both before and after Bacon's Rebellion, but the household itself was dramatically redefined in the process

Another potential criticism of gender historians' focus on household is that as a framework it tends to replicate the emphasis on planter class hegemony that dominates southern historiography. These feminist scholars affirm that white men, as masters of their household, were the only southerners granted access to civil and political rights. This household structure, as Stephanie McCurry eloquently argued in *Masters of Small Worlds,* worked to stifle dissent among classes and forced the submission of dependents, namely white women and slaves.

Laura Edwards, and more recently Stephanie McCurry, directly address this problem of agency. Edwards's "Law, Domestic Violence, and the Limits of Patriarchal Authority in the Antebellum South" examines violence to demonstrate that "the power of white male household heads . . . was neither complete nor stable in practice" in the antebellum South. According to theory, neither white women nor slaves had a public self. Antebellum law, Edwards states, "silenced domestic dependents and then turned that silence into acquiescence, affirming the 'natural' hierarchies that subordinated wives and slaves." Isolated by the law, these dependents took action and "stepped outside of their place" to leave their mark on the public order. Through acts of violence, gossip, and the building of social networks, white women and slaves subjected their husbands and masters to beatings, public humiliations, and slander. In the end, the law silenced these dependents. They were not members of the body politic, and by law, they were merely "extensions of their fathers, husbands, and masters who acted as their dependents' public representatives." But silence, Edwards reminds us, "should not be confused with acquiescence."

Peter Bardaglio, commenting on Edwards's essay, cautions that the framework of household and dependency threatens to gloss over important distinctions between marriage and slavery. He questions Edwards's statement that "Legally, slavery was a repressive extension of household heads' established rights over other domestic dependents." Bardaglio asks, "At what point does a difference in degree become a difference in kind?" Indeed, this new scholarship, with a few notable exceptions, does a poor job addressing the lives and experiences of African Americans. Slavery remains a closed institution, serving as simply a model or expression of household. Edwards addresses this issue, at least in part, by recognizing the agency of enslaved African Americans and by discussing the legal and social conditions under which they acted.

In "Citizens, Soldiers Wives and 'Hiley Hope Up' Slaves: The Problem of Political Obligation in the Civil War South," Stephanie McCurry radically broadens the political landscape by examining the "political subjectivity of the disenfranchised." This represents an important breakthrough in household studies. Southern historians Elsa Barkley Brown, Robin Kelley, and Tera Hunter address this question of political consciousness, but by and large historians working within the framework of household are stymied by the institution's seeming hegemonic force over all dependents.[6]

McCurry explores the political subjectivity of citizens, soldiers' wives, and slaves by focusing on the problem of political obligation in the Confederacy. The study of politics traditionally examines the steady progression of citizens' rights, ignoring the other half of the equation—the citizen's obligation or duty to the state. The Civil War mobilized both home front and battlefield, demanding that both citizens and the disenfranchised fulfill obligations to their country. As McCurry convincingly argues, the Confederacy's emphasis the obligations of both slaves and soldiers wives forced the state to recognize the political identity of the disenfranchised. Although McCurry's analysis in this essay remains focused on the government's reaction to noncitizens rather than focusing on the political subjectivity of white women and slaves, her work does demonstrate that "the disenfranchised make political history" and that gender is central to its telling.

Brown, Edwards, and McCurry each advance our understanding of gender and politics by addressing some of the potential criticisms of household. Each goes beyond her previous published work, pointing to new directions in scholarship. If household is to remain a model for understanding the relationship between domestic relations and political power, its emphasis on the tools of the politically powerful needs to be reexamined. In some ways, this history has replicated the master narrative by repeatedly turning to how power is constructed and employed by the political authorities. Brown, Edwards, and McCurry suggest ways out of this conundrum. Their essays focus on the unfixed nature of household, the agency of its dependent members, and their political subjectivity. These subjects provide necessary insight into how white women and slaves experienced household hierarchies and used them to articulate their unique understanding of rights and obligations.

The repression of the African American experience reflects the limits of household as a framework for analysis. But as Jacquelyn Hall suggests, it also reflects a failure of historical imagination on the part of some historians. Hall's essay "You Must Remember This: Autobiography as Social Critique" speaks to this when she states that "Turning memories into stories—whether humble life stories or pretentious master narratives—is also a potent form of forgetting." History, she reminds us, is politics used as "a technique of power and the search for a past that provides a sense of agency and a lever for critique." Politics, she continues, must be leavened with poetics which "demand that we hold seemingly

contradictory beliefs at the same time, that we embrace multiple
levels of meaning , that we think metaphorically. . . . That we
acknowledge the ways in which beauty and tragedy, good and
evil are entwined."

Perhaps no subject reflects the need for the use of poetics better than the Lost Cause. Focusing on the lives of three sisters,
Katharine Du Pre Lumpkin, Grace Lumpkin and Elizabeth
Lumpkin Glenn, Hall suggests that this conservative movement
which relied on the suppression of traumatic experiences and the
repression of dissenting voices also "carried with it possibilities
for revision . . . contestation . . . and change." Nowhere is this
more evident than in Katherine Du Pre Lumpkin's *The Making
of a Southerner*. Ignoring the boundaries between memory, autobiography, and history, Lumpkin was able to "speak to readers
beyond the academy" and "to demonstrate, through her own example, that even the most lethal and tenacious social memories
have their fault lines, contradictions, and emancipatory purposes." By not smoothing away contradiction, Lumpkin's writing
respects the "common condition" suggesting a new model for
rethinking how we construct historical narratives.

While Hall emphasizes the importance of subjectivity, Bryant
Simon examines the importance of the object—in his case the
male body in the 1930s. In "'New Men in Body and Soul': The
Civil Conservation Corps and the Transformation of Male Bodies
and the Body Politic," Simon argues that the state physically reconstructed male bodies to build a national identity and a military
force during the Great Depression. Seeing male bodies as "sites
of state action," the government used the Civil Conservation
Corps to build a nation of men who were strong, fit, and white
out of a hodgepodge of urban, ethnic, hollow-chested proto-revo-
lutionaries. Employing concepts of virile manhood developed at
the turn of the century, the government set out to physically construct middle-class manhood out of the flesh of working class immigrant men. As Louise Newman states in her comments, "Simon's work demonstrates how gender is a constituent of other

forms of social power—how gender is both implicated within and central to projects of nation-building and identity-formation."

Like Simon, Nancy MacLean also turns to the role of the state in remaking, or in her words "redesigning," social relations. In "Redesigning Dixie with Affirmative Action: Race, Gender, and the Desegregation of the Southern Textile Mill World," MacLean asks why the desegregation of the southern textile industry was relatively peaceful when compared to the desegregation of other industries, schools, and public places in the 1960s. She credits grassroots movements, strong government policy, worker consciousness, and gender relations for easing racial tension in the work place. The fact that the textile industry hired primarily women workers, she argues, affected the response to affirmative action. Avoiding simple dichotomies, she does not claim a sisterhood among women. Instead she quotes Elsa Barkley Brown's statement that "all women do not have the same gender." She is also careful to state that she is not "suggesting that women's interracial contacts were somehow better than men's." She continues, "The key point is that they were different, in ways that likely had broader consequences." Less likely to use violence and more likely to avoid conflict, white women "performed hostility in more insidious ways." They closed ranks around the areas of life over which they had the most control—courtship, family, and church life." White women, she argues, used family to construct race by "erecting a border between public work and private life." MacLean thus demonstrates the continuing efficacy of family metaphors up to the present day. Compared to the other essays, though, MacLean's work more openly recognizes women's investment in upholding the boundaries between public and private by emphasizing the "work of kinship [as] a female responsibility."

Each of these essays expands our definition of southern politics and substantially revises our understanding of political history. More significantly, however, these authors challenge our conceptualization of history itself. In her conclusion, Nancy MacLean "put[s] us on guard against the misleading dichotomies that . . . proclaim progress while discounting reverses, assert continuity while slighting ruptures, split race from gender, invoke class while ignoring race or pit struggles from below against the actions of the national state." MacLean, like Hall, questions the way history is written. "Integration," she asserts, "is not a thing but a complex and contradictory process, less a noun than a verb open to many modifiers." The same could be said about history. In her eloquent essay, Jacquelyn Hall calls for a new form of writing that questions the tired boundaries of public and private. As she writes, "we have invested too much energy in maintaining or reversing these hierarchies and too little in Katharine [Lumpkin's] project: writing that emphasizes not our expertise but our common condition, writing that troubles the boundaries between poetics and politics, memory and history, witnessing and writing, acting and research." In questioning politics, these and other historians have opened our eyes to new ways of seeing and practicing the art of history.

GENDER AND THE SOUTHERN BODY POLITIC

"You Must Remember This": Autobiography as Social Critique

JACQUELYN DOWD HALL

> There was the glamorous, distant past of our heritage. Besides this, there was the living, pulsing present. Hence, it was by no means our business merely to preserve memories. We must keep inviolate a way of life.
>
> —Katharine Du Pre Lumpkin,
> *The Making of a Southerner,* 1946

> History is perpetually suspicious of memory, and its true mission is to suppress and destroy it.
>
> —Pierre Nora, "Between Memory and History:
> *Les Lieux de Mémoire,"* 1989

Critics often lament a decline in historical literacy and worry about how little Americans know about the past. And yet, in the United States and throughout the world, historical memory has become both a cultural obsession and a powerful political weapon. The people of South Africa, to take just one example, have staked their hopes for reconciliation on the conviction that memories of atrocities must not be erased; the victims' testimony must be heard and acknowledged, and the perpetrators must admit what they have done. At the same time, in Rwanda, in the former Yugoslavia, in Ireland, and elsewhere around the globe, narratives of supposedly ancient grievances and hostilities can justify brutality, knitting people together in "imagined communities" that can exclude and kill, with no sense of guilt. [1]

Such narratives, like all memories, depend upon forgetting. To function at all, we must forget most of the scenes and sensations

1

that constitute the vast rush of "experience" or overlay them with
what Sigmund Freud called "screen memories," memories that
protect us from fear, anxiety, and pain. Turning memories into
stories—whether humble life stories or pretentious master narratives—is also a potent form of forgetting. For every narrative depends on the suppression and repression of contrary, disruptive
memories—other people's memories of the same events, as well
as the unacceptable ghosts of our own pasts.[2]

We are what we remember, and as memories are reconfigured,
identities are redefined. Indeed, we are never outside memory,
for we cannot experience the present except in the light of the
past ("all beginnings," writes Paul Connerton, "contain an element of recollection"), and remembering, in turn, is an action in
the present. The pressure of events puts a chain of associations
in motion; these ongoing reconstructions help secure the identities that enable us to navigate, legitimate, or resist the present
order of things. And yet when we speak and write *as historians*,
we tend to position ourselves above and beyond memory, which
we devalue as self-serving and inexact.[3]

Memory, according to Pierre Nora, is organic and continuous,
"affective and magical." It "only accommodates those facts that
suit it; it nourishes recollections that may be out of focus or tele-
scopic, global or detached, particular or symbolic. . . . [It] takes
root in the concrete, in spaces, gestures, images, and objects."
History, in contrast, is an "intellectual and secular production."
It "calls for analysis and criticism." It "belongs to everyone and
to no one, whence its claim to universal authority." Suspicious of
"myth" and "legend" as well as of the vagaries of personal memory, historians take it upon themselves to piece together a plausible narrative from scattered, surviving shards. In that sense, as
Nora argues, historians can represent a past that seems discon-
nected from living memory. And yet, for better and for worse,
history can also serve as a stay against forgetfulness, perpetuating
memories that secure a murderous sense of group identity or that

totalitarian regimes try murderously to stamp out. Even when memory and history clash, they are still intertwined.[4]

Indeed, history commonly receives its guiding impetus from memory. Try as we may to break free from the overarching narratives of our time, they persist in the underlying structures of the stories we tell. To challenge those narratives, we often turn to countermemories—memories that resist the biases, exclusions, and generalizations embedded in official versions of the past. History is animated by memory in other, more ineffable ways as well. We bring to our writing the unfinished business of our own lives and times; moreover, the experience of traveling so long in the country of research *becomes* our past, for our stories grow from a process of remembering and forgetting our encounters with the relics, fragments, whispers of an always already-recollected time. In all these ways, we live both the history we have learned through reading and research and the history we have experienced and inherited, passed down through the groups with which we identify, sedimented in the body, and created through talk.[5]

This essay springs from my own engagement with the interplay between history and memory in the American South. It is about the politics of history—by which I mean both the use of history as a technique of power and the search for a past that provides a sense of agency and a lever for critique. It is also about the importance of leavening politics with poetics. Politics demand that we choose a side, take a stand. Poetics demand that we hold seemingly contradictory beliefs at the same time, that we embrace multiple levels of meaning, that we think metaphorically (glimpsing "connections on the basis of a deep logic that underlies any use of words"), that we acknowledge the ways in which beauty and tragedy, good and evil are entwined. The politics of history usually entail an Olympian stance toward our subjects, who cannot talk back, who are dead and gone. Poetics require a different stance, one that acknowledges how history is entangled with memory and that implicates us in the history we write.[6]

The book from which this essay is drawn revolves around politics and poetics, memory and history in the lives of three remarkable sisters: Katharine Du Pre Lumpkin (1897–1988), author of *The Making of a Southerner* (1946), a classic coming-of-age autobiography; Grace Lumpkin (1891–1980), a proletarian novelist best known for *To Make My Bread* (1932), a novel about the famous Gastonia, North Carolina, strike of 1929; and Elizabeth Lumpkin Glenn (1881–1963), the eldest, a celebrated orator of the Lost Cause at the dawn of the twentieth century. Here I will tell two interwoven stories. First, the story of the South's Lost Cause, the re-remembering of the past that the Lumpkin sisters absorbed. The Lost Cause, I will argue, relied on two kinds of repression—the burying of traumatic or unacceptable experiences in the unconscious and the silencing of dissident voices and competing social memories. But it also carried with it possibilities for revision, footholds for contestation, contingency, and change.[7]

My second story turns on Katharine Lumpkin's rewriting of southern history in the 1940s, a rewriting that lay at the heart of her autobiographical project. Grace's fiction too drew on such rewritings, but in this essay she plays only a supporting role. The main characters are William Lumpkin, the father who made of the Lost Cause not just a story told but a cult enacted, Elizabeth, the true believer, and Katharine, the scholar, the heuristic value of whose work I want to explore. I end with a meditation on history and memory, remembering and forgetting, politics and poetics in historical writing today.

My structure is recursive; like memory, it does not move in a straight line. For example, I rehearse the story of the Lost Cause from a succession of points of view: mine, as a historian of the South; Katharine's, as an autobiographer; and then mine again, as I reflect on the possibilities that Katharine's project suggests. And I am concerned less with unraveling the complexities of biography (I can only gesture toward those here) than with exploring the phenomena that travel under the sign of "memory and history." First, personal memories (the chains of association that seem to come unbidden to the mind, rely on concrete images, and split and telescope time); second, social memories (the shared, informal, contested stories that simultaneously describe and act on our social world); third, history (the accounts we reconstruct from the documentary traces of an absent past); and finally, political imagination (the hope for a different future that inspires and is inspired by the study of the past).[8]

Katharine Du Pre Lumpkin was the seventh and youngest child in a family that produced some of Georgia's most prominent planters, lawyers, and politicians. Her father, William Wallace Lumpkin (1849–1910), came from a relatively modest branch of the Lumpkin clan. But the distinction hardly mattered. For, long after the children of slave owners had abandoned the plantations and thrown in their lot with the New South's railroads, towns, and textile mills, lineage mattered—more so than we can easily imagine, so much so that when William Lumpkin died, his obituary ended with a litany of famous "relatives and predecessors" while omitting the names of his children entirely. So much so that even Katharine would always fear bringing "disgrace on the family name."[9]

The South seceded from the Union when William Lumpkin was twelve years old. A few months after his fifteenth birthday, with General William Tecumseh Sherman poised to take Atlanta, he joined the army, spending the final months of the war as a private in Fighting Joe Wheeler's ragtag cavalry, harassing Sherman's troops as they abandoned their supply line north and cut a gash of destruction from Atlanta to the sea. William's parents had named him William *Pittman* Lumpkin. By the time he returned from war, he was calling himself William *Wallace* Lumpkin after the thirteenth-century Scottish patriot, known to late-twentieth-century moviegoers as "Braveheart," who died fighting against English rule. Straggling homeward after the surrender at Appomattox, he cast himself as a romantic hero and stored up tales of the "mad carnival of destruction" perpetrated by Sherman's troops. Studying history, Katharine would come to see Sherman's march as her father never could—as a military maneuver that quickly ended a terrible, costly conflict, the bloodiest conflagration the country had ever known. But as a child she had only her father's stories, which could still fill him with cold fury and, beneath that, a smoldering memory of impotence and disgrace.[10]

Slavery, as William Lumpkin remembered it, was a domestic idyll, peopled by African Americans who willingly catered to his needs and whims, images from a child's dream of unstinting availability and unconditional love. We are all fugitives from childhood, "never completely escaped," and the desires and anxieties of his generation were marked forever by the intimate relations between slaveholder and slave. They were also marked by war and emancipation, which shattered William's childhood Eden. Reconstruction, he believed, dealt it a final blow.[11]

When her father spoke of the "dark days of Reconstruction," Katharine remembered,

> it was as though his words were wrung from him, for he obviously hated the memories. Yet it seems that he felt he must tell the story, lest we have no concrete images such as haunted him. "Lest we forget," he would say to us. . . . We were told how our world . . . was ruled by . . . rank outsiders who had come in, so it was said, to feast like harpies upon a prostrate country, to agitate and use for personal aggrandizement the hapless black man, to dare to rule in place of the South's own foremost leaders. And to be ruled by Negroes! Ruled by black men! . . . The slave ruling over the master!

William himself "was spat upon, and his Mother insulted to his face." Summoned to membership in the Ku Klux Klan, he helped smash Reconstruction and restore white Democratic rule.[12]

Still, as Katharine put it, "the South might be 'restored,' but not the old life for Father." He married well, choosing Annette Caroline Morris (1856–1925), a beautiful, accomplished girl from

a middle Georgia planter family like his own. But by the time
Katharine was born, William had been reduced to working for
the railroad, an obscure lieutenant in the army of salesmen, dis-
patchers, and ticket sellers that sped the South's new transportation system along its ever-multiplying tracks. Transferred to Columbia, South Carolina, at the turn of the century, the Lumpkins
found themselves expelled from the magic circle where their
name carried weight. In exile, William's identity came to rest on
two props: first on his family, where he was, Katharine said,
"head and dominant figure, leader, exemplar, final authority,"
and then on the movement to commemorate the South's Lost
Cause. In practice, the two were inseparable. William's role in
the movement gave him stature in his children's eyes; their participation, in turn, demonstrated his success as a father. The pag-
eantry of the Lost Cause and the social relations of the family
reinforced one another. Each cultivated race, class, and regional
loyalties where they could grow most virulently: in the hearts of
vulnerable and idealistic children.[13]

The celebration of the Lost Cause began almost as soon as the
Confederacy surrendered, led by the Ladies Memorial Associations that took up the work of public mourning in a society
blighted by fratricidal war. The movement reached its apogee,
however, not in the postwar backwash of bitterness, uncertainty,
and raw, dazed, inconsolable grief, but during Katharine's turn-
of-the-century childhood, when it was shaped by quite different
needs and circumstances. Inchoate and often contradictory at
first, the narrative of the Lost Cause now gained a new cogency
and persuasiveness.[14]

Despite the demise of Reconstruction, African Americans
across the South had continued to vote and even to hold political
office. At the same time, the capitalist reorganization of agriculture fanned the resentments of poor farmers and up-country
whites, sparking an interracial Populist movement, the most powerful threat to white solidarity and elite rule that the South—

and, arguably, the country—had ever seen. "Here," Katharine wrote, "were white Southerners pitted not against outsiders, but battling among themselves. . . . Conservative men would not, if they could prevent it, let overtake them this threat to the white South's solid front."[15]

It was, many feared (or pretended to fear), "Reconstruction all over again." And across the South, Democratic politicians, many of whom were too young to have fought in the Civil War, blamed their ineffectual, nostalgic fathers—aging soldiers such as William Lumpkin—for what had come to pass. Rallying their forces against "Negro domination," they made white women the centerpiece of violent disfranchisement campaigns. Manufacturing rape scares, they whipped up support by charging that black men's access to politics, however limited, had aroused their desire for that other perquisite of white manhood: access to white women. Campaign parades featured floats bearing girls dressed in white with banners crying, "Protect Us," fluttering above their heads. African American men, politicians everywhere thundered, "must never be strong enough to threaten white women"; and white women, they implied through rhetoric and action, "must never be strong enough to protect themselves." Through propaganda, terror, and manipulation, New South leaders succeeded in doing what the men of William Lumpkin's generation had never quite had the stomach or the freedom from national scrutiny to do. They drove blacks out of politics altogether, locked a system of legal segregation into place, and destroyed even the memory and thus the possibility of an interracial opposition.[16]

Emerging victorious from the white supremacy campaigns, white leaders turned with fresh self-confidence, energy, and conviction to commemorating the region's past. Disfranchisement, segregation, and the battle for memory went hand in hand. Spearheaded by voluntary associations such as the United Confederate Veterans (UCV) and the United Daughters of the Confederacy (UDC), supported by small-town elites, buttressed by the South's first generation of professional historians, and amplified by new technologies of mass communication and entertainment, this effort created a landscape of memory that still surrounds us today. Dotted with what Nora has famously called *lieux de mémoire*—sites for anchoring memories even as they threatened to slip away—that terrain sentimentalized slavery; reconfigured the Civil War as a noble lost cause fought, not to preserve slavery, but to uphold the constitutional principle of states' rights; lauded the courage and sacrifice of soldiers on both sides of the battle; and portrayed Reconstruction as a tragedy that justified disfranchisement and segregation.[17]

It goes without saying that neither the trauma of slavery for African Americans nor their heroic, heartbreaking freedom struggle found a place in that story. But the Lost Cause narrative also suppressed the memories of many white southerners. Memories of how, under slavery, power bred cruelty. Memories of the bloody, unbearable realities of war. Written out too were the competing memories and identities that set white southerners one against another, pitting the planters against the up-country, Unionists against Confederates, Populists and mill workers against the corporations, home-front women against war-besotted, broken men.[18]

Brought to life on the screen in *The Birth of a Nation*, the Lost Cause narrative made its way, with amazing speed, not just into southern public memory but also into American popular culture. Indeed, the Lost Cause offered "ironic evidence that the South marched in step with the rest of the country." For as migrants from eastern Europe transformed northern cities, industrialization sparked violent class conflict, and the United States emerged onto the world stage as a leading imperial power, embattled native aristocrats everywhere commissioned sculptures of American heroes and revived colonial and classical architectural themes, projecting an image of a unified Anglo-Saxon social order onto the face of an increasingly polyglot nation.[19]

In the South, white women stood at the center of this battle for public memory, just as they had served as centerpieces of the white supremacy campaigns. And together those intertwined movements both widened women's horizons and "ensured that they did not venture too far." Turn-of-the-century rape scares hedged white women about with a lingering and debilitating fear: fear of the black rapist, but also fear of what would happen if they broke the bargain of ladyhood, which linked the right to protection with the obligation to obey. The rhetoric of the Lost Cause, by contrast, pictured Confederate women as courageous, self-reliant, and strong. The UDC, the South's largest and most powerful women's organization, shared with its predecessors, the Ladies Memorial Associations, a commitment to bolstering vanquished and disheartened veterans and keeping the memory of the dead alive. But it was also committed to immortalizing the heroism of Confederate women, whose valor, its leaders believed, had been every bit as important as men's. It is telling, and typical, that when Katharine's mother published her reminiscences, she evoked a long procession of soldier's funerals but closed with a paean to the home front: "Truly, those were days not only to try men's souls, but to put to the test all that was greatest in the souls of the women!"[20]

UDC leaders were determined to assert women's cultural authority over virtually every representation of the region's past. This they did by lobbying for state archives and museums, national historic sites, and historic highways; compiling genealogies; interviewing former soldiers; writing history textbooks; and erecting monuments, which now moved triumphantly from cemeteries into town centers. More than half a century before women's history and public history emerged as fields of inquiry and action, the UDC, with other women's associations, strove to etch women's accomplishments into the historical record and to take history to the people, from the nursery and the fireside to the schoolhouse and the public square.[21]

Both Katharine's mother, Annette, and her older sister Elizabeth joined the UDC soon after its founding in 1894. Elizabeth quickly became a sensation on the veterans' reunion circuit.

Speaking throughout South Carolina, Georgia, and Virginia, she "electrified Confederate assemblies as has no other human being," or so the newspapers claimed. She was, reported one observer, "transcendingly superior to any man or woman I have ever seen in any role on any stage." At the close of her speech, "strong old men" supposedly "threw their arms around each other and wept."[22]

Only Jefferson Davis's daughter Varina Anne, "Winnie," had ever elicited such adulation. Known as "the daughter of the Confederacy . . . the war baby of our old chieftain," Winnie Davis never spoke in public, but simply by appearing on the stage she attracted adoring crowds. "Nobody but Winnie could be the 'Daughter of the Confederacy,'" Elizabeth remembered. But at their South-wide reunion in Louisville, Kentucky, in 1904, the veterans named Elizabeth the "Daughter of the United Confederate Veterans," thus awarding her "the nearest similar honor that it was possible to pay."[23]

It is easy to see Winnie Davis and Elizabeth Lumpkin as spectacles and objects of speculation, bodies onto which men could project fantasies of eternal vigor, sometimes even bodies that could be literally embraced. Elizabeth assured the elderly soldiers that, "old and gray and wrinkled" though they might be, they could still enjoy the love of a young girl, if only vicariously. "I love you," she proclaimed, "you grand old men, who guarded with your lives the virgin whiteness of our South." We daughters can only envy the "honor our lovely mothers gloried in. . . . *they could love and marry Confederate soldiers! . . . We can [only work for them] with tireless fingers . . . run with tireless feet.*" At a reunion in Georgia, a phalanx of guards was required to protect her "from the ardor of the enthusiastic and admiring veterans." When fifteen-year-old Grace began to take Elizabeth's place as a veterans' reunion speaker, her youth seemed to provoke the crowd even more. Told at a 1906 reunion that a woman was going to speak, the veterans sighed in resignation. A speech by a woman "in any assemblage where men are present," the newspaper admitted, "is generally regarded with a half sinister indulgence." "But there came a surprise. It was not a woman at all, but a. . . . child-woman. She appeared under the influence of an occult power, and as she spoke the soldiers stood upon their feet and cheered wildly." Then they rushed the stage, grabbed her hands and kissed her—congratulating her father, who stood at her side.[24]

The kisses of the father and the father's friends: a textbook example of the seduction of the daughter in the Freudian family romance. These "child-women," like the "protect me" girls on the white supremacy floats, told their fathers' stories and followed their mothers' fate. Like the sexualized racism that made rape and rumors of rape the folk pornography of the Bible belt, the Lost Cause thus surrounded women's bodies with a strange brew of lust and etherealization. Walter Hines Page, an expatriate who became one of the New South's sharpest critics, saw other similarities as well. Just as the architects of the white supremacy campaigns had recruited women to help them split interracial alliances and drive black men out of public life, so the "wonderful military relics" of the Lost Cause duped women into helping them cling to their waning power.[25]

True enough. But, like the Lost Cause itself, the presence of women orators signaled, not just the comforting persistence of tradition, but the unsettling swirl of change. The newspapers portrayed Elizabeth's flights of oratory as spontaneous outpourings of emotion. In reality, they were the polished products of education and practice. She had studied oratory at Brenau College-Conservatory, a tiny women's college in north Georgia. From 1903 to 1905, at the height of her speaking career, she headed the Department of Reading and Expression at Winthrop Normal and Industrial College, a school founded at the behest of South Carolina's militant farmers to train white women for teaching and other occupations.[26]

Like Athena, sprung from the brow of Zeus, Elizabeth was a classic father's daughter; she memorialized the veterans and promoted the Lost Cause until the day she died. But she also threw herself into a wide range of women's civic associations, admonishing the "brainy, helpful women in the South" to uplift the "helpless, hopeless people in the Southern mills," promoting public libraries, and chairing the Red Cross during World War I ("helping humanity" at the expense of her health and her family, or so her mother feared). After her husband's early death, Elizabeth managed the hospital he had founded in Asheville, North Carolina, ran an inn, and became the first woman in a long line of planter-lawyers to win admittance to the bar.[27]

In the years before World War I, women like Elizabeth Lumpkin Glenn thus summoned the Confederate dead for a new purpose: to sway public opinion in favor of social reforms. By idealizing the Old South as a society based not on New South materialism but on *noblesse oblige*, they sought to promote a more expansive sense of community responsibility. By documenting a heritage of women's strength and achievement, they hoped to inspire contemporaries to action and to silence critics of women's expanding public role.[28]

UDC leaders, like organized southern women generally, saw education as the region's best hope for progress and reform. Dedicating themselves to the generational transmission of memory, they pursued a vigorous censorship campaign, using their influence with local school boards to ensure that "pernicious histories" were banned and "true histories" adopted. By the turn of the century, the historical commissions of the UCV and the UDC could announce what they saw as a "historical awakening": New state history textbooks sympathetic to the Confederacy, many of them written by women, had infiltrated the schoolrooms of Katharine's youth. No less important to the UDC's mission was women's education, and it used its formidable fund-raising skills to establish scholarships for white women not only at the South's normal schools but at Vassar College, the University of Chicago, Teachers College, and Columbia University.[29]

After World War I, the influence of the UDC waned, along

with that of organized women generally. This was due in part to
the rise of a younger generation of women, including Katharine,
who began to search out new patterns in the tangled threads of
memory and history and to weave new futures from what they
found. But the erosion of women's authority was also a measure
of their success in prodding southern state legislatures to assume
responsibility for archives, museums, and other representations
of the past.

Along with this expansion of state responsibility came the professionalization of historical writing. Indeed, by the 1920s, a co-
hort of professional male historians trained in a new archive-
based, seminar-driven "scientific" history was revolutionizing the
study of the American past. Among the most influential of the
new professionals were two prolific southerners: William A. Dunning of Columbia University, whose disciples churned out monograph after monograph documenting the "criminal outrages of
Reconstruction," and Dunning's brilliant student Ulrich B. Phillips, whose adumbration of the plantation as a paternalistic
"school of civilization" made him the country's preeminent historian of slavery. These university-based historians, drawing a
sharp line between themselves and the amateurs, purged the
Lost Cause narrative of its rancor and exaggeration, its fierce at-
tachments to place and kin. In so doing, they transformed it into
a story that the whole (white) nation could accept. Women found
themselves identified with imprecise, dilettantish, nostalgic
"memory"; the new professional history belonged to men. The
authority of history, in turn, relied on the prestige of science and
the deployment of an impersonal voice, an innovation as critical
to historical writing as the discovery of perspective was to paint-
ing. Organized women had taken the lead in creating the South's
landscape of memory. But it was the new history, cleansed of its
association with "scribbling women," that stamped the Lost
Cause narrative with the authority of scientific truth.[30]

Two decades later, on the cusp of World War II, Katharine
Du Pre Lumpkin turned to autobiography as social critique. *The*

Making of a Southerner is about an escape from childhood. It could not have been written if Katharine had not sprung herself free from the past.[31] It is also marked by a "doubled subjectivity": The *I* of autobiography is both the narrator and the protagonist, the recollecting self and the recollected self, the teller and the told. Once Katharine was the book's protagonist, an impressionable, vulnerable girl who had, as she put it, "learned both behavior and belief at a time when those around us were peculiarly disturbed." Now, in the 1940s, as she writes, she has become the narrator, a woman who has completely altered her outlook, "rejecting as untenable on any ground whatsoever . . . the Southern system of white supremacy and all its works." Yet she takes pains to stress, not her uniqueness or the success of her flight, but her commonality with her readers. She is both an outsider and everywoman. Like us, she is steeped in memory, yet capable of freedom. Speaking in the first person, she seeks, not just to critique the past, but to perform her own movement from past to present. Her writing em-bodies a promise: Change can occur— has already occurred—from within.[32]

The Making of a Southerner pivots on a chapter entitled "A Child Inherits a Lost Cause." The book begins by retelling Katharine's father's, and even her grandfather's, stories: The action takes place before she is born. When her protagonist does appear, almost halfway through the book, Katharine presents her as *tabula rasa*. Although "saturated with words and phrases," she remains a virtually disembodied watching, listening child. That child gains a voice and a body when she is baptized in the sentiments of the Lost Cause at a veterans' reunion in 1903.[33]

Katharine tracks that event, and her family's starring role in it, not just through the byways of memory but also in the material traces of the past, discovering as she does so tensions, contradictions, and hypocrisies that she could never have perceived at the time. (She can see in the newspapers, for example, how veterans' reunions became "good business" as power shifted from old soldiers like her father to their chamber of commerce sons.) But her

goal is not to use the historian's privileged view of the past to
secure her own and her readers' sense of progress and superiority. What she wants is harder and less conventional: She goes
"back to the contemporary documents," seeking to "relearn from
the sources," both to provoke and to resituate memory by combining the adult's ironic backward glance with the remembered
sensations of how that long-ago pageant registered in the mind
and body of a wondering six-year-old child.[34]

Her account is a bricolage into which she builds her own memories, family stories, and contemporary newspaper accounts. The
crowd, she writes, surges forward, cheering the parade and punc-
tuating the speeches with "clapping, stamping, . . . singing." Men
doff their hats; women flutter their handkerchiefs; schoolchildren
spread the streets with a carpet of flowers. Katharine too sings
and claps and stamps her feet until her spine "could not stand
any more tingles." Then comes the crescendo, the moment, as
Katharine put it, that "a child would never forget": The parade
ends and twenty-one-year-old Elizabeth steps forward to address
the gathering on opening night. Then, as if that were not enough,
William Lumpkin stars in the tableau that crowns the final day.
"Lights were extinguished. We waited while the curtain descended and rose again. Gleaming through the darkness was a
bright camp fire with a kettle hanging from a tripod. Around the
fire one could see men in bedraggled uniforms. One soldier
lounged up to the fire—'Quaint reminder of long ago as he stood
in the half light, pipe in mouth, pants tucked into his socks, coat-
less and collarless.' He began to tell a tale of war . . . 'lights
gradually brightened . . . the speaker was recognized . . . Col.
W. W. Lumpkin, a soldier of the Confederacy again.' " (William,
of course, was only a private. Like many a southern gentleman,
he acquired the sobriquet of "colonel" in the after-echo of war.)[35]

"Their mother teaches them their prayers; I teach them to love
the Lost Cause," William always said. Indeed, in the Lumpkin
household the Lost Cause became a mode of education and an
emblem of intimacy and family love. Confederate reunions of-

fered the most impressive stage for the Lumpkins' pedagogical efforts. But they were not sufficient. William and Annette also seized the most quotidian moments of family life to forward their children's moral and political education.[36]

"To be sure," Katharine wrote, "much was handed on to us incidentally," conveyed in the rituals, ceremonies, and pleasures of family life, sifting into consciousness "as softly . . . as snow floats down on a still winter night . . . but it was not my father's way to leave our lessons to chance. Nor yet indeed my mother's." Annette Lumpkin had been educated in the classics by a beloved Irish tutor and had taught school briefly after the Civil War. Both parents solicited their children toward reading and writing. In the Lumpkin household, books signaled affection; they were also a gateway to the world. Each afternoon, under their mother's tutelage, the children spent an hour reading aloud: the usual suspects—the novels of Thomas Nelson Page, the poetry of Alfred, Lord Tennyson, and the life of Robert E. Lee, but also the works of Charles Dickens and all the great nineteenth-century realists, with their heroes caught up in history's narrative sweep.[37]

Every week ended with a family ritual called the "Saturday Night Debating Club." Days in advance the children prepared their arguments on the South's history and problems. "We would hurry through Saturday-night supper and dishes. A table would be placed in the parlor, Father seating himself behind it, presiding," with chairs for the debaters on either side. "And what a game! . . . And how the plaster walls of our parlor rang with tales of the South's sufferings, exhortations to uphold her honor, recitals of her humanitarian slave regime, denunciation of those who dared to doubt the black man's inferiority, and, ever and always, persuasive logic for her position of 'States Rights.' " At school, Katharine used that training to triumph in lopsided debates on the question "Are Negroes Equal to White People?" More than thirty years later, she could remember her own fervor and the burst of applause when she finished her peroration: "and the Bible says that they shall be hewers of wood and drawers of water forever!" She also remembered how she and her friends banded together in a children's Ku Klux Klan. With costumes made from worn-out sheets, cut to pattern by their mothers, they met in secrecy to plan "punitive expeditions against mythical re- calcitrant Negroes." Transmitting memory through movement, ritual, and play, sedimenting in their bodies the gestures of racial dominance, they performed the ideologies that adults' narratives conveyed. "It was," Katharine remembered, "truly a serious game, and in a sense we were serious children bent on our ideals."[38]

As soon as Katharine was old enough to contribute to the proj- ect of commemoration directly, her father took her by trolley to recite at a veterans' camp on the outskirts of town. But instead of the glamour she expected, she found a sad collection of lost and bewildered men. Unlike Elizabeth, who basked in her moment on the stage, Katharine gave only a perfunctory performance. "After the first time I went as a duty," she remembered, "but it held no lure for me." The grateful veterans gave her a portrait of herself, an enlarged photograph tinted and set in an ornate gilt frame. She, however, recoiled at the sight of her garish double. That eerily touched-up image was not who she wanted to be. Even her parents were embarrassed, and they never hung the picture on the wall.[39]

The self that Katharine's mother mirrored back to her was a different story. Annette's learning was a "proud family posses- sion, more particularly among her daughters. Perhaps," Katha- rine reflected, "we took peculiar pleasure in it, feeling our own prestige advanced, who were but females in a world of male su- periority." All three loved to tell the story of how Annette's tutor encouraged her to read the New Testament in Greek when she was eight years old and then, when she was ten, put her to work on John Locke's *Essay Concerning Human Understanding*. And all three remembered Annette as the one, in Grace's words, who "made me wish to write."[40]

"The situation," Katharine said, "was anomalous." Certainly,

William and Annette believed in hierarchy, deference, and difference, in men's authority and women's "secondary and supple-
mentary" role. Women were to "sit silent when men were speaking; not to pit our opinions against the more knowing males."
Women were "creature[s] of intuition" who needed "the firm,
solid frame of a male protector and guide." Yet even as they absorbed such precepts, the Lumpkin sisters were learning contrary lessons—from their mother especially but also, however in-
advertently, from their father. Chief among them was the belief
that "those who have brains are meant to use them," girls and
boys alike.[41]

The Lost Cause, mixed as it was with the pleasures of reading
and the provocations of debate, endowed Katharine with a sense
of mission: the preservation of the past in the present, the burden
of southern history, in all its *gravitas* and entangling self-decep-
tions. To her, growing up in the wake of Populism and the white
supremacy campaigns, there was no doubt that the Lost Cause,
whatever else it might mean, symbolized the struggle to reconstitute white supremacy on new grounds, to reinstate, under new
conditions, the proper "relation of superior white to inferior
Negro. . . . No lesson of our history was taught us earlier, and
none with greater urgency than the either-or terms in which this
was couched: 'Either white supremacy or black domination.' "
Soldiers might perish, slavery might end, mansions might crum-
ble, but as long as whites retained their dominance over blacks,
Katharine's whole world taught her, the South's cause "had not
been lost."[42]

Those lessons might have forestalled curiosity, trapping Katharine, as they trapped her parents, in the coils of a racism secured
by an iconic, nostalgic understanding of the past. Instead, she
acquired a love of history from which a devotion to critical inquiry could grow. What saved her, she believed, was not her own
will, intelligence, and pluck, but the contradictions and contingencies to which she was exposed. "Here was a South," she re-

flected, "that had made us what we were in my childhood; to all appearances, it was a highly fixed, stable environment, frozen in its ways. But this same South could and did refashion some of its children. Some of us, although molded in the image of a bygone day . . . yet found the South itself so dynamic, so replete with clashing incongruities, that these could start us down the road toward change." For Katharine, those "incongruities" began in childhood, in the anomalies of her upbringing in a household where girls were expected both to excel and to defer; in the experience of exile, which gave her an outsider's ability to see things that she otherwise might not have seen; in the turn-of-the-century anxieties that the Lost Cause myth could not erase; in her position as the youngest child, the one who was different, who looked on from the sidelines, thrilled by the spectacle of the Lost Cause but not quite taken in.[43]

Looking back on her childhood from the vantage point of the 1940s, Katharine stressed two moments of rupture on which that child's refashioning turned. The first was, as she put it, "traumatic for me": an innocent sun-dappled morning, the sound of screams, a glimpse of her father beating the family's black cook. In her writings, biographical as well as autobiographical, racial violence lay at the heart of southern families. She opened her 1974 biography of the feminist-abolitionist, Angelina Grimké, with Grimké's memories of the cries of slaves, the sight of a boy her own age so crippled from a whipping that he could barely walk, and the wild rages of her beloved brother, so extreme that she feared he would beat a slave to death. These scenes from Angelina's childhood provided a source of "disturbing knowledge" upon which she, like her biographer, would later act. When I met Katharine in the 1970s (just as her study of Grimké was going to press), the memory of violence in her own family, refracted now through her long engagement with Angelina Grimké, had, if anything, gained in psychic charge. She spoke of the beating in a whisper, explicitly comparing herself to Grimké, who had also cringed at the sight of "someone helpless, in the throes of those who rule." For both women, remembering was a conscious political act.[44]

The second point of rupture, which supplemented Katharine's consciousness of racism with a perception of grinding class inequity, was what she called "A Sojourn in the Sand Hills": the family's move to a hardscrabble farm, where she found herself for the first time in intimate contact with black and white rural poor. By the time she left for college in 1912, Katharine claimed, "I was by no means entirely at home with my old heritage. Enough had gone on in the time-and-place limits of my short lifetime to disturb this seeming rapport. It could have come to nothing, of course—a passing flurry of doubts, and then forgetfulness. Perhaps it would have come to very little if I had chanced to be a student in less dynamic years."[45]

Following Elizabeth to Brenau College, Katharine encountered the action-oriented, optimistic message of the Social Gospel as it was spread through the region by the traveling secretaries of the Young Women's Christian Association (YWCA). It was these "far-sighted professional women," Katharine remembered, who "propelled . . . me . . . into this whole fascinating outside world." Hungry to "unravel the mysteries of why men behaved as they did and perhaps what could make them behave differently," she made her way to New York in the wake of World War I, tracing a path well worn by aspiring southern women at the time. Grace soon followed, and while Katharine studied sociology at Columbia University, her sister reinvented herself among the romantic young Communists and bohemians who flocked to the Lower East Side. Grace stayed on through the 1920s and 1930s. Katharine, however, felt a call to home. Hired as a YWCA student secretary, she plunged into the post-World War I peace movement, with its increasingly radical linkages to social reform. At the same time, she helped lead the YWCA's pioneering effort to build an interracial student movement in the Jim Crow South. Traveling with her black YWCA colleagues through a region that now seemed both familiar and strange, she saw the privileges

and deprivations that had always surrounded her, hidden in plain
sight. She also glimpsed the possibility of solidarities that transcended the claims of memory and kin. Eventually Katharine left
the South again, first to complete a doctorate in sociology at the
University of Wisconsin and then, on the cusp of the Great Depression, to take a one-year job at Mount Holyoke College. There
she met a radical economist named Dorothy Wolff Douglas. By
the time the year ended, they had moved to nearby Northampton, Massachusetts, and committed themselves to a partnership
that would last for almost thirty years.[46]

From the Social Gospel, with its dream of creating the King-
dom of God on earth, Katharine had taken a sense of agency, a
conviction that she could resist her world's "mores" and intervene in its institutions. Sociology—the science of society—had
extended that lesson: It gave her a secular angle of vision from
which to question the common sense of her place and time. It
also offered her the independence of a professional career devoted, not to the prescriptions of womanhood, but to the seemingly genderless life of the mind. There was, however, a price to
pay. Fleeing her father's stories, seeking a career in teaching and
research, she found herself still speaking in a patriarchal tongue.
The objectivist, scientistic assumptions of her discipline screened
out moral urgency, muted political passion, and discouraged her
regional and race concerns. Her early writings (focused on delin-
quency and the working-class family and generally couched in
bloodless prose) bore the marks of exercises undertaken less from
passion than from expediency: an outsider's attempt to get past
the gatekeepers and win acceptance in a highly exclusive club.[47]

By the late 1930s, however, Katharine had begun to see herself, not as a potential insider in the academy, but as a permanent
outsider—with all the penalties and advantages her welter of regional, sexual, and professional marginalities entailed. Entering
the job market just as the stock market crashed, she could not
find a teaching job; over the next two decades, professionalization
and discrimination pushed women and radicals to the margins of

the academy and stamped both sociology and history as masculine domains. In response, and with Dorothy's backing, she
helped found alternative institutions: first a Council of Industrial
Studies at Smith College, whose work foreshadowed the new
labor history of the 1970s, then an independent Institute of Labor
Studies that tracked labor relations during World War II. The
depression, meanwhile, inspired a new left-wing political movement, which Katharine and Dorothy wholeheartedly embraced.
That movement helped to realign the South in the American
imagination—as "the Nation's No. 1 economic problem." South-
erness, for Katharine, acquired a more positive meaning. It became a location from which to speak with authority about the
burning issues of the day. Seizing that place and that moment,
she began to write less cautiously and more politically. As the
thirties gave way to the war years, she "came out" as a southerner, first in a book called *The South in Progress* and then in
The Making of a Southerner, the autobiography that became her
most enduring work.[48]

The Making of a Southerner, although concerned with the long
arm of the past, took as its point of departure "the fact of change."
That point, to Katharine, was critical, for she believed that white
supremacy was alive and well, not just in the South, but throughout the country and the world. She also believed that the South
in the 1940s stood at a crossroads similar to the one it confronted
in the 1890s. Her parents' generation and their successors had
opted for reaction and repression, fastening upon the South a
system of class and race domination that her generation now had
a chance to undo. The New Deal, the rise of the Congress of
Industrial Organizations, the impact of the war—all, it seemed,
were propelling southerners into a freer postwar world. It was to
those citizens in transition that *The Making of a Southerner* was
addressed. By describing her upbringing as a white southern
woman, Katharine sought to persuade them to identify with her.
Then, by taking them step by step through her own transformation (as she re-remembered, re-searched, and represented it), she

hoped "to deepen and clarify [the] process of aroused thinking" in which they were already engaged.[49]

She used the tools of history to read new meanings into childhood memories and to question the stories on which she was raised. She took her cues from a small group of radical scholars—including W. E. B. DuBois and C. Vann Woodward—whose work on black history and Populism was beginning, by the 1940s, to challenge the authority of Phillips and Dunning, the towering figures who had helped give the Lost Cause narrative the ring of scientific truth. Through them, she discovered a new regional past—that of the "white millions whose forebears had never owned slaves" and the "Negro millions whose people had been held in slavery." But, unlike the revisionists, she placed a woman, herself, at the center of southern history. Categorically rejecting the racism and censorship that underlay the "historical awakening" of her youth, she nonetheless returned, albeit perhaps unconsciously, to the project initiated by her mother's and sister's generations: the project of etching women into the historical record and using that history to change the world. She chose as her heroes brave black politicians and white Populists (all men, to be sure), but also the black and white women reformers who, in the 1920s, had helped her see the world anew. Her history, like that of her predecessors, was driven by an urgent sense of mission, not by a quasi-scientific search for objective truth. And, like theirs, her narrative had a utopian dimension: It aimed, not just to describe the world as it was, but to bring into being "what has never been."[50]

The Making of a Southerner resonates with Katharine's foremothers' efforts in another way as well. It is—to borrow Studs Terkel's phrase—a "memory book" in which she layers her own memories into other traces of the past: her parents' stories, her older sisters' writings and memories, historical documents and newspaper accounts, the histories and sociologies she read. Throughout, she deploys history against memory, but she also gives memory its due, by showing not only how it can cripple the present, but also how it is always in process, always emerging in the present, and therefore always open to emancipatory uses. Her stance combines the critical perspective of the modern scholar with the forbearance of the autobiographer who keeps faith with other times, other selves.[51]

The new histories that began in the 1970s—social history, labor history, African American history, women's history—have been wildly successful in transforming the theater of the past. They have created entirely new scenes and filled them with actors who played no role in the Lost Cause narrative that Katharine learned. And yet, for all the innovations and advances, the conventions of historical *writing* have hardly changed at all. In that regard, even feminist scholars have tried to use the master's tools to dismantle the master's house. Katharine Du Pre Lumpkin struggled mightily in her time to acquire and deploy those tools—to use the weapons of social science and revisionist history to demystify the memories and histories that she absorbed as a child. But as long as she remained entirely within those disciplinary frameworks, she could not speak with political effect. In the 1940s, she cast aside those conventions and that impersonal voice. Daring to speak in the first person, she tried to create a new kind of writing, a new way of interweaving memory and history, poetics and politics, without blurring the distinctions between the two.[52]

The 1990s has seen a striking and unprecedented turn to first-person writing, especially among feminist literary scholars. Historians have met this phenomenon—and the "return of the author" more generally—with a mixture of hostility, anxiety, and relief. For Katharine, the *I* of autobiography was an embodied, remembering, reading, and writing self, a self participating with others in the reconstruction of social memory. She asked not, "Who am I?" but, like so many black and white southern writers before her, "Who are we and how can we use both memory and history to reinvent our regional identities?" That approach is the antithesis of "narcissism," the charge that is sometimes leveled at the turn to autobiography today. As such, it may prove particularly useful to historians, who care so much for the social and depend so much on the warrant of facts.[53]

Katharine's rewriting of the Lost Cause, together with my rewriting of her project, may also suggest directions for the study of memory even as they show just how urgent and difficult that study can be. There is no doubt that the Lost Cause dominated the social memory of the "white South" and, indeed, of much of "white America." Hegemonic, in this case, is not too strong a word. Here, if anywhere, was an understanding of the past that evoked intense emotion, provoked action, and worked evil in the world. But the Lost Cause was not a replication of an old original, a banner mechanically transferred from one generation to another. It was a retelling in a new context in which white southerners used history as a resource to fashion new selves and a new society from the materials of the old. William Lumpkin's stories, for example, were bent to the political moment even as they drew on living memory and on unfinished mourning for a childhood cut short. Those twice-told tales could still evoke powerful emotions in the postwar generation, but as they traveled they became ever more malleable. Appropriated by a younger generation of businessmen and politicians, they served to promote national reconciliation, to forward modernization, and to wrap a mantle of Old South legitimacy around a New South elite. Yet even this party of remembrance, effective as it was, could not know in advance, nor control, what would happen when its stories were retold. Even at its height, moreover, the Lost Cause could not stamp out countermemories. The ex-slaves created their own sites of memory. Black historians fought persistently to make sure that such memories survived. And even the planter class produced sons and daughters like Katharine Du Pre Lumpkin, who, thinking first through their families and then through the ever-widening circles in which they were involved, struggled to rewrite, re-remember, and spring free from—while also honoring—their vexed and painful yet precious pasts.[54]

To comprehend such a contested, multileveled process, we need both poetics and politics, imagination and critique. We cannot, for example, see William Lumpkin's longings simply as utilitarian covers for political ends. Nor can we see history—whether written by the self-styled scientific scholars of the turn of the century or by our own late-twentieth-century selves—simply as the enemy of memory. As we abandon such reductions and dualities, ever more challenging questions will emerge. How, in practice, is memory transferred from one generation to another, impressed in the body, and sustained by the everyday performance of self? What is—or should be—the relation between individual memory, social memory, and history, between how people in general make sense of their personal and collective pasts and how historians practice their craft?[55] And, most important perhaps, how can we explain why some pasts triumph, motivating actions, shaping societies, maintaining their emotional charge, while others flicker into burnt-out meteors, spinning hollow shells?

Katharine Du Pre Lumpkin fashioned autobiography into history and, at the same time, used her professional knowledge of the past to re-remember her childhood, resituating her memories in a new perspective derived both from research and from the left-wing politics of her time. She made history a weapon for dismantling social memory, but she also used memory (and autobiography) to breathe life into history. Her aim was to speak to readers beyond the academy in a believable and compelling voice and to demonstrate, through her own example, that even the most lethal and tenacious social memories have their fault lines, contradictions, and emancipatory uses.

We too could benefit from at once questioning and *using* the differences between memory, autobiography, and history. "Historical sense and poetic sense should not, in the end, be contradictory," wrote Robert Penn Warren, "for if poetry is the little myth we make, history is the big myth we live, and in our living constantly remake." Too often in our living, unspoken hierarchies prevail: historical sense overrules poetic sense; modes of explanation that highlight structure (or discourse) eclipse agency; written texts trump oral sources; master narratives override local knowledge.[56] If, as some critics suggest, we have lost our audience, perhaps it is because we have invested too much energy in maintaining—or reversing—these hierarchies and too little in Katharine's project: writing that emphasizes not our expertise but our common condition, writing that troubles the boundaries between poetics and politics, memory and history, witnessing and writing, acting and research.

Nathaniel Bacon and the Dilemma of Colonial Masculinity

KATHLEEN M. BROWN

In October 1674, just eighteen months before the outbreak of hostilities that came to be known as Bacon's Rebellion, a skirmish erupted between longtime resident and secretary of the colony Thomas Ludwell and Giles Bland, a royal commissioner of the Customs and fellow member of the Governor's Council. Ludwell and his brother Philip were among Governor William Berkeley's most powerful cronies and staunchest supporters. Born in the same parish in Somerset, England, Berkeley and the Ludwell brothers were also related by marriage. Although his grandfather had owned land in Virginia since the days of the Virginia Company, Bland was new to the colony. Sent by his father to attend to the estate of an uncle, the younger Bland became mired in a property dispute with the Ludwell brothers. He soon found himself at loggerheads with the Berkeley-Ludwell "Green Spring" faction, named for its headquarters at the governor's home.[1]

By all accounts, the disagreement erupted after an evening of drinking at Thomas Ludwell's house. Insinuating that the Bland family's property claims were based on forged documents, Ludwell appears to have provoked the conflict with his guest. "Heated with too much Wine and Brandy," the younger Bland responded angrily to the imputation against his family's honor. Bland, Ludwell recounted to the General Court, "most Barbarously and Contrary to the Laws of Hospitallity and humane Society abused and Called [him] *pittyful fellow* [,] *puppy* and *Sonn of a Whore*." When Ludwell refused to accept Bland's challenge to a duel, Bland took one of his host's gloves "without his knowlidge or Consent" and "did Ignominously p[re]sumptuously and Un-

worthyly nayle the Same upp a the State house Doore with a
most falce and Scandalous Libell which Contayned these words
that the owner of the Glove was a Sonn of a Whore [,] mechannick fellow [,] puppy and a Coward."

Bland mounted the purloined glove in a public place where all
Assembly members would be sure to see it. Compounding the
enormity of his crime, Bland "Dared to fix his Glove an the afore-
said Libell at their Gates on a *Sunday.*" Although Ludwell clearly
sought personal redress from the General Court, he observed
that Bland's action also constituted "a Publique Affront as well
because the Said Secretarie was Publique minister."[2]

With one gesture, Bland had offended colonial sensibilities on
a number of fronts. By calling Ludwell "Sonn of a Whore," he
impugned the family lineage of the colony's second most powerful officer, thereby casting aspersions upon the entire planter
elite for suffering one of such debased origins to rise to the top
of their ranks. "Mechannick," an epithet suggesting one who per-
forms manual labor, likewise implied lowly birth and the incon-
gruity of Ludwell's background with his current high status in
the colony. Ludwell's manhood did not escape Bland's withering
commentary; a "pittyfull fellow," "puppy," and "Coward" who
had allowed Bland's challenge to go unanswered, Ludwell violated the etiquette of conflict that underwrote the elite English
culture of manly honor. Compounding his insults to Thomas
Ludwell, Bland treated the governor and the General Court
scornfully when ordered to apologize for the "Horrid Injuries"
and refused to cooperate with the governor's effort to conceal
customs abuses from the commissioners of the Custom House in
England.[3]

Bland's behavior toward the colony's elite governing faction
exposed a growing crisis of political authority in the colony,
rooted in slumping tobacco prices, Anglo-Indian clashes over
land in the backcountry, the threats of foreign invasion, and the
new Stuart interest in managing the colony during the 1660s.
Wealthy immigrants like Bland, of whom there were many in the

royalist influx of the 1650s and 1660s, had the potential to become powerful rivals unless incorporated into the governor's circle. Once allowed to enter the inner sanctum of colonial power, however, newcomers such as Bland and his better-known contemporary, the rebel leader Nathaniel Bacon, were in a position to expose the venality of the governor and his friends. Such revelations of corruption might not have been so politically explosive had there been no questioning of political authority among ordinary male citizens, who faced mounting impediments to their ability to establish and maintain themselves as heads of independent households, the foundation of English manhood.

My subject is the relationship between these impediments to male domestic authority and the political and military struggles traditionally ascribed to Bacon's Rebellion. In choosing to focus on the connections between domestic and political authority, I am consciously allying myself with a new wave of feminist scholarship that is no longer content to leave the writing of political and military history to political and military historians. Unlike a previous generation of women's historians who sought to write about forgotten women, this new generation has broadened its agenda to include men, with particular attention to the social roles, privileges, and responsibilities that gave historically specific meaning to manhood. Bacon's Rebellion presents a unique opportunity to study one of these formations of masculinity and to situate it within both the conditions of everyday life and the momentous political events that still largely determine historical periodization.[4]

That women's historians are only now turning their attention to Bacon's Rebellion can be explained in part by the longevity of two scholarly interpretations of colonial Virginia's history, Winthrop Jordan's *White Over Black* and Edmund Morgan's *American Slavery, American Freedom*. Jordan adopted a cultural approach to the history of race, eschewing lengthy discussions of well-known political events like Bacon's Rebellion to focus on literary, scientific, and legal sources. For years, his analysis of the embeddedness of racial attitudes in English and Anglo-colonial culture was the only book-length study of the colony to include material on gender and sexuality. Not surprisingly, *White Over Black* became a favorite text of feminist scholars interested in the links between gender and slavery. Bacon's Rebellion, which barely received mention in Jordan's study, appeared irrelevant to scholars with those interests.[5]

In contrast to Jordan, Morgan represented Bacon's Rebellion as a central and defining event in the colony's history. Morgan depicted the rebellion as a turning point in Virginia's transformation from a society divided along class lines and reliant upon the labor of white servants into a society divided by race in which African slaves provided most of the strenuous field labor. His account of Bacon's Rebellion continues to have broad appeal because it offers a provocative analysis, resonant with twentieth-century U.S. race and class relations, of how racial animosity can serve class interests by protecting the property and political hegemony of an elite ruling class from the challenges of lower-class white people. But Morgan's account of white planters fanning the flames of racism in reaction to Bacon's Rebellion is a narrowly political view of what Jordan has shown to be a complex psychological and cultural phenomenon. *American Slavery, American Freedom* does not explain why a shift in racial attitudes would necessarily spread beyond the group of white men most directly concerned with the outcome of the rebellion. Morgan offers few clues about white women's stake in the postrebellion political settlement or about how family law, racial ideology, and the division of labor might have been implicated in the emerging racial order. Jordan comes closer to explaining how a politically useful concept of racial difference might have taken hold in late-seventeenth-century society, but his cultural approach makes a political upheaval like Bacon's Rebellion of little interest in and of itself.

Casting the net wider than these two influential interpretations of colonial Virginia does little to help the historian interested in the connections between gender and politics, narrowly defined.[6] Efforts by women's historians to document the lives of women in the colony and female participation in the rebellion, moreover, have done little to alter these basic interpretive frameworks. Julia Cherry Spruill incorporated some anecdotal information about Bacon's Rebellion in her *Women in the Southern Colonies*, but her portrait of white women's lives transcended any political chronology. Lois Carr's and Lorena Walsh's important article about the demographic trends affecting white women in the Chesapeake similarly aimed at truths about the colonial female experience that were largely impervious to political upheavals and military conflicts. More recently, Susan Westbury has provided convincing evidence that a dozen or so women were materially as well as politically involved in the rebellion. But treatments such as Westbury's are largely additive in their approach and do not result in a reconceptualization of the colony's history or of the rebellion itself. Knowing that a handful of women participated ultimately does very little to change our basic understanding of the conflict and its impact unless that knowledge points to some previously overlooked cause or consequence of the rebellion.[7]

The interpretation that follows builds on the work of all of these scholars. Morgan's identification of a postrebellion political alliance among white men remains a valuable starting point for assessing the significance of Bacon's Rebellion. Jordan's exegesis of race reminds us that meaningful concepts of racial difference could not simply have been conjured up by white men hoping to forge a political alliance but drew from the deep well of racial knowledge in Anglo-American culture. For race to have political meaning in the final quarter of the seventeenth century, it had to have a greater legal and cultural foundation than what Morgan has allowed—one that grew out of labor arrangements, definitions of family, licit sexuality, marriage and household, and concepts of honor and gender privilege, as I have argued elsewhere.

Taken together, Morgan's focus on the political concerns of

embattled planters and Jordan's sensitivity to the institutions and cultural traditions that made racial difference meaningful to them compel us to expand our view of the politics of the rebellion and the complexities of the participants' political identities. As I will argue, such an expanded view should include attention to the specific social location of participants as householders, frontier dwellers, property owners, and English settlers. Although many historians have discussed the economic motives of male participants in the rebellion, few have stopped to consider the impact of colonial conditions that undermined traditional gender privileges or transformed the meaning of Englishness. This paper, in contrast, places manhood and English ethnic identity, which would subsequently become whiteness, at the center of the analysis of participants' motives and attempts to use these two concepts to bridge the gap between the political outcome of the rebellion, narrowly defined, and its broader impact on gender, family, household, and society.

Focusing on masculinity and white ethnicity is not without pitfalls. First, there is the danger of undermining two decades of effort by women's historians to document the lives of women in the past. If we place men at the center, we might ask ourselves, aren't we simply recreating the problem that provoked feminist scholars to enter the fray in the first place? A second problem with focusing on masculinity is that recent work on the topic already seems to be moving in a predictable direction. Masculinity, as defined in these new studies, is perpetually in crisis, leaving the historian to wonder about its explanatory power. Similar kinds of questions can be raised about focusing on whiteness when African Americans are still only partially included in the historical canon. It worries many people that we seem to have come full circle to a newly masculinized and racially exclusive history in which, for somewhat different reasons than in the past, we privilege the experience of white men and make it central to our analysis.

These are all legitimate concerns. I certainly don't advocate replacing histories of white women and black people with histories of white men's embattled masculinity. Rather, I think we need to apply the feminist theory and the critical race theory of the last ten years to the history of white manhood—to examine its historical contingency, its embeddedness in relationships with groups it defines as "other," and the foundation of its privilege in the law, the distribution of property, the Judeo-Christian tradition, and early modern theories of political power. In the absence of such an effort, white male historical subjects retain their exclusive claim to an unqualified humanity. Even the cliche of masculinity perpetually in crisis, which threatens to undermine the usefulness of studying manhood, can be avoided with proper attention to the historically specific conditions under which white men exercise their privileges and successfully perform their identities.

Giles Bland's conflict with Thomas Ludwell is a suitable place to begin our inquiry, as it offers us a glimpse of some of the issues confronting elite masculinity on the eve of the rebellion. Bland, the relative newcomer, who scorned the efforts of the colonial elite to gentrify their social position, insulted Ludwell, a member of the governor's inner circle, by suggesting he was not an honorable or honorably descended man. Reading between the lines of Bland's insult, we find that his indictment of Ludwell focused on a failure of performance that included references to ungenteel labor as well as to a lack of courage. Significantly, the conflict between the two men arose over an ambiguous title to property in a colony where all titles and claims were new and the transformation of Indian land to English property continued. This confusion over the authenticity of a property claim, as much as the content of the insults themselves, reveals the difficulty of performing English manhood outside of England.

In the remainder of this essay, I focus on the specific context for masculinity in Virginia. What factors altered the performances and foundations of English masculinity in the colony? What conditions undermined English manhood and what reaffirmed it?

What groups served as foils for defining manhood in the colony and what groups competed with English men for privileges settlers defined as traditionally male? To what degree did Englishness and manhood overlap in their meanings in the colony? At what points were they at odds? Throughout the essay I use evidence from Bacon's Rebellion to shed light on what ordinary male colonists thought it meant to be a man. But since Bacon's Rebellion also provided colonial settlers with a unique opportunity to communicate about the meaning of manhood in the colony, I also treat the rebellion as a crucible for a new configuration of colonial masculinity.

MANHOOD IN ENGLAND

When he nailed Thomas Ludwell's glove to the Assembly door, Giles Bland invoked a code of conduct that distinguished members of England's elite from ordinary men. Making sense of his public act as a display of gentility as well as of masculinity requires that we consider its English context. Bland's defiant expression of honor derived from one of several English cultures of manhood that crossed the Atlantic to take hold in somewhat altered form in colonial Virginia.

For most English men, manhood was less a matter of dramatic flourish than of consistent daily performance, rooted in labor, property ownership, and relationships with legal dependents. Legal treatises, household advice books, and sermons held up the example of the independent householder as an ideal for men. The economic independence of small farmers and lesser yeomen, according to many of these authors, allowed manhood to reach its fullest and most natural expression. As masters of households and the land they leased or owned, independent householders achieved political visibility in their communities. Recognized legally as the household's public representative, the head of household assumed economic, legal, and moral responsibility for all its members. In exchange for his responsibility, the community

supported his authority over dependent members of his household, including his wife, his children, and his servants. The
householder's domestic authority reinforced his claim to be admitted to public life and became the defining feature of his civil
manhood. In contrast to women, children, and those in servitude,
whose social roles and identities were defined primarily by their
domestic focus and allegiance, the master of the household belonged to an imaginary public community of male property holders that extended all the way to the king.[8]

Of the English householder's numerous responsibilities, provision was the duty emphasized the most by advice book authors
and communities. If a householder failed to feed, clothe, and provide medical care for his dependents, that duty, along with the
expense, would fall on the parish. Householders who proved unable to carry out this charge relinquished one of the primary
foundations of their domestic authority, public existence, and
male identity. Authors of household manuals from this period
warned that a man's failure to provide for his household might
lead to marital problems such as disobedience, nagging, scolding,
and adultery, which often spread beyond the household to involve neighbors and kin, ultimately threatening the harmony of
the larger community.[9]

Basic economic provision was a less weighty responsibility for
members of the English gentry and aristocracy than for yeomen
and other small property owners. Instead, public displays of gentility, manners, and honorable conduct dominated elite performances of manhood, as Giles Bland's and Thomas Ludwell's conflict illustrates so well. Like their yeomen counterparts, English
gentlemen adhered to a concept of manhood defined by a combination of privilege, authority, and responsibility. In the case of
the gentry, however, the responsibilities to the community were
not simply a matter of providing for one's household, but of be-
having justly towards lesser men, from whom one could expect
deference and loyalty in return. The need to distinguish oneself
from ordinary farmers, smallholders, and even members of the

minor gentry motivated elite men's attention to public performance, display-oriented ritual, and honor. The material trappings
of gentility, including stately homes, carriages, and accessories
like hats and gloves, became crucial props in the public theater
of honor. Reputation and status depended to a great extent on
adherence to a code of conduct to which all true gentlemen sub-
scribed.

Clearly, if these ideals had been within easy reach of most
Englishmen, there would have been little migration across the
Atlantic. Economic crises, inflation, and crop failures uprooted
many young men from their villages and towns in search of
steady wages. In an age of diminishing opportunities for gentry
sons to engage in honorable pursuits at home, voyages of adventure, the settlement of new colonies, and military campaigns
overseas provided elite men with new opportunities for bringing
glory to their families and enhancing their reputations with their
peers. Even in England, the meaning of manhood was subject to
challenge and impediment.

Yet it is doubtful that any of these obstacles to masculinity in
England would have sufficiently prepared a male settler for the
situation in Virginia. Whether he came to the colony with the
financial resources to establish himself as a gentleman or hoped
merely to survive his term of service to set up his own household,
an individual who measured his manhood by English standards
faced unprecedented challenges in the New World. Not only
were households in Virginia situated in a different economic context, but the very process of setting up a household through marriage was fraught with obstacles unique to the colonial setting.
Even the concept of Englishness, a major premise of the colonial
venture, seemed inadequate as years of settlement came to separate the interests of veterans of the colony from those of new
arrivals.

Before we look more closely at the conditions under which
English settlers attempted to transplant familiar concepts of manhood, we need to remind ourselves of the reasons for their attach-

ment to these concepts. In the late twentieth century, an over-weening need to prove one's manliness is easily and sometimes glibly dismissed as pathology, but such a judgment about seventeenth-century manhood would be grossly anachronistic. For English men in the colonies, the quest to achieve manhood represented an effort to gain a very real set of privileges. Property-holding men not only enjoyed material advantages over women and non-property-holding men, but also achieved a measure of respect and recognition in their communities not available to those without property. Invested with titles to land and the legal authority over household members, a seventeenth-century man had about as great a degree of control over the circumstances of his life as one could hope to have in a century in which life-threatening disease, famine, warfare, and poverty might make regular appearances. English-style masculinity represented, in short, the main embodiment of personhood for a non-noble individual in the seventeenth century. That colonists might cling tenaciously to the particular rights and privileges that signified manhood in England is not to be wondered at.

MANHOOD IN VIRGINIA

At first glance, Virginia would seem to come out ahead of England as a place offering young men opportunities to buy property and establish independent households. Compared to England, Virginia had plentiful land. Scarcity of labor, moreover, created conditions for high wages, presenting a sharp contrast to late sixteenth- and early seventeenth-century England with its glutted labor market, unemployment, and wages that were unable to keep pace with inflation. Beginning in the early 1620s, however, tobacco altered the relationship of land to labor and with it the context for English settlers' pursuit of their vision of manhood. Capable of depleting the soil in just a few years, tobacco, compounded by the price of labor, led settlers to abandon their vision of subsistence farms as well as their agricultural traditions of replenishing the soil and conserving resources like timber. To deal with the short supply of labor and the cost of moving it across an ocean, planters devised a system of indentured servitude in which laborers ultimately paid for their own transportation through additional years of service. The labor they were expected to perform in the colony's tobacco economy, moreover, tended to be more arduous and less skilled than in England. To a young settler, there was little mystery or mastery attached to pounding Indian corn by hand or working tobacco fields with a hoe. Equivalent tasks in England—putting wheat to the grindstone to make flour or guiding the plow to make straight furrows—required great skill and had strong associations with adult male identity.

Reliance upon indentured servant labor and the colony's peculiar demography combined to retard the progress of young men seeking to establish their own households. Before 1675, more than half of the colony's population was either servant or slave, with English men making up the vast majority of both the unfree and the newly free. For these individuals, the political recognition that normally came with adulthood and property ownership had been deliberately deferred to make their labor available to already established planters. That the labor itself may have been perceived by male servants as more demeaning and physically taxing than what they would have performed in England was an undoubted irritant. But the fact that a large proportion of these young men would die before they completed their service, which sometimes lasted as long as six or seven years, added an element of desperation. Many seem to have felt that they had little to lose by running away. During the decade and a half before the rebellion, planters from various counties frequently complained about the problem of runaway servants. The slow climb in the average annual numbers of runaways in several counties suggests that it was an ever-present problem.[10]

That nearly all the runaway servants were men, as was to be expected from an overwhelmingly male labor force, pointed to another impediment facing these young men. Although the Virginia population at large had been slowly moving toward a more balanced sex ratio, the ratio of male to female servants remained sharply skewed. By 1670, English men still outnumbered English women by approximately three to one, with the greatest imbalance appearing among the newest arrivals, the unfree and newly free men with the fewest financial resources with which to compete for a wife. Compounding the obstacle to adult manhood created by servitude, therefore, was the difficulty of finding a wife in a colony with a shortage of marriageable English women. This feature of the colony's demography diminished the chances that a newly freed man could set up his own household, benefit from his wife's labor to achieve any measure of prosperity, or assume his rightful place in the community.

Even if he managed to overcome these impediments to manhood by surviving his term of service and finding a wife, a young householder in Virginia faced the uncertainties of mastery. Two plots by servants in the early 1660s to break out of their bondage left planters on edge about the security of their work force. Throughout the late 1660s and 1670s, planters brought complaints to both their county courts and the colony's General Court about the problem of runaways, the importation of jailbirds, and the growing visibility of African and Indian servants in all of these forms of unrest. In addition to this literal challenge to mastery, institutions that traditionally defined the boundaries of public life and enhanced the authority of men conducting public business appeared shaky and compromised in Virginia. In county after county, vocal women ignored the distinction between domestic and public business with slanders of prosperous planters and their wives, local officials, and even county justices themselves. The General Assembly's efforts in 1662 to silence them by allowing their husbands to choose to have them ducked failed ultimately to solve the problem, although it did reduce it. Governor Berkeley fared no better in his attempt to suppress religious dissenters, many of whom were women, who continued to hold secret meetings throughout the 1660s and 1670s. In all three of these instances, masters of households proved unable or unwilling to keep members of their households in check.[11]

The weakness of domestic authority within individual households was part of a larger problem of transporting English concepts of social order to Virginia. In England, political theorists described the nation as a body of male property owners bound together like links in a chain. The king, who was usually equated with the head of the body, ruled over all but also protected smaller property owners from the greed and exploitation of bigger men higher up in the body. Although this model undoubtedly had its problems in England, it simply didn't work in Virginia. With the head of the body over three thousand miles away, there was little to check the greed and dishonesty of the colony's big men. A group of servants in York County, Virginia said as much in 1661 when they reviewed their options for presenting grievances about their treatment. Men throughout the colony reiterated this complaint in the immediate aftermath of the rebellion when asked to name the factors that provoked them to take up arms.[12]

Being part of a political body with an absentee head might have been bearable but for persistent evidence that the big men of the colony were taking advantage of the situation to line their own pockets. Tax rates shifted erratically between 1662 and 1675 to pay for the colony's defenses against the Dutch and for the mounting expenses of the General Assembly, known as the "Long Assembly," that sat uninterrupted during those years. The decision by assemblymen to restrict the pool of eligible voters in 1670 to landowners and housekeepers was perceived as irksome by many newly freed men. Some of these men would have been unable to acquire land, marry, or set up their own households but would still have been required to pay taxes. That tobacco prices remained low throughout the period 1660–1680, with larger planters better equipped than their smaller neighbors to diversify their crops and wring lower shipping costs and higher selling prices from their factors, only deepened the frustration of ordinary men. In 1673 and 1674, protests against levies and the burdens of militia service erupted in at least three counties, with several others experiencing episodes of disobedient and disrespectful behavior directed at local officials and prominent planters. Distrust of the colony's government and discontent over the combination of unpredictable taxes and depressed tobacco prices were aggravated by the fact that the governor called no elections to reconstitute the Long Assembly during the fifteen years before the rebellion.[13]

It is relatively easy to see how conditions in Virginia during the 1660s and 1670s might have thwarted male settlers' expectations of setting up independent households and participating in the public business of their communities. Many of the aforementioned obstacles to manhood prevented these men from becoming providers, the male social role most emphasized in the social commentary and advice books of the period and most integral to the daily performance of manhood for ordinary men in England. When we look beyond the general case of male settlers to consider the particular situation of frontier dwellers, however, we begin to see that English-style manhood was not only thwarted in Virginia, but significantly altered in its expression. This, too, was a factor contributing to rebellion.

English men living in Virginia's frontier counties, which made up over half of the colony in the early 1670s, faced a problem that was without precedent in England and of less consequence in the older counties of the coastal Tidewater and Northern Neck regions of the colony. Situated at the farthest remove from the center of colonial government and closest to the interior regions still inhabited by Indians, frontier residents represented the latest wave of settlers whose insatiable need for new lands was resulting in the forced dispossession and relocation of Indian peoples. If we use the term "frontier" not in the Turnerian sense of the front line of civilization but in the more recent anthropological sense of a dynamic meeting ground for two or more cultures where conditions and rules for conduct could change rapidly, we

begin to understand it as a zone where the institutions and fundamental principles of English society could be dramatically transformed. Much to their dismay, frontier dwellers found it difficult
to compel all Indians to acquiesce to English concepts of property in the form of absolute ownership of land and livestock. As
the frontier lands were still literally contested terrain, moreover,
male heads of household needed to be prepared for eruptions of
violence. The consequence of these frontier conditions was that
male settlers had to concern themselves as much with the *protection* of household and property as with provision. For a people
whose main defense against external foes consisted of their location on an island, living in close proximity to a non-European
enemy, particularly one that could claim prior residence, was a
shockingly new experience.

In the responses of frontier dwellers to the Indian presence, a
new configuration for colonial manhood began to emerge that
would reach its fullest expression during the rebellion. During
the 1670s, Governor Berkeley had attempted to stabilize relationships between settlers and Native Americans by distinguishing
between the groups with whom the colony's leading men could
do business and form alliances, and those believed to be hostile
to English interests. His distinction between so-called "friendly"
and "enemy" Indians derived from decades of conflict and bloodshed and represented the interests of a powerful group of Tidewater planters who were more concerned about the threat of a
Dutch invasion than an attack upon frontier settlements. For
frontier settlers, the most pressing danger came from the Indians
who occasionally killed English men and their livestock but could
not be held accountable for their actions the way an Englishman
could. In their outrage over their vulnerability to these non-En-
glish foes, much of it recorded in the petitions and investigative
reports of the rebellion, frontiersmen voiced a militantly English
identity in which their rights as Englishmen to own property,
unmolested, justified taking up arms to slaughter not just those
who had done them wrong, but anyone who failed to abide by

English laws or respect English property rights. In a petition to the governor in 1676, settlers complained that "the Indians hath already most barberously & Inhumanly taken & Murdred severall of our brethren & put them to most cruell torture by burning of them alive & by cruell torturing of others which makes our harts Ready to bleed to heare & we Yor poore subjects are in dayly dandger of our lives by the Heathen in soe much that we are all afraid of goeing about our domisticall affaires." Forced to choose between obeying the law of "Nations," as they referred to the authority of the colonial government, and the law of "Nature," many frontier dwellers declared their readiness "to take armes in defence of our lives." At the core of their justifications was a traditional duty of English manhood, provision, given new militance by the settlers' sense of collective suffering and the widespread ownership of guns.[14]

Men on the frontier expressed a male identity whose main foils had been transformed by the colonial setting. Like their counterparts in England, frontier dwellers continued to define their duties as men in relation to women and children. But whereas in England the gender opposition emphasized women's and children's alleged inability to provide for themselves, on the Virginia frontier men described women and children as needing their protection from Indians. English enmity with Indians thus not only reinforced the importance of property ownership and authority over an established household of dependents, but served as a foil for colonial manhood. As they described their anger at the injuries done them by Indians and their desire to subject Indian offenders to the full power of English law or, barring that, English vengeance, Virginia's frontier dwellers put greater weight on the Englishness that underpinned English masculinity. Manhood, these angry men implied, was an ethnic as well as a gendered privilege, reserved for English men whose relationship to the land conformed to English concepts of property ownership and use.

Compounding this shift in the meaning of English manhood

was the availability of guns. Although by twentieth-century U.S. standards gun ownership was still relatively rare in colonial Virginia, compared to early modern England guns were everywhere, especially after the early 1670s, when Governor Berkeley distributed them widely to improve the colony's defenses against the Dutch. For ordinary men, the value of a gun consisted of its usefulness for hunting, for protecting livestock and households, and, during periods of military alert, for required militia service. Guns appear to have had more than a functional value, however. Virginians showed great enthusiasm about the ceremonial uses of guns, shooting them off whenever there was a celebration of a royal birthday, anniversary, or funeral. Men appear to have accorded guns the same place in their wills that women accorded childbirth linens, moreover, making special mention of the gun and its disposition to an heir, usually an eldest son. Even when guns were in disrepair, which the estate inventories of York County suggest was not uncommon, they seem to have retained some of their material and symbolic value.[15]

As tools of protection, provision and military participation, guns developed a much stronger association with masculinity in Virginia than had been the case in England. Although efforts to restrict the availability of guns to English freemen and keep them out of the hands of enslaved Africans, Indians, and English servants were never completely successful, the exclusion of women from the community of gun owners and users appears to have been nearly universal. Englishmen in the tobacco colony may have lost their ancient association with the mysteries of the plow, but they seem to have gained a new association with the destructive technology of the gun.

Although frontier masculinity represented the most dramatic reconfiguration of English manhood, elite masculinity also underwent adaptations that would prove significant to the way the rebellion unfolded. Saddled with the burden of recreating the aura and mystery of the English aristocracy, with its hereditary claim to political authority, but lacking important props such as

manor houses, sacred burial grounds, ancient churches, and cas-
tles, elite men adapted English traditions selectively and recre-
ated the props as best they could. In an attempt to replicate the
material culture of the aristocracy, Berkeley built himself a large
brick house that stood out in a landscape dominated by small,
hastily constructed wooden dwellings. In the decade of the
1670s, there were probably only four or five other houses like it
in Virginia, three of which belonged to men who would take the
governor's side during the rebellion. Notable among these distinguished householders was Thomas Ludwell, in whose residence
Giles Bland became "overheated" with alcohol and abusive to his
host. Brick structures not only connected these men to the English landscape, which bore the imprint of the social hierarchy
that legitimated their political authority, but displayed their
greatness to smaller planters, who would have been familiar with
the prohibitive costs of building in materials other than wood.
For newcomers like Bland and lesser men who resented the
wealth of the governor's faction, however, brick houses might
also become symbols of pretense and exploitation, irritating reminders that one's social betters had succumbed to greed and
abandoned their duty to protect men more vulnerable than themselves.

Other aspects of elite masculinity appear to have been selectively transplanted to Virginia, where they became sources of
conflict for elite men during the 1670s. That Ludwell did not
deign to respond to Giles Bland's challenge to a duel reveals the
subtle changes in the code of male honor taking place in Virginia
with successive waves of well-heeled migrants. For Bland, the
imputation that his family had gained colonial property illegally
could only be remedied by proving his honor through a duel.
Lacking that opportunity, Bland nailed Ludwell's glove to the
Assembly door accompanied by a note derogating his manhood,
perhaps believing that public exposure of his opponent's coward-
ice would demonstrate the falsehood of the allegations against
the Bland family. Indeed, the glove mounted on the door did

provoke Ludwell into action. His decision to take his fiery young opponent to court, where the governor and other friends presided, rather than to participate in a duel, suggests that Ludwell may have valued political advantage over the rituals of manly honor. Although he expressed concern over the public nature of the insult, its appearance on a Sunday, and the content of the note, Ludwell sought public remedy for his damaged reputation not on the open field of a dueling ground, but in a courtroom.

The lack of consensus about the etiquette of elite manhood in the colony weakened Berkeley's alliance with recent wealthy immigrants like Bland and Bacon, leaving the Green Spring clique ill-prepared to deal with the rage of frontiersmen. Having failed to reinvent itself to meet the twin challenges of internal dissent and irrelevance on the frontier, the elite was in no position to present a united front in a moment of crisis. Concepts of elite honor and manhood that ordinarily would have provided wealthy men with a common world view became a source of division during the rebellion, giving ordinary men the "persons of quality" they needed to turn local discontents into a colony-wide conflict.

REBELLION

The rebellion that erupted in Virginia in 1676 grew out of this rift between the culture of the elite, which had lost its grounding in timeless ritual, and the volatile manhood of the frontier, where violence and bloodshed held sway. Yet it is doubtful that there could have been much of a rebellion without the leadership of Nathaniel Bacon, who bridged the distance between these two cultures of masculinity to create a new alliance of elite and ordinary men. Combining honorific nobility with frontier populism, the formation of colonial manhood that emerged from the conflict featured ethnic exclusivity and a renewed respect for the authority of the English householder. As the events of the rebellion unfolded, masculinity provided a traditional yet flexible set of

values that could be used to justify innovative behavior and do-
mesticate otherwise treacherous activities. As a set of privileges
believed by many contemporaries to be grounded in the natural
order, masculinity also enabled participants in the rebellion to
lay claim to the benefits of a traditional social order even as they
refashioned the meaning of that order in Virginia.

The trigger for rebellion came, not surprisingly, in a frontier
county in July 1675 with the killing of an English overseer by a
Doeg Indian. Conflict between frontier settlers and Indians
quickly escalated after militia leaders indiscriminately killed Sus-
quehannah Indian allies, Berkeley's "friendly" Indians, along
with the Doegs alleged to have committed the offense. Berkeley's
hesitation in pursuing the alleged Indian perpetrators of the violence deepened the discontent of white inhabitants throughout
the winter of 1675 and the spring of 1676, until it finally burst
forth in April of that year under the leadership of Nathaniel
Bacon.

Bacon, who was but twenty-nine years old in 1676, had his
own reasons to bear the governor ill will. He and his friend William Byrd I had been shut out of the profits of the fur trade that
had contributed to the wealth of Berkeley and his allies. In the
recent military conflict with the Susquehannahs, moreover,
Bacon had lost an overseer to an Indian raid. Having allied himself with backcountry protesters, Bacon began to challenge
Berkeley's Indian policy publicly, bypassing governor and legislature with direct appeals to the people. Instigating racist, carth-
artic campaigns against any and all Indians, he sarcastically denied Berkeley's distinction between friends and enemies and
accused the governor of failing to protect the lives of his English
subjects. This strategy, more than any other, enabled Bacon to
appeal to the anger of frontier dwellers without compromising
his own elite status. Outfitting himself as the protector of those
neglected by the governor, Bacon clothed his illegal and innovative behavior in the traditional garb of elite responsibility to
lesser men. Outflanked by Bacon's rhetoric and the young man's

ability to satisfy frontiersmen's desires for bloodletting, the governor was forced to mobilize popular support for his policy. He declared Bacon a rebel and reluctantly initiated elections in May 1676, only to discover, to his surprise and dismay, that the voters had been "seduced and carried away by soe young, unexperienced, rash and inconsiderate p[er]son as the said Nath'll Bacon junr."[16]

The conflict between Bacon and Berkeley was fought not only with troops of armed men, but in the language and ritual of elite male honor. Much like his counterpart Giles Bland, Bacon viewed the men who ruled the colony with disdain: "Trace these men in Authority and Favour to whose hands the dispensation of the Countries wealth has been committed; let us observe the sudden Rise of their Estate compared with the Quality in which they first entered this Country Or the Reputation they have held here amongst wise and discerning men, And lett us see wither their extractions and Education have not bin vile." Bacon urged ordinary Virginians to observe whether Berkeley and his cronies were "spounges [who] have suckt up the Publique Treasure and . . . unworthy Favourites and juggling Parasites whose tottering Fortunes have bin repaired and supported at the Publique chardg." Rather than attempting to do away with the privileges of elite manhood, Bacon was claiming them for himself, arguing that the men currently enjoying them were undeserving. Essentially asking who the natural aristocracy are in a colonial society, Bacon and his followers rejected the governor's men and advanced their own claims to leadership. Only those of noble birth in England, according to Bacon, had a legitimate right to rule in Virginia.[17]

In public condemnations of his political rival, Berkeley defended his honor by contending that it was superior to that of the rebel. The governor described himself as a careful and cautious ruler who took "councel of wiser men then my selfe," but Bacon "boasted," acted "foolishly" and "Treacherously," and surrounded himself with the "lowest of the people." Whereas Berkeley was "conscious of humane fraylty" and could admit an error, it was "not for his [Bacon's] honor to Acknowledge a fault." Berkeley claimed to stand for God and Law, but Bacon "tend[ed] to take away al Religion and lawes." Worst of all, whereas Berkeley had represented the English honorably in his dealings with Indians, Bacon dishonored the English nation with his actions, losing more men in a single campaign than Berkeley had lost in three years of fighting.[18]

In his face-to-face confrontations with Berkeley, Bacon flagrantly violated elite conventions of male honor. Following the elections, he appeared in Jamestown, flanked by his supporters, to take his place as a burgess. After offering a ritual apology for his disobedience to the governor and pledging his word and estate as a "Christian" and a "gentleman" not to subvert Berkeley's orders again, Bacon promptly returned home to gather more men, this time with plans to assault Jamestown. Returning to the colonial capital with more than four hundred foot soldiers, Bacon again confronted the governor in person. His refusal of the governor's offer to settle their dispute through man-to-man combat with swords, like his earlier breach of his pledge, revealed that many of the traditional codes for gentlemanly conduct were irrelevant to the concept of honor driving him and his men. Too late, Berkeley recognized the unique challenges of political leadership in Virginia: "How miserable that man is that Governs a People when six parts of Seaven at least are Poore Endebted Discontented and Armed and to take away their Armes now the Indians are at our throates were to rayse an Universal Mutiny."[19]

By the middle of the summer, Bacon began to appropriate the trappings of formal political authority in the effort to raise funds and recruit men to his cause. A convention in early August produced an ideological justification for the rebellion under the title "Declaration of the People." In it, Bacon condemned the governor and his followers as corrupt, irresponsible, and impotent policy makers who had sold their "Loyall Subjects to the Barbarous Heathen." Bacon also accused Berkeley of leaving his people vulnerable to the Indians and obstructing their attempts to defend themselves. He depicted himself as having stepped into a vacuum of leadership at a critical moment when people needed protection. Bacon also began to require that his followers take an oath of loyalty to their leader. Despite his scorn for Berkeley's appeal to the conventions of elite honor, Bacon clearly still placed some value on a man's word. Using oaths to identify his supporters and bind them together, Bacon attempted to legitimate actions normally considered illegal and dishonorable.[20]

Although all these rituals of association and rebellion helped to confirm the honor of Bacon's cause and the legitimacy of his leadership, the racism underlying his attack on neighboring Indians ultimately enabled the rebels to place their arguments within the context of English ideas of justice and liberty. Complaining bitterly in the "Manifesto" issued at the August convention, Bacon denounced the "protected and Darling Indians" whose close contact with settlers on the frontier resulted in predictable disputes over debts, crops, livestock and land. His greatest grievance was that so-called friendly Indians were not held accountable according to English law yet were "unjustly defended and protected" by it. Calling for all Indians to be outlawed, Bacon presented his own campaign against neighboring Indians as a remedy to the partial and inconsistent application of English justice.[21]

When offered the opportunity to identify the sources of their discontent, ordinary men, especially those living on the frontier, consistently echoed the two issues Bacon had made central to his leadership: their hatred of the Indians who threatened their lives and livelihoods, and their anger at the governor who had failed to protect them. Hoping to clear themselves of the charge of disloyalty to the king's government in Virginia, petitioners and those interrogated by the Royal Commissioners emphasized that their own motives had remained honorably fixed on the traditional duty of male subjects, provision, even as they had taken on the additional burden of protecting English lives and property. In

Charles City County, to take one example, petitioners explained their support of Bacon as an effort to "secure their wieves and children, whose daylye cryes made our lives uncomfortable." In Warwick County, petitioners similarly claimed to have "beene induced compelled and drawne to something that wee now finde to bee absolutely repugnant to the Lawes of his Vast Realme of England," as a consequence of their efforts to preserve their "p[er]sons families and estates from utter ruine."[22]

The active participation of women on the rebel side lends credence to the claims of male petitioners that their motives were primarily domestic in nature. As Susan Westbury has noted, rebel women appear to have taken a much more active role in the conflict than loyalist women, suggesting that the issues at stake for Bacon's followers were rooted in their households, rather than in a more narrowly defined political quarrel. By offering material assistance to the rebels, spreading the word of their triumphs, and refusing to be cowed by the governor's commands to desist, the women who participated in the rebellion demonstrated a more than casual interest in the outcome of the struggle.[23]

Blaming Indians for the colony's problems presented rebels with a convenient way of recasting their treachery as duty. In "The Virginians Plea for Opposing ye Indians without ye Governors Order," written in the middle of the conflict, apologists for the rebels defended their actions as the dutiful responses of Englishmen to the exigencies of life on the frontier. Rather than emphasizing the personal nature of their sufferings, the petitioners portrayed Indians as a threat to the entire colony's well-being, claiming that Virginia was daily weakened by "ye Rapines, Theftes and Murders they Comit & ye Frights they put us into." Seen in this light, the rebellion was not the act of self-interested householders, unmindful of the greater good of the colony, but of activist men with a heightened sense of duty. "We of the Frontier Plantacons are in the most imediate danger of suffering by them [the Indians]," the authors reasoned disingenuously, "so we counted ourselves accordingly oblig'd to offer our Service in ye first place ye more readily against them."

Ultimately, however, the authors of "The Virginians Plea" attributed the behavior of the rebels not to the frontier environment but to hereditary qualities exhibited by all true and honorable Englishmen. "Having still so much English Bloud," the petitioner observed, frontier residents "account it far more Honoble to adventure o[u]r Lives in opposing them [the Indians] wherever we finde them, to ye last drop of o[u]r Blouds for ye security & Defence of this His Matie Colony & whatever is therein dear unto us, than to be Sneakingly Murder'd by them in o[u]r Beds." More than a simple act of self-preservation, killing Indians became the honorable pursuit of ethnic Englishmen devoted to the service of their King, the colony of Virginia, and the dependent members of their households. The duty to protect one's household and provide for one's dependents had become not just the mark of manhood, but a mark of Englishness, defined by an identity that coursed in the "bloud."[24]

Other commentators on the rebellion echoed the focus of ordinary men on their Englishness. In a petition that offered a lengthy summary of the troubles in Virginia, including detailed accounts about the burden of taxes, one author laid out a set of directives that he believed would help restore order. Second on the list, following a recommendation that titles to property be secured to the present owners and their heirs, was an injunction to the king to enlarge "their Liberty, in declareing that all such as are born there shall bee free borne Subjects of England to al intents and purposes." Decades of settlement and distance from England had left many residents of the colony insecure about their rights as Englishmen. As hostilities with Indians intensified and resentment of the governor's policy grew, settlers responded with vigorous reassertions of their Englishness.[25]

Nathaniel Bacon's ability to grasp and exploit the anger of frontier dwellers paved the way for the postrebellion convergence of elite and frontier manhood and for the revitalized concept of

Englishness that was to become so important by century's end. That the resolution of the rebellion rested on more than a political maneuver by the colony's elite planter class, but had deep roots in English traditions of manhood, we can glean from the frequent references made by petitioners to their duties to their king and to their households. That the meaning of colonial manhood shifted in Virginia from a set of privileges and responsibilities defined in relation to women and children to one more broadly defined in opposition to Indians, we can also glean from the documents that survive the rebellion and subsequent investigations by the Royal Commissioners. This theme might be profitably explored with reference to the female participants in the rebellion, whose interests in preserving their husbands' abilities to protect and provide frequently drew them into the conflict. Their participation, like that of their menfolk, testifies to the broad category of politics connecting issues of taxation, Indian policy, and elite corruption to the so-called domestic issues of protection and provision.

Examining Bacon's Rebellion from the perspective of manhood ultimately helps us to understand the complex realignment of the racial landscape during the final quarter of the seventeenth century because it reveals the compromised and uncertain position of English men that lay at the root of subsequent legal and political efforts to define the privileges shared by white men. In attempting to secure their own ill-defined position as English men, living in an English colony on land they had to defend against the original inhabitants, male participants in the rebellion took a major step towards defining themselves as a group of colonial propertyholders with distinct political and economic interests. Like all interest groups before and after them, they summoned their political identities into being and justified their interests with reference to nature and tradition. In the traditions of English masculinity, they found a suitably flexible set of arguments for reaffirming their privileges as Englishmen, even as they actively redefined the meaning of these privileges for the colonial setting.

Commentary by Winthrop D. Jordan

Kathleen Brown's astute, imaginative, and sophisticated paper has opened up a new and most revealing view of an important and puzzling set of historical events.

When I was in graduate school, concentrating on early American history, Bacon's Rebellion remained a mystery to me, and I am eternally grateful to my Ph.D. oral examining committee for not asking me about it. Thomas Wertenbaker's book, *Torchbearer of the Revolution*, had raised conceptual problems because it reeled the film of history backwards from the American Revolution, in chronologically reverse order, to a small conflict in what seemed to me a marginal and demographically unstable frontier society. Wilcomb Washburn's book, *The Governor and the Rebel*, then recently published, seemed a welcome departure, since it emphasized the importance of interracial conflict, but it did not fully explain how the deliberate burning of Jamestown was connected with persistent hostility toward Indians. Considerably later, Stephen Webb's discussion of Bacon's Rebellion shifted the focus from Virginia to policies that appeared to emanate from London's coffeehouses and royal court, but I still remained confused about what happened in Virginia in 1676.

Owing to Professor Brown's paper, I am now much less at a loss for understanding, but I still feel somewhat uncertain as to why events transpired as they did. Previous explanations, which have often focussed on all those guns out there among a large populace of discontented males, do not seem entirely satisfactory. Kathleen Brown emphasizes that those guns were "tools of protection, provision and military participation" and that they had become more "associate[d] with masculinity in Virginia than had been the case in England." Those guns were indeed frightening and could indeed be deadly, but they were inefficient and dangerous to the users, especially in comparison with the ease and efficiency of Governor Berkeley's twin weapons, Authority and Rope. And would it not be equally fair to say, without reference to the word "masculinity," that guns in seventeenth-century England were firmly associated with males of the upper classes and that when in frontier Virginia they came into the hands of the lower sorts, there was conflict between those who traditionally were supposed to have them and those who traditionally were supposed (or hoped) not to? (This matter of guns has had remarkable persistence, especially in the American South, and on this matter Bacon's supporters seem to have become "Americanized" very rapidly.)

In a paper that so often uses the word "manhood," it would have been preferable to have some recognition that the so-called "men" were of very different ages. The point is not trivial, since in the seventeenth century English traditions about the proper age for militia service and the proper age for voting, property ownership, and other legal privileges were transplanted pretty much wholesale to the New World. The minimum age for political privileges was twenty-one, but for obligatory militia service it was sixteen. Since then, these ages have been buffeted about during the history of this nation, at least from the time of the American Revolution, when the song *Yankee Doodle* referred to the "men and boys" in the army of that "glorious cause," right down to the present day. For many years the minimum and maximum ages for military service have fluctuated considerably and sometimes rapidly. More than a generation ago, the question of military age interacted with other developments to result in an amendment of the U.S. Constitution concerning the voting age. And of course, in very recent years this nation, in its variegated collectivity, has been tussling with matters of age concerning such issues as drivers' licenses, liquor consumption, and court systems.

My hope here is that the recent enormously important and

productive attention to genderizing history will not result in the exclusion of attention to the life cycle. In this connection, seventeenth-century English society was dissimilar from many others which have regarded age-grades as absolutely fundamental units of their social structures. At the time of its overseas expansion, English society lacked a clear demarcation point and accompanying important rituals for a boy to become a man and indeed for a girl to become a woman, except for the rather weak one of "confirmation" in the Established Church. Yet later, in the late nineteenth century, with Huckleberry and Tom and Penrod, the notion of boyhood emerged as a romanticized version of a more ancient, nearly atavistic, and thoroughly ambivalent human sense that during intergroup conflicts ten-year-old males were not as yet useful or qualified for much of anything except to be cared for and watched carefully. Today, ten-year-olds can and do easily carry and use very deadly firearms, but in the seventeenth century they could scarcely lift them off the ground, let alone fire them.

Even with firearms set aside, the importance of the life cycle among other qualities becomes apparent when one recalls the races, genders, and ages of Aunt Polly, Pap, Jim, and Huck. For emphasis, one only needs to try imagining Huck and Jim as being the same age.

But Kathleen Brown has written about Bacon's Rebellion, not about a society that developed two centuries later. Her use of the word "masculinity" in this paper stands at its heart. So far as I can see, the genderizing of this episode in early American history works quite well and results in much better understanding of what actually transpired. Yet I think there are still difficulties, especially as to causal relationships. If one poses the question, "What were the causes of Bacon's Rebellion?", we are left wandering among a bewildering variety of possibilities, including personality conflicts, two loose cannons named Bacon and Berkeley, class conflicts, ethnic hostilities, imperial gaffes, and now testosterone and estrogen. My particular point on this matter is that the author does not focus on what the historical participants thought they were doing. To impose contemporary understanding upon people's actions is an ordinary procedure in historical practice, but it often serves to avoid the difficult task of getting inside the heads of people now long dead. Is the asserted "masculinity" something they were trying to achieve, or is it a valuable lens through which we can view their own specific thoughts and actions? Is it our concept or theirs?

These are easy questions for so sophisticated a historian as Kathleen Brown. Those men knew what they wanted to be, and they went about their business of being it quite successfully. Their inner concepts of "provision" and of "protection," so eloquently described in this paper, help greatly in explaining Bacon's Rebellion. In my opinion, this is genderized history of the very best sort, and there ought to be no need to justify such a point of view explicitly.

But points of view matter, and I remain troubled by what seems to me imposition of present concerns upon the rather distant past. The word "manhood" is very old, but it originally had no relationship with the concept of "independence," which is a largely eighteenth-century concept. Professor Brown does not use "manhood" often. But she does use the word "masculinity" very frequently, and also in the title of her paper. It is a word that did not exist (at least according to the *OED*) until seventy-five years after Bacon's Rebellion, which makes one wonder about consciousness of the concept in 1676.

Two other portions of the title of the paper also give one pause. The title is: "Nathaniel Bacon and the Dilemma of Colonial Masculinity." So far as I can make out, there seems to be no "dilemma" in the paper's eloquent description of the differences between English and Virginian handling of gender roles nor in the perceptions of those roles among the participants in Bacon's Rebellion. In short, what was this "dilemma"?

In addition, presumably here the word "Colonial" refers to British-dominated North America though some readers might rightly read the term more broadly as properly applying as well to southern Africa and Asia and Central and South America and the Caribbean. In these other arenas, will similar analysis yield similarly satisfactory results?

Professor Brown's paper is fundamentally about Virginia. No matter how powerfully persuasive a gender-oriented argument can be—and is most certainly in her hands—it does not shift gears easily into other, and especially broader, levels of generalization. Can such a perspective be profitably applied to all the disparate outbreaks of rebelliousness that occurred in the English-speaking world during the last quarter of the seventeenth century? While not often called such, surely this was indeed an "age of revolution." In addition to Bacon's Rebellion, one thinks of the nearly simultaneous Indian counterattack and the Anglo-American response which is commonly known as King Philip's War in southern New England, of the Glorious Revolution in England, and of its reverberations as Andros's Rebellion in Massachusetts and Leisler's Revolt in New York. Was the battle against Metacom in "King Philip's War" at all influenced by the fact that there were so many more women in New England than in Virginia? Especially during that devastating war, many households were headed by women, whose roles as surrogate heads of households were so strongly emphasized by the Puritan minister Mr. William Gouge in his earlier but still popular English tome, *Of Domesticall Duties* (1622)—which work I appreciated Professor Brown's citing as we are probably the only two scholars at this conference who have read Gouge's book in all its refulgent six-hundred-page entirety.

More important, can a gender-oriented perspective help explain such a clustering of separate rebellions during a single fifteen-year period? My guess is: probably not.

Perhaps, looking in a slightly different direction, it would be well to bear in mind that these events all took place during the course of only two generations after English rebels killed their king and thereby horrified the rest of Europe and many of their compatriots overseas. This regicide was justified at the time of John Milton and also, exactly a century after Bacon's Rebellion, referred to approvingly by Thomas Paine in connection with the independence of the British colonies in North America. In more direct connection with Professor Brown's fine paper, surely we ought also to keep in mind precisely what particular portion of King Charles I's anatomy was whacked off by the swing of the Axe.

Law, Domestic Violence, and the Limits of Patriarchal Authority in the Antebellum South

LAURA F. EDWARDS

In 1846, James Meadows, a free white man, was brutally murdered. As his son later testified, Meadows was dragged from his North Carolina house in the middle of the night. After his Achilles tendon was cut so he could not run away, he was beaten lifeless. Then, in what seemed like a final act of rage, his penis and testicles were brutally "squeezed and pressed." After the inquest, James Meadows's wife, Mary, and a neighboring slave named George were arrested. George was charged with murder and Mary, as his accomplice, with conspiracy to murder.

Was an ill-fated romance behind this case? It certainly seems possible, given the two people accused, the fury so evident in the murder, and the sexually explicit forms the violence took. Perhaps Mary and George had been involved in an illicit affair that progressed to the point where they decided to rid themselves of Mary's husband. Of course, murder was a poor solution, even if they did get away with it, because George was a slave who could never marry his beloved or be a husband to her in the same way that James Meadows could. Maybe this was why George's rage boiled over when he confronted James Meadows that night in 1846. Not content with eliminating his rival, George inflicted a punishment reserved for slaves and then emasculated his victim's body.

It would be a tragic, compelling story. The evidence, however, does not support it. In fact, there is nothing in the existing documentation to suggest that George or Mary had any hand in James Meadows's death or any connection to each other beyond being neighbors. The evidence linking George to the murder scene was highly questionable. At his trial, one Meadows son testified that George was one of three men who had taken James Meadows from his house the night of the murder. But at the inquest on the day after the murder, he claimed that he could not identify any of the men. Only after George was arrested did the son "recognize" him—a fact that made his testimony suspect enough to constitute grounds for one of two appeals made on George's behalf. Even if George had taken James Meadows from his house, there were no witnesses to connect him to the actual murder. To confuse matters further, the local authorities made no attempt to find the other two suspects. There was no direct evidence to tie Mary Meadows to the crime at all. She apparently came under suspicion because of threats she made against her husband. The trial transcript does mention a "guilty connection" between George and Mary Meadows, but it neglected to explain the nature of this connection. The justices of the North Carolina State Supreme Court were puzzled and frustrated by this omission when they heard George's first appeal. Such a connection, they pointed out, could be any number of things. It could be sexual. Or it could refer to a plot to murder James Meadows. But without any additional explanation, it was impossible to assume either.[1]

Interpreting the Meadows case as an interracial sexual romance ultimately says more about current historiographical assumptions than events in the past. Southern historians have had a longstanding fascination with illicit sexual liaisons, particularly those between white women and black men. Until recently, they also have had a tendency to displace women and African Americans by centering their analyses around white men. Both propensities are evident in an interpretation that focuses on a presumably sexual "connection" between Mary and George and then identifies sexual tension as the motivating force in James Meadows's death. Such a reading turns Mary Meadows into a prize over which two men fought, a view that duplicates antebellum views of white women. Similarly, the characterization of George as a slave whose ultimate demise was the result of his desire for the things that free white men had also defines him primarily in terms of contemporary white racial stereotypes of African-American men.[2]

Southern historians' assumptions, in turn, are shaped by the sources they use. Antebellum law marginalized and silenced women like Mary Meadows and slaves like George. Scholars of the antebellum South have studied legal records and documented the inequalities that the law imposed on both wives and slaves. The Meadows case affirms the racial and gender biases that other historians have found in southern law. Antebellum gender conventions apparently made it difficult for court officials to imagine a white woman capable of such a brutal murder. Although initially arrested as an accomplice, Mary Meadows was acquitted. Her acquittal was not determined by lack of evidence alone. The evidence against George was equally thin and circumstantial. But George, who could not mount the same kind of defense that a white man or even a white woman could, was ultimately hanged for James Meadows's death.[3]

The courtroom, however, did not represent the entire South. What neither the historiography nor the legal sources fully acknowledge are the limits of this arena in describing the operation of power relations. The law did not merely reflect social relations or, conversely, impose its will on society. It was a tool of power, to be sure. The law determined the fates of Mary Meadows and George. In fact, legal categories were so effective at hiding and diffusing the actions of wives and slaves in most cases that it is difficult to imagine Mary Meadows and George outside the roles laid out for them in law. But the law was an imperfect tool, an unwieldy one that could produce multiple meanings and was difficult for any one group to control completely. Even within the legal arena, the law could never completely contain domestic dependents within private space.[4] The evidence in the Meadows case, for instance, indicates that the fit between legal categories and the events surrounding James Meadows's death were far from perfect. The testimony reveals Mary Meadows as a foul-mouthed, quarrelsome woman who had boasted to her neighbors that she would have her husband beaten or killed. James Meadows, never far from a fight himself, supplied all sorts of people with all sorts of reasons for wanting him dead. His wife, whom he beat, was one. George may have been another. If so, sexual competition was only one among many possible points of contention. George and other slaves in his neighborhood had the opportunity to mix with James Meadows in a crowd of free blacks, slaves, and whites who drank, gambled, traded, fought, and drove respectable whites to distraction.[5] This South was not the orderly one upheld in law. In this arena, wives and slaves like Mary Meadows and George acted and spoke for themselves, just as free white men like James Meadows did. The upshot was often violence, as those who were supposed to be domestic dependents—white and black women and African American men—fought to establish borders around their own bodies and, by extension, some authority over their own lives. Their battles are documented in local legal records, the vast majority of which involve violence of some kind and a significant number of which involve women of both races and black men.[6] Indeed, if the South were the one described in law, populated by powerful white, male household heads and passive domestic dependents, there would have been no need for court officials to intervene on behalf of patriarchal power at all.

Focusing on local and state legal records in antebellum North and South Carolina,[7] this article argues that antebellum law had to continually assert the power of white male household heads in the antebellum period precisely because that power was neither complete nor stable in practice. The argument is not that the law was irrelevant in understanding social relations or that patriarchal power and domestic dependency were merely legal fictions. To the contrary, the law was obviously powerful. It buttressed the power of white patriarchs, who exercised their authority in ways that wives and slaves could never overcome, either inside or outside the courtroom. But not all white men were equally powerful or equally competent in exercising the power allowed to them by law. The historiographical focus on the legal affirmation of patriarchal power, moreover, has obscured the social conflicts that made the decisions necessary in the first place. These conflicts reveal an important debate, centered around the proper expression and substantive limits of patriarchal power, in which white and black women and African American men played active roles.

At times, this debate became too lively for the comfort of antebellum court officials. James Meadows, for one, never secured the obedience of his own wife, let alone the respect of his neighbors, white or black. When the law finally intervened, it affirmed the gender and racial inequalities that defined domestic dependency and patriarchal authority. But it did so because James Meadows, like so many other white men, failed to keep order himself. James Meadows's murder and the legal handling of it thus reveals the contingency and contestation that also defined patriarchal authority in the antebellum South. That contingency and contestation was precisely what antebellum law sought to control, to diffuse, and to hide.

Southerners, particularly free white southern men, are infamous for their fighting. Of course, not all brawlers wound up in court. But when they did, the legal treatment of their cases reflected their status as citizens with full civil and political rights and recognized members of the body politic. The law thus privileged violence against free white men, by assuming that such acts always affected the public order and, thus, had criminal status. The law not only treated a much wider range of violence acts against free white men as criminal matters, but also gave these men greater latitude in using violence against others. The implications are contained within the distinction between "civil" and "criminal" cases. In law, criminal offenses were "public" because they endangered the social order to the point where the King or, later, the state prosecuted the suit. By contrast, civil matters were "private" disputes, limited in their impact to the parties directly involved. A criminal case in which Henry Jones had injured Jane Smith would be designated *State v. Jones*, while a civil case involving the same parties would be called *Smith v. Jones*. The first involves the interests of the state. The second does not. Violence against free white men, by definition, involved the state because they were constituent members of the state.[8]

Violence against those people who were not members of the body politic was a different matter. In common law, all domestic dependents were extensions of their fathers, husbands, and masters, who acted as their dependents' public representatives and possessed property rights in their labor and bodies. Recent work has used gender to reveal connections between the legal status of slaves to that of those people who were supposed to be domestic dependents—women of both races as well as African American men. Changing the point of comparison has cast the institution of slavery in a new light. Scholars once took the experience of free white men as historically representative and thus compared the legal status of slaves to that of men with full civil and political rights. Given this basis of comparison, slaves' legal status appeared contradictory and the institution itself seemed anomalous in an otherwise "free" society. But only a small minority of the antebellum population, North or South, actually enjoyed the full rights of legal personhood that free white men claimed. The majority were subordinated in their status as domestic dependents. The legal residue of dependency still attached to white women and African Americans who were not wives or slaves because they were seen as people who, because of their sex and/or race, were naturally dependent. Once this dependent majority becomes the point of comparison, the legal status of slaves begins to look less anomalous and contradictory in the context of the time. Legally, slavery was a repressive extension of household heads' established rights over other domestic dependents. The institution of slavery magnified and even transformed that authority, but it did not create the legal concept.[9]

Of course, the theoretical connections in the laws relating to slaves and wives did not mean that the actual conditions or the legal treatment of these two groups was the same or even resulted in similar outcomes. The legal position of slaves was far worse than that of wives. Where nineteenth-century southern political theorists regularly invoked the theoretical links between marriage and slavery, jurists increasingly avoided direct comparisons between the actual position of wives and slaves. Apparently, they were troubled by similarities in the legal logic governing free white women and enslaved African Americans. Taken to its logical extreme, this reasoning might produce similarities in the lives of these two groups that would challenge jurists' commitment to both the racial superiority of white women and the inherent differences between all white and all black people.[10]

Still, by law, neither wives nor slaves were legally recognized persons who could act in their own names or bring their concerns directly to institutions of state governance. They were domestic dependents, stuck within the private sphere. Domestic relations were legally "private" in the same sense that civil issues were legally "private." This kind of privacy did not mean that domestic relations were wholly free from legal oversight. Rather, they were legally "private" in the sense that disputes between household heads and dependents were considered personal matters that should not, in theory, involve the public order. Antebellum law, for instance, sought to confine the effects of fights between a husband and wife or a master and slave to the parties directly involved. A fight between two free white men, however, was different. Here the law assumed that the dispute reached beyond the two parties. In such cases, the state intervened to regulate relations between public citizens, to ensure that their respective rights were maintained, and to set precedents involving other citizens' rights as well. In the process, the law made some kinds of violence more visible—and more legitimate—than other kinds.

In fact, the political implications of domestic dependency were nowhere more apparent than in the legal treatment of violence, where the status of those involved defined the very nature of the offense. Mary Meadows, for instance, had accused her husband of physical abuse before his death. But such violence was not assault or any other criminal offense in law. When husbands or masters beat their wives or slaves, the law considered it legitimate "discipline" necessary to household governance. In the case of slaves, the courts also justified such violence in terms of masters' property rights to their slaves' bodies.[11] Both husbands and masters could be tried for killing their wives and slaves. But usually, the charges were either reduced or dropped because the law defined legitimate discipline so broadly. Although writing about children and free servants, Tapping Reeve, an influential nineteenth-century legal commentator, outlined the principles that southern courts applied to all domestic dependents. According to Reeve, it was difficult to determine when punishment "exceeded the bounds of moderation" because parents and masters were supposed to prevent the development of "vicious habits" that might prove "a nuisance to the community." As long as parents and masters acted "from motives of duty," Reeve explained, "no verdict ought to be found against" them. Only if fathers or masters acted out of "wicked intent" could they be convicted of murder.[12]

In following these principles, courts in North and South Carolina allowed masters of slaves the most discretion.[13] The experience of Warner Taylor, a particularly brutal North Carolina slaveholder, is revealing. In 1819, an inquest jury found him guilty of beating his slave Betty to death. But Taylor's responsibility for the killing was a different matter in a court of law. The grand jury did not find evidence of "wicked intent" and charged him with the lesser crime of manslaughter. He was acquitted at trial. Just six years later, however, Taylor admitted to beating another slave to death. Charged again with manslaughter, he was convicted this time. Still, he did not receive the full punishment for his crime. Burned on the hand instead of hanged, he went back home to his other, unfortunate slaves.[14] Warner's treatment was well within the bounds of the law. The state supreme courts in both North and South Carolina upheld convictions against masters only when the agonizing details of "wicked intent" were so sadistic as to be, in one judge's words, "beyond the pale."[15]

When wives were beaten by someone other than their husbands, it was a criminal offense. Even so, the law did not treat wives in the same way as other assault victims. In 1814, for instance, a county superior court in North Carolina indicted four people for riot against George Byers, even though he had not been affected directly. The defendants had actually assembled to give "Sally Byers the wife of the said George Byers . . . great and gross abuse with foul and Blasphemous language." More than chivalry brought George Byers into his wife's assault case. Because wives were legally subsumed within their husbands, the law considered violence against them to be a crime against their husbands as well. Technically, Sally Byers could not file criminal charges by herself. Her husband could also initiate separate civil proceedings for any expenses incurred from her injuries and for damages sustained by the loss of her labor and sexual services.[16]

But wives still had more legal visibility than slaves. Where wives were recognized as parties in criminal offenses committed against them, slaves were not. In North Carolina, masters prosecuted their slaves' assault cases, as Benjamin Hester did in 1802 when he charged that Willie Howington "violently beat & also wound[ed] with a knife a Negro fellow belonging to the sd Hester." Hester's omission of his injured slave's name was unusual. More common was William Clay's 1815 complaint that Abington Kimbel "did commit an assault and battery on a certain negro man belonging to him . . . by the name of David."[17] But, whether named or not, slaves were not legally recognized parties to the suit. Masters gave the injured slaves' names to clarify which property had been damaged, much as victims of burglary listed the specific items stolen from them. Slaves' injuries, in other words, acquired status as criminal offenses only through their masters. They did not enter South Carolina courts as criminal matters at all. In the 1850s, the courts began interpreting a stat-

ute prohibiting "unjustified" abuse by masters to include violence by third parties as well. But for most of the antebellum
period, South Carolina considered violence against slaves to be
merely civil offenses that entitled masters to sue for damages to
their property. If the violence resulted in the slave's murder, the
state did allow the assailant to be charged with the criminal offense of murder. The same was true in North Carolina, where
masters could face charges of manslaughter as well. But legal
standards of proof similar to those applied to masters meant that
convictions were rare.[18]

As Mary Meadows and George discovered when they were
arrested for the murder of James Meadows, the principle of domestic privacy did not remove the violent acts of wives and slaves
from public view. Quite the opposite. Not only did antebellum
southern courts consider virtually all violent acts committed by
wives and slaves to be serious criminal offenses, but it also defined the category "violence" more broadly for them to include
speech and gestures. This double standard was based in the legal
fiction that domestic dependents should not be public actors. Of
course, southern jurists and lawmakers knew otherwise. It was
very clear that slaves and wives had wills of their own and that
they moved, spoke, and acted in public space. It was that knowledge that made the legal fiction necessary. By refusing to recognize the legitimacy of slaves' and wives' actions within the theoretical structures of law, antebellum court officials and politicians
limited the ability of a potentially troublesome population to affect public policy. If the law did not recognize the ability of wives
and slaves to act, then wives and slaves could not affect the law.[19]

By implication, then, lawmakers categorized the violent acts of
wives and slaves to be more serious than those committed by
people, namely free white men, who were already recognized
legal actors. When wives and slaves imposed their will on a legally recognized person, whether directly or indirectly through
his dependents, they stepped out of their place and left their
imprint on the public order. They became legally visible, politi-

cally active, and extremely problematic. The legal definition of provocation suggests the lengths to which jurists went to keep wives and slaves in their place. In fights among free white men, nineteenth-century courts in North and South Carolina insisted that provocation consisted only in actual threats of violence, such as drawing a knife within striking range. If provoked, a free white man could legally defend himself without bearing criminal responsibility for his acts. Not so with wives and slaves. The law considered their insults, disobedience, or suggestive gestures sufficient to provoke violence from husbands, masters, and other free white men as well. In 1821, for instance, Thomas Wright of North Carolina was indicted for the murder of his wife Anne, whom he had shot in the face at point-blank range. Despite the evidence against him, he was acquitted. Anne Wright, it turns out, had been having an affair with Barnett Jones. Giving a new twist to a husband's legally recognized, although "unwritten" exemption from murder when he killed his wife's seducer in the act, the judge and jury apparently considered Anne Wright's actions to be sufficient provocation. Certainly that was the implication the court gave later, when it indicted Barnett Jones for adultery and noted that his partner in crime had been "killed by Her Husband for Bad treatment from Her & said Barnett."[20] Neither wives nor slaves, however, could defend themselves in kind. The law was particularly restrictive for slaves, allowing self-defense only when death or permanent injury was imminent. North Carolina's Justice Richmond Pearson explained the double standard operative in both states: "If a white man, receiving a slight blow, kills with a deadly weapon it is but manslaughter; if a slave, for such a blow should kill a white man, it would be *murder*; for, accustomed as he is to constant humiliation, it would not be calculated to excite to such a degree to 'dethrone reason,' and must be ascribed to a 'wicked heart.' "[21]

Domestic dependency justified these legal restraints. Its effects were most visible in wives' and slaves' interactions with their husbands and masters.[22] But wives' and slaves' dependent status also shaped cases where their husbands and masters were not involved. Most obviously, dependency muted their voices in court. Because they were legal extensions of another person, the law treated their oaths with suspicion and required corroborating evidence to establish their claims. Its demands were most extreme in the case of slaves, who were barred from testifying against whites.[23] Dependency also shaped the legal treatment of violence in more subtle ways, as Justice Ruffin revealed in an 1847 discussion of the legal limits of self-defense in relation to slaves. Ruffin argued that violence, in the form of corporal punishment, was integral to all domestic dependents' subordination. By extension, he reasoned, the law assumed that domestic dependents responded to violence differently than did free white men. It also judged their violent acts by different standards. A child who killed a parent during punishment, for instance, was guilty of murder because the act could only seen as "a malignant and diabolical spirit of vengeance." Ruffin then extended this logic to cover slaves' dealings with all free people. "It is a just conclusion of reason when a slave kills a white man for a battery . . . that the act did not flow from . . . uncontrollable resentment, but from a bad heart." Then Ruffin betrayed how dangerous domestic dependents' violent acts were to his understanding of public order. In his words, slaves with "bad hearts" were "intent upon the assertion of an equality, social and personal, with the white, and bent on mortal mischief in support of the assertion." Wives, whose domestic status also followed them beyond the household, could be substituted for slaves. But their evil intent would be the "assertion of an equality, social and personal" with men.[24]

While unmasking the logic underlying state governance in the antebellum South, the law's abstractions can distort as much as they reveal. In fact, the legal decisions, particularly at the appellate level, suggest a level of political order that did not actually exist in practice. To be sure, nineteenth-century household heads exercised broad authority over domestic dependents in both law and practice. But that power was never as absolute in practice as it was in law. In fact, the courts mobilized the legal principle of domestic authority when it had broken down in practice—to decide cases, for instance, where a household head abused his power over his dependents or proved unable to keep them under control. To clarify the legal issues and weigh competing claims, the courts then distilled relations between household heads and dependents from other complicating social relations, creating the legal fiction of an isolated, self-contained household, abstracted from social context. Of course, no husband or master actually stood alone, unencumbered by other social ties. Nor was any wife or slave completely isolated within a single household. Of course, the courts employed this legal fiction in different ways with different effects at different points in time. In the nineteenth-century South, southern lawmakers applied the principle of domestic authority in particularly expansive ways. Marking off the household as an individual man's private domain and refusing to intervene in his domestic governance, the courts made each individual man sovereign at home.[25]

But the courts' insistence did not make it so, because the law did not simply reflect existing practices or impose its will on them. As both a product of and participant in social conflicts, the law actively intervened to shore up the authority of household heads and, by extension, a particular social order based on that authority. In the process, the courts suppressed alternate perspectives by denying their legitimacy. Domestic dependents, however, were neither as passive nor as silent as the law made them out to be. By all accounts, for instance, Mary Meadows was loud and opinionated. She was particularly vocal on the subject of her husband. One year before his death, she complained about him to several neighbor women while grinding corn at John Duncan's house. In the course of this exchange, Mary Meadows offered to work for Duncan for one year without pay if he would kill her husband. Susannah Duncan substantiated her husband's story and added to it. She had overheard a conversation between Mary Meadows and Thomas Murray, who had his own quarrel with James Meadows and gone as far as to load a gun to shoot him, but then decided against it. Mary Meadows reportedly said that "she wished that Murry had . . . blowed that load through him." She made a similar statement to Samuel Jackson. While arguing with her husband at a community gathering, she rebuked Jackson for not "knock[ing]" her husband's "brains out" when the two men had fought earlier. "If she was a man," Meadows had screamed as her husband pushed her down the hill towards home, "she would do it." Then, just one week before the murder, Mary Meadows told James Hobgood that she intended to have her husband beaten, boasting that he "would be the worst whiped [*sic*] man he (Hobgood) ever saw." The beating would be so severe, she claimed, that "his hide would not hold shucks."[26] Mary Meadows's words and actions do not fit into any of the expected historical categories. Those available would make her either a victim or a madwoman—images that ultimately say less about the motivations of Mary Meadows than about the law's power to marginalize the actions of wives and slaves.

Legally, people like Mary Meadows were supposed to be the recipients, not the instigators, of violence. But her willingness to use it was not unusual among slaves and white women, particularly wives in poor families. Despite their position in law, white women were not so subordinate that they would silently endure anything for the sake of their marriages, nor so dependent that they were helpless on their own. White women, married and unmarried, regularly challenged in court violent acts committed against them. In 1833, for instance, Mrs. Susannah Lansdale charged John Armstrong and Thomas Patrick with assault. As she claimed, they forced their way into her house, where they used "a great deal of very vulgar language and threatened her & did violently assault and abuse her by laying hands on her and dashing her across the house." "After being frequently invited to leave," she continued, they "swore they would stay as long as they pleased." The fight was over Susannah Lansdale's child, whom Thomas Patrick wanted to apprentice. Lansdale, however, defended the physical borders that defined her life, refusing either to give over her child without a fight or to accept violence silently.[27]

White women could be as brutal as their menfolk. Even those in the planter class, supposedly paragons of refined womanhood, regularly battered slaves and even their own children. Less restrained by class conventions, yeoman and poor white women also directed violence against other free adults for a variety of reasons: to defend themselves, to shame, to retaliate for perceived wrongs, or to assert their own interests. A combination of these motives seem to explain the actions of Mary Hester, Nancy H. Pullam and Rachel Hester, who assaulted a court official charged with seizing their property in default of a debt. Sometimes arguments involving women simply got out of hand, just as they did with men. Apparently, Abigail Guy's passion got the best of her when she "made an affray" at the Coe household in North Carolina, "wherein the persons of said Amos Coe & Betsy Coe was beaten & abused by . . . the said Abigale Guy." Sometimes women's violence was simply an extension of drunken revelry, as in the case of Patsy Dove and Fanny Davis of South Carolina. Apparently looking for fun and diversion, they woke Hannah Green, let her chickens out of the hen house, and then chased her around the yard, threatening to beat her.[28]

When necessary, wives used violence against their own husbands. Of course, all white women had a stake in their own dependency, which not only gave them rights to provision and protection, but also grounded their racial and, in the case of wealthy women, their class privilege. This investment mediated their use of violence against men, particularly their own husbands. Wives did not try to establish their own position as equal individuals in physical confrontations with their husbands. But they did use force when they thought husbands had pushed the limits of their authority too far or expressed it inappropriately. Barbara Davis's reaction to her husband's abuse of his mother is typical. She stood by as her husband "dashed [his mother] against the floor" and threatened "to whip her," but when he got a gun to "blow her brains out," she intervened. In fact, Mary Meadows may have acted similarly, feeling that her husband's abuse justified her own belligerence.[29]

With little stake in their own dependent status, slaves regularly used violence to challenge the authority of their own masters and other whites. Perhaps the most famous example is Frederick Douglass's fight with the man who was supposed to break him in. In Douglass's narrative, the victory is an isolated triumph—another step towards personal independence, but not necessarily representative of the slave experience. As local court records indicate, however, such fights were common in the daily routine of slavery, part of the ongoing, often failed efforts of whites to maintain control over slaves. Joe, for instance, was "in the habit of scuffling" with Jacob Mathis, the white overseer of the South Carolina foundry where Joe worked. One day, after a fight that Mathis himself called typical, he filed assault charges against Joe. Apparently, the balance of power had tilted too far in Joe's favor, making it necessary for Mathis to bring in outside reinforcements. Even this effort failed to demonstrate Jacob Mathis's power. The court acquitted Joe.[30]

As Joe's experience suggests, threats and physical blows allowed slaves to establish de facto borders around themselves that whites grudgingly acknowledged, even if they did not completely accept them. When Lease, a South Carolina slave, struck Eunicey Guthrie for interfering with her children, the three whites present did nothing to stop her. Apparently, they already knew not to cross that border with Lease. The experience of Violet, a slave given to the Burgess family by Thomas Burgess's father, is also suggestive. As the Burgesses later explained, Violet "generally done as she pleased" before she came to them. Polly Burgess, Violet's new mistress, decided to change that and struck at Violet with an ax handle to discipline her. Not about to begin taking such abuse, Violet turned on her mistress, "took the weapon out her hand and knocked her down and struck her again." It took

Polly Burgess, Thomas Burgess, their two daughters, and a loaded gun to wrestle Violet to the ground. The Burgesses tied her up and whipped her. But they were still unable to control her, so Thomas Burgess went off for assistance. While he was gone, Violet untied her bonds and left. Defeated, the Burgesses filed charges against Violet for assault, hoping that the court system would succeed where they had failed. In court, both Lease and Violet were convicted and sentenced to whippings. Still, the fact that so many whites found it necessary to call on neighbors, churches, and the courts for assistance in protecting themselves from slaves is significant. Such actions suggest slaves' persistence, if not always their success, in building barriers around themselves and claiming control over their own bodies.[31]

Wives and slaves also used social networks to limit their husbands' and masters' authority. Although Mary Meadows's efforts backfired, she actually followed a common pattern of publicizing husbands' and masters' excesses in the hopes of mobilizing outside aid. To be sure, social ties outside their households could never alter wives' and slaves' institutional subjection to a single master or husband in law. Still, the law defined the nature of patriarchal power in the abstract by overstating the authority of individual patriarchs, who were always subject to other men and, sometimes, other women in their own families and communities.

White women's ties to other families were particularly effective in disciplining their own husbands. Wives in the planter class, for instance, fled abuse through extended visits or invited relatives and friends into their own homes to moderate their husbands' behavior. Marion Singleton Deveaux Converse, a well-placed South Carolina widow, used both tactics in an effort to escape her second husband's tantrums, beatings, and heavy-handed pressure to sign over large portions of her estate to him. When Augustus Converse refused to alter his ways, Marion's sizeable, influential family closed ranks around her. Of course, it was not just Marion that concerned them. With his flagrant, public abuse, Augustus had embarrassed them and compromised their own reputations. Worse, he threatened their patrimony by grasping at property entrusted to Marion's care. Although patriarchal, the ties which bound Marion to her father's and first husband's families, gave her effective weapons to wield against a tyrannical, but penniless and socially unconnected husband. With family support, Marion managed to procure a legal separation in a state where divorce was impossible. Her husband fared even worse in the court of public opinion, where Marion's family made him a social outcast and finally drove him out of the state altogether. With every trace of Augustus Converse gone or suppressed, Marion dropped his name and lived the rest of her life as if he had never existed.[32]

Poor wives were far less circumspect about publicizing marital disputes than those of the planter class. Like Mary Meadows, they made their husbands' failings known, demanded shelter and provision, and even rebuked neighbors for failing to discipline errant husbands. Complaining of her husband's abuse and neglect, Mrs. Woodruff of South Carolina begged a neighbor woman for food and asked that word be sent to her father so that he could help her. Mrs. Littlefield, who also lived in South Carolina, regularly sought shelter with her neighbors to escape her violent husband. Mrs. Watkins did not suffer in silence either. She told at least two women that her husband "whipt" her. These women, in turn, told several others who passed on the story as truth, based on what they already knew about her husband.[33]

The requests of poor white wives often became demands, suggesting the extent to which they felt entitled to aid from neighbors and kin. Mary Meadows's efforts to have her husband beaten or worse may have been attempts to shame her neighbors into disciplining him. If so, her demands were not unprecedented. Community members regularly intervened when masters and husbands abused their power and abandoned their responsibilities, because they had to pick up the social and economic pieces of broken domestic relations, whether they liked it or not. Churches regularly mediated domestic disputes for these reasons, seeing intervention as part of their mission to promote harmony among all their congregants. So did family members, as North Carolina's Westley Rhodes discovered. Rhodes, who had long "indulged himself in the habits of intemperance and abuse to his wife," beat her "in a most cruel manner." Mrs. Rhodes "fled to her father's house." In this case, it was Mrs. Rhodes's mother who came to the rescue. Marching back to Westley's house, she "reprimanded him for his conduct" and "struck him with a tobacco stem which she had picked up on the road."[34]

Slaves could not use their social networks against masters in the same way. But they, too, had ties outside their masters' households and the slave community. Slaves, for instance, occasionally fled to white neighbors' houses to evade beatings and to seek shelter afterward. In so doing, they expected more than a temporary haven. Exhibiting the bloody results of their own masters' brutality could prompt white neighbors to intervene. If direct action did not occur at that time, slaves still set the rumor mill in motion.[35] The experience of Judy, a South Carolina slave, suggests how innuendo could work its way through the neighborhood and find its way back to a master's doorstep. In 1823, Judy's master, Brother Johnson, charged her with disobedience and lying at their Baptist Church. Worst of all, according to Brother Johnson, was Judy's assertion that she had "good backers in the church to do the Evel she had done, or Else she wood not have done it." In her defense, Judy explained that she gave "ill Language" to her master and mistress "because she had not anough to Eat." She "did not humble herself" afterward, because she feared they would "tung lash" her. While hedging on the question of whether she had threatened action against the Johnsons through her church allies, she finally admitted that she might have said words to that effect. Although "backers" is too strong a word, Judy had effectively turned existing doubts about her master and mistress against them. Apparently congregation members

knew enough about the Johnsons' abuse to make their denial of
Judy's charges impossible. Instead, Brother and Sister Johnson
apologized not just for this act, but for their past mistreatment of
Judy as well. How the congregation knew about Judy's difficulties is unclear. Maybe some members saw or overheard for themselves. Or maybe Judy made sure that they knew. Either way,
she stood firm in her refusal to admit any wrongdoing toward her
master and mistress. Ultimately her recalcitrance got her excluded from the church. But neither was the congregation satis-
fied with the Johnsons' apology. It continued to investigate, sub-
jecting the couple to continual scrutiny. Several months into the
matter, Brother Johnson complained of the church "leving him
behind and working over his head." The church conceded it had,
and the issue cooled somewhat, but not completely. Four years
later the matter was still open and unresolved. Although Judy
was never received back into fellowship, the cloud of suspicion
that hung over the Johnsons never completely dissipated either.[36]

Local courts could operate as an extension of community authority as well. Wives, who had more legal presence than slaves,
occasionally brought their complaints to local courts and, in the
process, subverted stated legal practice at the appellate level.
Mary Meadows, for instance, had intended to file charges against
her husband just before his death. There is no record that she
ever did file charges. Perhaps her husband's death eliminated
the need. But court records, particularly those in North Carolina,
contain other women's complaints. Usually wives swore out
peace warrants, an action that brought their husbands under public scrutiny by forcing them to appear before a magistrate and
enter into bond to keep the peace toward their wives. Peace warrants were not an ideal solution. After posting bond, husbands
returned home in no mood for a cheerful reconciliation. If they
could not make bond and were jailed, wives could suffer econom-
ically. Still, peace warrants ensured public monitoring of husbands and penalties for further abuse. By implication, although
not by design, peace warrants also allowed wives a way out of the

confines of domestic privacy. When pressed, some wives used this opening to seize some control over their bodies and push concerns about their husbands' unchecked, absolute authority into the public arena. In the process, they legally transformed their husbands' legitimate governance into illegitimate violence that endangered the public order. Occasionally, local officials went one step further. Ignoring the law, they prosecuted husbands for the criminal offense of assaulting their wives.[37]

Local officials never relaxed the law in the same way for slaves. But their unwillingness to do so says as much as about the similarities as the differences between wives and slaves. Local officials only allowed wives to proceed with charges when the husband in question was poor and troublesome. They acted to limit the rights of her husband, not to recognize a wife's claims to legal personhood. Similarly, slaves were generally only acquitted of violence against a white person when the alleged victim was poor or otherwise socially marginal. In these instances, the courts protected masters by acquitting slaves. No one, for instance, was disposed to believe Lucressy Campbell, a poor white woman who charged a slave named Sam with rape. Campbell came alone to trial. She had no father, husband or other male relative to add his name to her case. Nor did she have any witnesses to the crime or to recommend her character. Her word amounted to little against the claims of six upstanding white citizens who lined up beside Sam's master to testify for Sam. Sam's acquittal, however, did not move him or any other slave closer to legal personhood. But it spoke volumes about Lucressy Campbell and, in a larger sense, the legal insignificance of a poor woman's word when she acted in her own name against the property of a wealthy, established master.[38]

Once the wheels of outside intervention were set in motion, wives and slaves often lost control and fell victim to the proceedings. Even neighbors and kin were not always sympathetic. Mary Meadows's repeated, increasingly desperate appeals for assistance fell on deaf ears. When assistance was forthcoming, it did not always promote the particular interests of those wives and slaves who made their complaints known. In South Carolina, neighbors resolved the problem of destitute and abused women by prosecuting their husbands for vagrancy. An open-ended charge that covered a wide range of "disorderly" conduct, vagrancy convictions gave communities the leverage to force more responsible behavior from husbands and, by extension, their wives as well. In North Carolina, which lacked South Carolina's rigid vagrancy laws, neighbors sent needy wives to the poorhouse instead.[39]

Wives and slaves found it even more difficult to articulate their views in terms recognized by the law. Forced into existing legal categories, their voices grew fainter or were eliminated altogether. The divorce petitions filed by husbands provide a good example. Hidden behind men's efforts to establish legal grounds for divorce are dissatisfied and obstinate wives who acted in ways not allowed in law and discouraged in practice. John Moore, for instance, had "expected meekness and pliancy of disposition and temper" from his wife, Lovey. Instead, he "met with opposition" and "suffered the most continued and violent torrent of invective that ever flowed from the mouth of a female." In another case, eight neighbors claimed that they often saw Ann Jane Bryan abuse her husband "in a most extravagant and outrageous manner."[40]

Just as a wife's wilfulness became "extravagant and outrageous" abuse for the legal purposes in divorce, her decision to leave her husband became adultery or even prostitution. Exercising a time-honored form of self-divorce, some women left their husbands and started over as if they had never been married. This is exactly what Mary Ann Clawson did when she left James Mills after just fifteen days of marriage and returned to her father's house; apparently she had second thoughts about the marriage after she learned that she would have to live with her in-laws. Mills tried to reconcile with her, proposing "to take her to the 'West' or any place she would choose for a residence." But

Mary Ann Clawson was happy where she was. She "not only refused" to go with him, "but on the last occasion drew a knife from her bosom and said that if he insisted on his right to make her return she would cut his throat!" Other women entered new relationships that passed as marriages. Although accused of prostitution by her husband, Rebecca Farrow had actually been living with William O'Neal for two years "as if they had been man and wife." Even women who claimed abandonment in their divorce petitions may not have been entirely truthful. By law, it was more difficult for wives to establish grounds for divorce if they were the ones who left. Mary Southwick, for instance, invoked the properly pathetic image of the abandoned, destitute wife in her divorce petition. But her husband countered with his own version of the story, claiming that she had left him, taking "all the property that originally belonged to her and also a considerable part of his property."[41]

It is even more difficult to locate slaves' voices in the legal records. Trials usually went forward as if the accused slave were not there at all. George's trial for the murder of James Meadows was typical. The documentation of the case is extensive, including two appeals that produced lengthy opinions. But there is no record of any word uttered by George. Legally, nothing he said could have altered the outcome of his case anyway. His fate rested entirely on the testimony of others. If anything, the appeals process marginalized him even more because it dealt with points of law, not the interpretation of the evidence. Sometimes, state supreme court justices pondered the theoretical balance between slaves' dual status as property and people and placed limits on masters' and other whites' power over slaves. Yet, while recognizing slaves' humanity, these decisions still denied them legal personhood. Where legally recognized people had rights to protect their bodies from others, the law defined slaves' acts of self-defense as a "natural" response exhibited by all animals when their lives were endangered. Like most cases where slaves were accused of violence, George's fell outside the legal category of

self-defense. In the first appeal, the state supreme court over-
turned his conviction on a procedural error. Although granted a
new trial, he was convicted again. This time the court turned
down his appeal, and George was hanged for the murder of James
Meadows.[42]

But George's silence should not be confused with acquiescence. That was the law's ploy. In the nineteenth-century South,
it silenced domestic dependents and then turned that silence into
acquiescence, affirming the "natural" hierarchies that subordinated slaves and wives. Their unruly actions became isolated,
criminal acts, the product of evil and demented minds, not of
legitimate complaints with the South's social structure. By contrast, violent acts committed against them were regrettable, but
necessary means to keep subordinates in their place. The court
personalized domestic dependents' complaints about unlimited,
arbitrary power as "private" disputes of no broad social consequence. The law thus contained domestic dependents within the
privacy of domestic space and placed limits on ideological cur-
rents that posited all people's capacity for self-governance and,
by extension, the necessity of their consent to the social contract
and their place within the body politic. But the law was never
completely successful. It gave men like James Meadows the
upper hand in dealing with their domestic dependents. But
James Meadows, for one, clearly had his work cut out if he
wished to play the patriarch. Ultimately, he and others like him
failed because domestic dependents fought back, physically
pushing their way into public space. That free white men, particularly those who were poor, continually fought amongst themselves suggests their insecurities as well as the actual contingency
of their authority. Only through constant struggle could they defend the physical borders theoretically allowed them in law.

Commentary by Peter Bardaglio

One of my most vexed memories, to use a phrase from Jacquelyn
Hall's eloquent keynote address, is a story that my father first

told me as a child. It involves his cousin Glenda from North Carolina and her husband Willie.[1] One evening Willie and his father
got into a fierce argument; what the dispute was about and
whether they had been drinking I don't remember. In any event,
things spiraled out of control and Willie's father went down the
street to his house and returned with a gun. Right there, in Glenda's kitchen, in front of her and the children, Willie was shot
dead by his father. To this day my father shakes his head in disbe-
lief when he recounts seeing the hole in the kitchen floor where
one of the bullets hit.

The story of Willie and his father made a big impression on
me. In my world, the kitchen was a safe place, protected from
this kind of violence. In my world, fathers did not shoot their
sons. The world that Glenda and her children lived in seemed
unimaginable to me, and yet there it was: they were family.

Laura Edwards, in this provocative paper, explores the role
of violence in southern households, examining in particular how
violence helped delineate the border between private and public.
Together with other scholars, among them Stephanie McCurry,
Victoria Bynum, and Martha Hodes, Edwards has transformed
the ways we understand and classify political actors, political debate, and political conflict in the antebellum South by showing
that the struggle over what gets categorized as private and what
gets categorized as public is political.[2] This new approach challenges the exclusive focus of traditional political history on events
such as the rise and fall of party systems, the nullification crisis,
the controversy over slavery in the territories, and the secession
movement. It promises to provide us with a richer and subtler
understanding of how southerners exercised power, challenged
power, and negotiated power, an approach that asks whether
what happened in Glenda's kitchen was simply a family tragedy.

Examining a wide array of local court records in North Carolina and South Carolina, Edwards shows how what we now refer
to as "domestic" violence involved issues at the heart of the

South's social and political order. By recognizing only certain kinds of violent acts as threats to the public order, the law ignored or downplayed the bulk of the violence encountered by southerners, especially wives and slaves. In doing so, the legal system buttressed a political and social system deeply committed to notions of hierarchy and inequality, a system that acknowledged "only certain people as public actors and only certain issues as public matters," as Edwards stated in the original version of this paper.

It will come as little surprise to those familiar with *Reconstructing the Household* that I support Edwards's call for a more expansive understanding of domestic dependents, one that includes slaves as well as women and children.[3] Only when we comprehend that southern lawmakers, planters, and other elites viewed slavery within a larger web of domestic relations that included husbands and wives, parents and children, and masters and servants will we fully grasp the interplay of race, class, and gender in the antebellum South. Nonetheless, I have to confess to a certain ambivalence about considering slavery as merely "a repressive extension of household heads' established rights." If bondage was simply an extension of a dynamic already at work in other domestic relations, and no more, then why did the southern legal system develop a separate set of procedures and rules for the prosecution of crimes involving slaves? At what point does a difference in degree become a difference in kind? Is it accurate to characterize the status of slaves as similar to that of wives and children (in the sense of being dependents) but worse? Or did slaves occupy a distinctive niche in the southern social structure? I don't pretend to have answers to these questions, but I do feel the need to sound a cautionary note: Even as we explore how the principle of domestic dependency threaded its way through southern ideas about both marriage and slavery, we should keep in mind the crucial ways in which these two institutions diverged. As Edwards herself recognizes, the auction block left far less room for negotiation and contestation than the altar.

The central contribution of Edwards's work, including her recent book *Gendered Strife and Confusion: The Political Culture
of Reconstruction,*[4] is its insistence on the agency of domestic
dependents. In contrast to Eugene Genovese's emphasis on the
effectiveness of planter hegemony, Edwards stresses the cracks
and fissures that erupted as southern slave holders sought to impose their authority.[5] Like the seventeenth-century system of
royal absolutism, the paternalism of household heads was never
as perfect in practice as it was in theory. Very few planters at-
tained the success of a Louis XIV; most more closely resembled
James I, whose absolutist pretensions rarely matched his actual
ability to fulfill them. Still, except for perhaps James Meadows
and a handful of other white southern men, few ended up experiencing the fate of a Charles I. In Meadows's case, of course, it
was not his head that was separated from his body.

Especially intriguing, I think, is Edwards's analysis of how
wives and slaves employed social networks to constrain the
power of husbands and masters. In a culture where one's standing rested in large part on the question of respectability and reputation, the power of peers to influence one's behavior should
not be underestimated. As Bertram Wyatt-Brown, Edward Ayers,
and others have pointed out, community sanction sometimes provided an even more effective tool than the law for enforcing social norms in the antebellum South.[6] Most suggestive here is Edwards's examination of how a local church in South Carolina
mediated a dispute between the slave Judy and her master,
Brother Johnson, compelling the latter to apologize for his abusive treatment of the slave. I would urge Edwards to look even
more closely at these sorts of church records, which are a relatively untapped source of information about social relations in
the Old South.[7] I would also like to know more about the different ways in which women and slaves used the social networks of
southern towns, where presumably the behavior of husbands and
slaveholders came under closer scrutiny than in the countryside

and where the pressure of community sanctions could be applied more readily.

By enlarging our notions of public agency, Edwards makes it possible for us to see issues like expanded grounds for divorce in a new light. As Jane Censer has noted, Southern lawmakers passed new divorce laws during the antebellum period that included cruelty clauses. In North Carolina, Tennessee, Arkansas, Louisiana, and Texas, the legislative language embraced not only physical cruelty as a cause for divorce, but also what were termed "personal indignities."[8] With a perspective that views women in divorce suits as public actors, we can now see that wronged wives who insisted that they be protected from abusive husbands helped to shape the judicial doctrine of mental cruelty. These women seized on the open-ended nature of the indignities clause and managed to persuade the courts to apply it in a way that recognized cruelty without physical violence. Thus Justice Christopher Scott declared in 1849 his manly resolution to retain a strict construction of the law, but then went on to enumerate the following acts as constituting a "personal indignity": "rudeness, vulgarity, unmerited disdain, abusive language, malignant ridicule and every other plain manifestation of settled hate, alienation and estrangement, both of word and action." Seeing her opportunity, Nancy Rose, the plaintiff in the case, took it: she obtained a divorce on the basis of testimony that her husband had encouraged her slaves to disobey her, that he had called her a liar as well as a "lazy white woman," and that he slept in one of the outbuildings during the last five months of their relationship.[9]

Although Edwards calls our attention to the previously overlooked ways that wives and slaves participated in nineteenth-century political debates, her paper does little to explore the agency of children. As the writings of Robert Coles remind us, however, children do have moral and political lives,[10] and as historians committed to reconstructing the past in all its complexity, we have a special responsibility for examining the experiences of people whose labor was so crucial to the building of rural society.

Here the recent work of Elliott West on growing up in the American West, Wilma King on slave youth, and James Marten on children in the Civil War suggests how we can begin to think about nineteenth-century youngsters as historical actors.[11]

Marten, in particular, writes about the ways in which the violence of the Civil War influenced the lives of children in the South. In one North Carolina community during the summer of 1863, the children's activities took on a distinctively martial spirit, one informed by the ideology of southern liberty and individualism. Forming a militia company of sorts, a band of about a dozen boys ranging in age from six to twelve decided to launch a raid on a local watermelon patch. The owner of the patch, according to Marten, "had broken with community tradition and banned poachers." Keenly aware of this infringement on their customary rights, the boys armed themselves with shotguns loaded with peas. Although the owner and his son fired off shotguns, the rain of vegetable pellets drove them from the field; the boys grabbed five of the biggest watermelons and went off to celebrate this defense of their "watermelon rights." The boys' readiness to employ violence to resolve conflicting claims clearly reflected the world around them, a world in which their elders had rushed to arm themselves against what was perceived to be a northern assault on their personal liberties. For these boys, violence and politics went hand in hand.[12]

Besides the experience of children, another aspect of violence in the southern household that needs fleshing out is a sense of change over time. Edwards asserts in the original version of this paper, for example, that "in the antebellum South, free black women could never inhabit the legal category wife . . . because their husbands never had the rights of legally recognized persons." The status of free blacks, both male and female, was not static during this period, however; in the 1850s it worsened dramatically due to the intensifying antislavery movement in the North and the growing sectional conflict.[13] Complicating matters further is the fact that the late antebellum period saw significant improvements in the law of married women's property rights, divorce and child custody.[14] How did these developments shape the encounters of blacks and white women with violence?

Part of any commentator's job is to provide a sense of context. Well, what's the big picture here? Laura Edwards has rightly underscored the centrality of domestic violence as a political issue and has made us question how the modifier "domestic" influences our perceptions of violence directed against household members. This is a topic that few of us are comfortable with, making it hard to focus on for long. But when we do, as Edwards does here with an admirable combination of balance and controlled outrage, it becomes obvious that wife battering, child sexual abuse, and rape are not just individual misfortunes; they are expressions of power relations that embody the social constellation of race, gender, and class in American society.

In part because it makes us uncomfortable and in part because it provides such a clear window on the dynamics of coercion that shape so much of our daily lives, domestic violence has long been dismissed as a valid subject for historical inquiry. Put another way, a sophisticated analysis of domestic violence like that carried out here by Edwards threatens the status quo because it has the potential to unmask one of the most powerful ways that American society produces and reproduces patterns of domination and subordination, structures of inequality and hierarchy. This is not the sort of narrative that has much appeal for those invested in the historical story that has occupied center stage for so long: the rise of the American nation and the progressive unfolding of liberty, equality, and democracy that supposedly accompanied this rise. Anyone who thinks that the American public is ready to abandon this story need only tune into the ongoing battle over efforts to tell a more ambiguous and nuanced history in high school textbooks to be convinced otherwise.[15]

Despite continued support for what might be thought of as the master narrative, there is an emerging counter-narrative, one that illuminates the extent to which the republic has been a contested body politic rather than an abstract set of principles whose potential has been gradually but steadily realized by the harmonious consent of the American people. Domestic violence should be a crucial element in this counter-narrative. The questions that Laura Edwards's thoughtful paper and other recent studies pose about the politics of domestic violence promise to open up new ways of integrating the histories of elites and ordinary people, of what is often thought of as "high politics" and the struggles of everyday life, of what we all too blithely refer to as the public and the private.[16] By revealing the socially constructed character of these categories, such work creates the space for the telling of stories that have been neglected or suppressed for far too long, stories that may indeed prove to be vexed memories, but which transform the way we view the present and the future, as well as the past.

Citizens, Soldiers' Wives, and "Hiley Hope Up" Slaves: The Problem of Political Obligation in the Civil War South

STEPHANIE McCURRY

> The Negroes is very Hiley Hope up that they will soon
> Be free.
> —William H. Lee to Jefferson Davis, May 4, 1861

As early as May of 1861 William Lee, a yeoman farmer from Alabama, pointed out to Jefferson Davis what was destined to become one of the great considerations in the political and military contest of the Civil War: slaves' pursuit of freedom. "[t]hire is a Nother question to rise with us," he informed Davis, "the Negroes is very Hiley Hope up that they will soon Be free so i think that you Had Better order out All the Negroe felers from 17 years oald up Ether fort them up or put them in the army and Make them fite like good fells for wee ar in danger of our lives hear among them."[1]

Lee was a good deal ahead of the game in worrying about the loyalty of slaves. Since the campaigns of the previous fall, secessionist politicians had focused on mobilizing free white men, struggling to articulate their stake in secession and southern independence. It was the voters they worried about, and especially nonslaveholding ones, those first class citizens invested with the right of the franchise, the power to decide the question of nationhood, and, not inconsequentially, the obligation to bear arms in

its defense. Would voters embrace secession? Would they fight
to defend the new nation? Thus was the problem of political obligation first confronted in the Civil War South.

But if it was first defined around the constituency politicians
knew they had—adult white men—then that antebellum construction of the body politic soon showed signs of strain. For as
"the crisis of our destiny" was met and passed and secession gave
way to war, state and Confederate governments were forced into
a growing recognition of the political relevance of the previously
marginal: white women now soldiers' wives, and William Lee's
"Hiley Hope up slaves." However unlikely the prospect of success, securing the allegiance of this diverse southern majority—
not freemen but their dependents—became an imperative of
Confederate discourse and policy. When state officials attempted
to harness the political agency of the disfranchised to the pursuit
of its own goals, however, the problem of political obligation acquired startling new dimensions. For if it was difficult to articulate the citizen-freeman's obligation to the state and to command
his body in military service, how could that obligation be articulated and extracted in the absence of the rights and privileges
that were its usual corollary?

In raising the possibility of military service for slave men, William Lee's letter to Jefferson Davis directs our attention to the
complexity of the southern body politic, to the political subjectivity of the disfranchised, and to the problem of political obligation
in the Confederacy. It challenges us to write a new kind of political history.

CITIZENS

While the preoccupation with rights has been unflagging since
the eighteenth century, the whole issue of citizens' obligation
has been underdeveloped in American political theory, as Linda
Kerber has recently pointed out. "The federal constitution was
remarkably silent on obligation," she reminds us, and "the Civil

War amendments continued in the same spirit," with citizenship described in terms of its privileges and immunities, not duties and obligations. Political history, too, has followed the liberal framework by focusing more on the progressive expansion of citizens' rights than on the means by which governments articulated citizens' obligations at particular historical junctures. If we now understand "the extent to which the meaning of rights has been linked to gender," Kerber muses, we have hardly begun to consider that there is a "history of gendered obligation."[2]

When southern advocates of secession made their case to "the people" in the fall of 1860, they acted in a fashion preeminently American, talking obsessively about "rights": rights imperilled, invaded, violated. In ways historians have usually failed to recognize, however, secessionists' litany of Black Republican abuses constituted as well the state's claim on its citizens for defense. Rights and duties, white southerners had been told repeatedly, existed in reciprocal relation. So although most radical politicians denied that secession would bring on war, they still cast the sectional struggle in martial terms, dwelling on the citizen's duty to defend or "protect" the state to which he was indebted for all the rights and immunities he customarily enjoyed. As always, political mobilization did the early work of war. Unknowing of the burden it would have to bear, then, secessionist politicians worked out the pieces of the "glouris cose," as one yeoman farmer put it.[3]

Even popular shorthand versions of "the Cause" point to the discursive work women and gender did in the secession crisis. "A call has been made upon the young, brave and chivalrous sons of Georgia and the South to leave home and the endearments that bind us to our families to defend the rights and interests of our mothers and sisters and homes." So young Edwin Bass put it to his sister in the high days of April 1861. "Tis glorious to die for one's country and in defense of innocent girls and women from the fangs of lecherous Northern hirelings," William Plane wrote to his wife in June of the same year. "Whenever Yankee

feet tramples upon Georgia soil and I am called upon to expel
them, I shall fight as if they were entering your dwelling or ready
to give the deadly blow to my dear wife and child." So D.T.
Pound put it to his parents in September 1861. "I tell you," he
finished, "I shall feel like I am fighting for home sweet home."
"We have everything to fight for—our wives, children, land and
principles," Tulius Rice wrote from Richmond in 1863.[4]

The absolute centrality of gender and sexuality to secessionists'
early construction of the Black Republican threat and of white
men's obligation to serve the state is striking—and long overdue
of analysis. So cryptic as to be almost insensible, of proportions
simultaneously mythic and minute, the Confederate cause as
white southern men represented it invites a different kind of
scrutiny than it has yet received. "The conviction that they fought
for their homes and women gave many Confederate soldiers remarkable staying power in the face of adversity," James McPherson has recently argued. But where he treats those sentiments
transparently, as evidence of soldiers' idealism, a closer interro-
gation yields both more precisely historical and more problematic conclusions about "What They Fought For."[5]

The analysis begins properly not with soldiers but with politicians and voters, not in 1863 or even 1861 but in 1859 and 1860.
Only in the longer view do white men's wartime utterances reveal their mimetic quality. For in consistently linking their duty
to the state with their duty to protect white women Confederate
soldiers literally echoed secessionists politicians' earlier call to
arms. Soldiers' talk about protecting women and womanhood
cannot, therefore, be taken simply as truth—a transparent explanation of why they "really" went to war—nor can it be treated
cynically as meaningless repetition of high-sounding ideals. It
should, rather, be taken for what it was: an indication of the
power of gender in public discourse and of the complicated relationship between public rhetoric and private consciousness. Seen
in this light, then, the specifics of the secessionists' case for political obligation are revealing of southern politics, both past and yet

to come: the troubling cleavages in the late antebellum southern body politic, the way in which gender as well as race was used to breach them, and the matrix of manhood, citizenship, and military service as southerners understood it in the era of Civil War.

Louis Malone Ayers, a South Carolina politician, showed how the radicals' case usually worked. The task, Ayers instructed the newly formed district Minute Men's Association in early November 1860, was "to inform every man (nonslaveholder as well as slaveholder) of the deep and vital interests that are involved in our slavery institutions," to convince them "to strike as men strike, who strike for their hearths and firesides." "There is a principle involved in this contest as important to one of these classes as the other," another planter politician declared: as "freemen" you are called upon to "save your country's honor and that of your families." By mid-November 1860 the shorthand was already fully comprehensible to popular audiences. "The election of a Black Republican President should be the signal for the dissolution of the Union," the planter-politician John Palmer told his audience at a rural Charleston muster field. "Only under a Southern Confederacy" will we find "security of our rights and the very safety of our hearths and firesides."[6] Even before federal troops put foot in the South, long before Sherman burned his path across Georgia to the Sea, every "freeman's" personal domain was put in imminent danger of invasion.[7] The language of invasion was conventional by the time it was descriptive of military reality.

The political calculus is not difficult to discern. Enumerating the dangers to slavery and slaveholders' interests clearly would not do the job. The "circle of ownership" was just too narrow. On the hustings wealthy planter politicians chose their words carefully, worried about anything "calculated," as one put it, "to widen the breach between the slaveholder and the nonslaveholder." "When the battle comes in earnest," Daniel Hamilton, U.S. Marshall for Charleston, had written to his friend, the United States Senator William Porcher Miles, in January 1860, "you will find an element of great weakness in our own nonslave-holding population." "I mistrust our own people more than I fear all of the efforts of the abolitionists," he added a few weeks later.[8] A deep anxiety about the political loyalty of nonslaveholders, including propertied yeoman farmers, revealed itself in every political venue, not least in loud assertions of class unity.

By the fall of 1860 everyone spoke as and for "the people." With rare exception the "rights of slavery" and slaveholders became the "rights of the South," or in planter-legislator Oliver William's expert phrase, "the rights of freemen" to the constitutional "protection of person and property" against the "tampering thieves of abolition." Like the "mom and apple pie" American men said they were fighting for in World War Two, the folksy "hearts and firesides," "families and homes," proved a winning construction of what was at stake in the struggle over slavery, secession, and southern independence, and served as touchstone for an ever more militaristic state politics. "He who will not protect his property will soon have none to protect," Williams warned at a meeting in May 1860. Nothing short of a redefinition of "the aristocracy of possession," as one editorialist aptly put it, was at work in the representation of the Black Republican threat.[9]

But what exactly was that property on which abolitionists had designs? What was the nature of the threat they posed to the ordinary yeoman voter? Certainly that property was racial, whiteness itself, as John Townsend of South Carolina, J.D.B. DeBow, Joseph Brown of Georgia and countless other southern politicians and intellectuals rushed to point out. But something as fundamental as race—and inseparable from it—constituted the property rights at risk in Lincoln's election.

When Joseph Brown, the Governor of Georgia, identified the sufficient justification for secession in his public letter of December 7, 1860, he pointed to the Republican Party's avowed "purpose to take from us our property, so soon as it has the power." Asking why nonslaveholders should help defend slaveholder's property, he answered rhetorically: "If our *right of property* are assailed by a common enemy, shall we not help each other? Or if I have a wife and children and a house, and another has neither wife and children nor house. Will he, therefore, stand by and see my house burned and my wife and children butchered, because he has none." For Brown, as for more radical men, property in women constituted the fundamental case of property rights themselves; a man had an obligation to protect what he by right possessed. Nor was the adversion to women as property simply analogical to slaves. For populists like Brown, exclusive possession of white women was at the heart of whiteness and freedom itself. "The [poor white people] are a superior race, and they feel and know it," he insisted. "Abolish slavery and you make the negroes their equals, legally and socially." Then, "the negro and the white man, and their families must labor in the field together as equals . . . very soon their children must marry together as equals." Brown's references to "amalgamation" were more restrained than some others but the meaning was clear. "Wealth is timid and wealthy men cry for peace," he proclaimed. "When it becomes necessary to defend our rights against so foul a domination, I would call upon the mountain boys." No one should doubt the capacity of mountain men," he proclaimed, "their patriotism and valor to defend their rights when invaded."[10]

Others were more hysterical than Brown in exploiting popular conceptions of the rights of manhood and the property in women on which they were based. "Vigilance," a South Carolina fire eater, used the opening afforded by John Brown's raid to cast the threat of invasion in explicitly sexual terms.[11] The scenario he sketched was explicitly sexual; it focused centrally on the rape of chaste southern women; and it confused utterly the racial identity of the rapist."History teaches us that the most effective mode to rouse an ignorant people is to appeal to their superstition and lust," "Vigilance" asserted in clear reference to slave men. "Nat Turner" appealed to superstition, he noted, and so do the "travelling agents" of abolition currently "put[ting] the devil in negros heads." "Blacks have been tampered with in this district," he continued, asking "[W]hat man," after hearing William Seward's Rochester speech, "who is himself a father of grown daughters can vote for such a brute to be President." Now thoroughly conflating the actions of Black Republicans and the slave men they were inciting with prospects of success to rape and murder, he finished ominously: "Forewarned—forearmed! Let us teach our daughters how to defend themselves against his [Seward's] threats of negro rape."[12] The "brute" was obviously white, but was the rapist black? By the time "Vigilance" was finished metaphorical and corporeal blackness were so fully conflated as to make the question unanswerable if not wholly irrelevant.[13]

A few things are clear, however: how radicals used race to confuse and inflame the sexual threat presented by the Republican ascendancy in federal politics; and how freemen's property in their "own" women—wives, daughters—was put at risk in the struggle over slavery and southern independence. "The enemy is at the gateway," George Elliott, another South Carolinian, proclaimed a month later. "The honor and purity of the hearthstones are not safe [and] lovely dependent woman at our own fireside is not free from death or pollution." It is only what is due to our manhood, he concluded, "to act decisively against those who wage a war of extermination against our institutions."[14]

In attempting to bind up the weak spots in the southern body politic, secessionists like "Vigilance" and, belatedly, Joseph Brown drew on and exploited deeply held but usually unarticulated assumptions about the "natural" positions of men and women in gender and (hetero)sexual relations—assumptions saturated, as were all relations of power in the Old South, by the institution of slavery. The freeman was master of his own household and the dependents it enclosed in purportedly protective embrace: violation was spatial (the dwelling, the hearthstone, the fireside) and sexual ("pollution," rape, "foul domination" of chaste woman). In the constant references to "our property" and "our institutions," to the "hearths and firesides" on which Black Republicans had designs, it was not so much on slaves and slav-

ery that fire-eaters put their emphasis but on chaste women and
southern womanhood; not on the property in slaves which constituted a minority of voters as masters, but the property in white
women which constituted the common patrimony of freemen in
the slave republic.

Cast in terms of property rights invaded, white men's protection of women appears in a new light indeed. It renders more
problematic that central part of the glorious cause, and it rescues
from nature and grounds in history the conventional gender
script of protected and protector. To protect one first had to pos-
sess. It was, not inconsequentially, the free (white) man's ability
to claim a right of property in his wife's body—that is, exclusive
sexual access—that distinguished him from a slave man, or a dishonored one.[15] Slave men had been routinely denied "the privilege of appropriating to themselves those of the other sex," federal officials would explain during the war in a bald admission of
the propertied character of marriage and manhood both.[16] But if
the references to Black Republican "brutes" exploited a deep-
seated popular belief in man's predatory sexual nature then they
also expressed ambivalence about whether slave men possessed
the same nature as freemen. All of the contingencies of slavery—
and the discursive necessities of its defense—can be read in the
particular rape complex secessionists deployed.

Thinking about men's predatory nature was not new in 1860.
As early as 1835, Thomas Roderick Dew had offered southern
readers his conservative version of modern scientific thinking
about "The Characteristic Differences Between the Sexes." His
long treatment included a portrait of man "in all races" so violent
and aggressive in nature, so driven to contests for domination
over other men, that they turned the world into a battleground
and women into booty of war. In Dew's rigidly binary construction of sexual difference, man was the warrior and assailant on
the fortress of chastity, woman the guardian of chastity and se-
ductress of man. Woman, then, was simultaneously chaste and
seductive, man simultaneously protector and predator. So preva-

lent were such views among southern whites that the planter and
one-time governor, James Henry Hammond, felt justified in
using them to (publicly) explain the rape [not his word] of slave
women as an "irregularity natural enough" among men. Nor was
this a view conditioned exclusively by race, for Hammond used
the same argument (privately) to justify his own sexual abuse of
his teenage nieces: it was only natural, he explained, given "the
greatness of my temptation."[17] Ella Gertrude Clanton Thomas, a
plantation mistress, shared men's view of the matter: When she
referred in her diary to men's "natures but one degree removed
from the brute creation and with no more control over their passions," she was talking about sex, and she was talking, without
exception, about white planter class men.[18] But if manhood "in all
races," as Dew put it, had universal properties it was no essential
entitlement. Slave men could not lay claim to manhood; as slaves,
black men could be denied sexual access to white women, and
exclusive sexual access to particular black women. As freemen,
however, the matter might stand rather differently.

Fevered contemplations of that possibility characterized the
articles that poured into radical papers just before the 1860 elections. John Townsend, a recent convert to the radical cause, articulated clearly the matrix of manhood (including sexual right), citizenship, and military service as southern white men understood
it—and the particular fear of emancipation it involved.[19] There
were two possibilities under Black Republican rule, Townsend
declared in late October. The first was the predictable one: "The
midnight glare of the incendiaries torch will illuminate the country from one end to another, while pillage, violence, murder, poi-
son and rape will fill the air with the demonic revelry of all the
bad passions of an ignorant, semi-barbarous race, urged to mad-
ness by the licentious teachings of our northern brethren." If
they did not secede, in other words, southern freemen would live
to see their women seized as booty of war by Black Republicans
or in victorious revelry (not revenge) by emancipated black men,
formerly their slaves. But the second scenario Townsend envi-

sioned was less predictable and even more revealing of the free-man-citizen's imperiled prerogatives. "It is possible," Townsend pondered in concluding his article, "that no antagonism will arise between the two races—and harmony and identification will take their place." Then, "Amalgamation must be the result." The last and worst thing white freemen had to face was not that slaves would be rapists but rather that white women, their "own" women, might make consensual sexual arrangements with black men, now freemen, victors of war, and the new protectors. Women could not be trusted; they would always revert to sexual type, trained to the arts of seduction as their politics of survival in the world of predatory males. Black men would emerge from slavery fully possessed of the rights of manhood—including its characteristic sexual and political rights—earned, as was custom-ary, by military service. This most frightening of possibilities was the one most relevant to the post-emancipation South and it eerily foretold the New South career of the politics of protecting white womanhood. From this perspective, as Townsend put it to rural Charleston voters, secession and southern independence was the only manly expression of "your duty to your families and to the state."[20]

In ubiquitous references to "invasion," "pollution," rape and the protection of white womanhood, fire-eaters skillfully invoked the spatial arrangements of masterhood as yeoman farmers and planters alike understood them in the South, and linked the viola-tion of the state and its rights to the violation of the household and its masters' rights. The strategy was not exclusive to South Carolina. "I think I see in the future a gory head rise above our horizon," T. R. R. Cobb declared in the midst of Georgia's heated debate. "Its name is Civil War. Already I can see the prints of his bloody fingers upon our lintels and door-posts. The vision sickens me already and I turn your view away."[21] In Georgia as in South Carolina, "the sovereignty of the state" and the sovereignty of the home were one and the same.[22] When you vote, Cobb urged his fellow legislators, "remember the trembling hand of a loved

wife, as she whispered her fears from the incendiary and the as-
sassin. Recall the look of indefinable dread with which the little
daughter inquired when your returning footsteps should be
heard. And if there be manhood in you, tell me if this is the
domestic tranquility which this 'glorious Union' has achieved."
"As brothers, as friends, as Georgia's sons, let us come and take
counsel together how we shall avenge her wrongs, promote her
prosperity, and preserve her honor."[23] Georgia, like the other
women a freeman loved, now required his protection.

"Georgia," "Mother Carolina," "[o]ur political mother," "insulted mother"—images of the state as chaste woman violated
proliferated across the South. Here, as in other republican regimes, such "psychosymbolics" (to borrow Lynn Hunt's phrase)
served quite transparently to root the political and martial duties
of male citizens not in an abstraction, the state, but in the intimate body of the mother ("the soil which gave him birth," as one
man put it) and in men's already acknowledged responsibilities to
women closer to home.[24] It was in the pertinent and emotionally
charged connection between political issues and personal ones
that radical discourse worked and that the case for political obligation was made in 1860 and early 1861. "The aid of every loyal
son is now needed to defend the rights and honor of his political
mother, where nestles the home of his wife and children, and
where is deposited all his property for their support." So John
Townsend made the case for southern independence in the late
fall of 1860.[25] It was, then, in specifically gendered terms that the
popular case for secession was made; yeoman farmers and their
planter neighbors were urged to prove their manhood in defense
of vulnerable woman, symbolic and real.

Would-be Confederates were hardly the first to make recourse
to a gendered politics of nation-making and war-making. And indeed, their particular tactics (the symbolic representation of the
state as woman, the invocation of rape, and the necessity of protecting women and womanhood) are strikingly like those in evi-

dence in revolutionary France and World War One Britain, to take but two examples. Discrete parts of Confederate rhetoric— the rape complex and the protection of white woman, most specifically—also proved their staying power in southern politics, appearing repeatedly and ever more malevolently until the 1880s and 1890s when they carried much of the discursive weight of the movement for black male disfranchisment.[26] Viewed in comparative perspective, the very sameness of the images and discursive moves becomes meaningful, pointing up the power of women, gender, and male "sex-right" to fabricate unity in moments of political crisis. Yet it is only in comparative perspective that the particularity of any one case comes into clear focus. For if would-be Confederates invoked the specter of rape to call yeomen to arms, and if they used the references to "black" Republicans to racialize that threat, their rape complex was decidedly more metaphorical and less corporeal than the one Jacquelyn Dowd Hall and Glenda Gilmore have described in the making of the Jim Crow South or of the British propagandists Susan Grayzel has described in World War One Britain. Secessionists neither fingered particular black men as rapists or identified particular white women as victims, nor did they try to fabricate "real" documentary evidence of the rape threat as their latter-day southern counterparts would; they didn't talk about rape in reference to the impregnation of particular women or dwell on the miscegenous issue of rape as the British did in World War One propaganda.

That all politics has a "family model," every revolution its "family romance(s)," and that every state attempts to harness forms of deference, loyalty, and obligation customary to households and family relations now seems entirely plausible; Lynn Hunt's argument about the French Revolution has applicability far beyond that particular case. But the Confederate case highlights one feature of this gendered politics not central to Hunt's analysis: that the family is not simply the model of state politics but provides, more concretely, the line of connection between citizens and the state.

"The institution of heterosexual marriage," Nancy Cott has recently pointed out, is "the most direct link of public authority to gender formation, [is] the primary institution that makes the public order a gender order." As such, "marital status has, traditionally, not only defined individuals' household and sexual relationships but has also shaped their civil and even political status." So in the western political tradition, it was "a man's headship of a family, his responsibility for dependent wife and children, [that] qualified him to be a participating member of a state."[27] But if that headship of a family endows a man with the full complement of citizen's rights—or excludes him from them, as the case of the slave man pointedly reminds us—it also constitutes the means by which the state secures the individual citizen to the pursuit of its own political ends.[28]

Faced with the problem of political obligation in the secession crisis, secessionist politicians and the Confederate states and central government after them, turned women into "objects of obligation," to borrow Robert Westbrook's apt phrase, and figured the state around the body of the woman—wife, daughter, mother.[29] The duty of the citizen-freeman reiterated the duty of the husband; the state reiterated the family or, more specifically, marriage, its foundational relation. By the time secessionists had finished it really could seem, as so many ordinary white soldiers would later say, that "the glouris cose" they fought for was the protection of woman.[30]

The success of this solution to the problem of political obligation is hardly in question: one voter and soldier after another reiterated its claims, sometimes verbatim. Its consequences, however, have not fully been considered. By articulating the relationship of individual citizens to the state through the constituent element of the family, secessionists saddled Confederate officials with a never-ending struggle over local loyalties and political authority. Mobilized to the cause of southern independence by an obligation to protect hearth, home, and womanhood, freemen-citizens might well wonder to which state, precisely, they owed loyalty and military service: to the immediate locality and its militia; to the state in which they lived—Georgia, for example—and its political and military authorities; or to the newly created Confederate state and its political and military authorities? "We are composed mostly of married men of families, therefore we want a place in our state," volunteer John Allen informed Governor Joseph Brown of Georgia in September 1861, and "feel that twelve months will be best for us and our families." [31] Throughout the war white men of military age attempted to define the state to which they owed military obligation, empowered by the original terms of mobilization.

Much certainly has been written about the conflict over state rights in the Confederacy. Not much noticed in the discussion, however, is the way in which secessionists' gendered call to arms authorized a very local notion of defense—literally home protection—thus rendering the task of nation-making the more difficult. Men who went into the army happily in 1861 proclaiming their duty to "protect your interests and rights, my mother and sister," were trying to get out by 1863, motivated by the same concerns. "Oh Mollie," William Stillwell wrote his wife in August 1863, "I think of the thousands of widows and fatherless children all over our land," and understand why "hundreds of our men are deserting;" William Moore couldn't write his wife, but he did swear out a petition detailing the ages and sexes of his nine children (7 girls) to appeal for exemption from state military service on the grounds that his wife and children "are solely dependent on his labor for their support;" 53 people from his neighborhood signed the petition.[32] Family sacrifice and the vulnerability of their women became the currency of Confederate petitioning. Jacob Blount put it plainly to Joseph Brown in 1863: "I am willing to defend my country but I as well as other men want my wife and children protected."[33] The protection of womanhood and the defense of their "rights and interests" was soon at odds with military service, the private duties of husband and father antagonistic to the public political obligation of the citizen-soldier.

SOLDIERS' WIVES AND SLAVES

All legitimate governments "rest upon the consent of the governed," Jefferson Davis acknowledged in his inaugural address as President of the Confederate States of America.[34] The full import of those words, and the contradictions into which they plunged the C.S.A., would emerge only over time. The gender and racial politics of nation-making did not end with secession. Far from it. Secessionists' solution to the problem of political obligation—to mobilize citizens in reference to their property in household dependents—left those dependents themselves beyond the direct reach of the state. Initially, that was not a matter of much political consequence. Nobody, including Jefferson Davis, was worried about securing the consent of white women or slaves. But as the now substantial literature on the home front, Confederate "morale," and the destruction of slavery suggests, it was not long before individual state and Confederate governments were forced to contend with the political desires and actions of the dependent and disfranchised majority. In ways entirely different and by no means complementary, white soldiers' wives and slaves "Hiley Hope up" for freedom, seized the opportunities the war offered to figure themselves as subjects, of politics and political history in the Civil War South.[35]

Secessionist and Confederate representations of white women as objects of political obligation were entirely consistent with conventional understandings of married women's legal and domestic identity in the mid-nineteenth-century United States. The state itself could not reach the married woman, Linda Kerber has recently reminded us, without disturbing coverture: marriage was woman's state, her husband the authority to which she owed duty. Most of the resistance to women's suffrage in the nineteenth century, she points out, rested on this fact.[36]

Any significant variation that the antebellum and Civil War South offered on the national theme built upon slavery. The region's virulent practice of coverture reached deep into white households and utterly ignored black ones. The Presbyterian minister Benjamin Morgan Palmer put it plainly: In the "family, that model state, subjection to law" originates with the authority of man as "the head of the woman." By the time subjection is proscribed to the "servant" [read slave] it had "already been exemplified not only in the headship of the husband but in the wifely obedience which is its commentary. Submission . . . will yield all that is incumbent upon the wife."[37] Whatever their official legal status, then, adult white women were not regarded as citizens: "This Constitution was made for white men—citizens of the U.S.," T. R. R. Cobb of Georgia proclaimed in November 1860, and the "right of suffrage should be given to none but citizens of the U.S." Cobb wasn't thinking about white women—he was objecting to the enfranchisement of some free black men in the 1860 elections—but his view of the matter applied as well to women, governed by coverture and notions of household representation. In August 1863, then, a group of men and women from Bullock County, Georgia, reflected the common sense of the matter in a petition that divided their signatures neatly into two columns: "Citizens names" and "Soldiers wives names."[38]

Clearly adult southern white women's political identity and status was defined through marriage. As such it reflected their own particular property in whiteness. Slave women's marital status had no legal or public meaning in the Civil War South and even in federally occupied areas black soldiers in the Union Army fought a difficult battle to have their wives recognized, much less compensated, as "soldiers' wives."[39] White southern women made the most of their second-hand standing in relation to the state. Though conforming entirely to the substance of coverture and holding white women at a distance from the formal political sphere, "soldiers' wives" was a political identity with possibilities. Confederate state governments had incurred a political debt to soldiers and the women they were mobilized ostensibly to protect; it was not long into the war before women, empowered now as "soldiers' wives," moved to redeem it.[40] Their loyalty, their allegiance, and their support for state policies—especially military service—had to be considered; individual state and Confederate governments had acquired a new and undesired constituency.

The wartime recognition of white women's political significance was not entirely unprecedented. In the antebellum period, the idea of household representation through the white male franchise had little substance; households were not little democracies. But at critical moments in antebellum campaigns, politicians had revealed a fear of female influence in trying to harness it to partisan ends. Secessionists' flattery of white women's influence as wives and mothers expressed that kind of anxiety. "[A]t this time of threatened difficulties, it is the women who have been foremost in the cause," the editor of the *Charleston Mercury* proclaimed in November 1860, in what would become the standard public line about the war and a staple of the Lost Cause. Elite women's show of support for secession and southern independence was critical to the radicals' construction of the "manly" cause and women's bodies and voices were commandeered to that end in every public venue. "I would rather die than hold a position of inferiority and vassalage to the North," one country lady is reported to have said in a letter to a city friend. "And the dominant feeling of my heart is to *leave* a state where men are too cowardly to protect their women, and too mercenary to risk their money." Louisa McCord, one of the South's few female public intellectuals, issued a sterner warning to elite women to prove themselves "fitting wives and mothers of freemen" through their willingness to sacrifice beloved sons and husbands.[41] That passive construction of women's political role ("giving up" for the cause) has had long currency in southern myth and history, dubious though it always was in a descriptive sense. Most women were not consulted by "their" men; most husbands, and sons too, did precisely what they wanted, as more than a few women later complained to Confederate authorities in seeking the discharge of their menfolk.[42]

White women had a role in antebellum southern politics, a largely symbolic one that culminated on the eve of war in the gender ceremonies of flag presentations, public leave-takings at train stations, and the ubiquitous cheering of soldiers by the "ladys." [43] "We had a fine time of hit," one yeoman farmer delighted in a letter to his brother and sister about his trip to camp in August 1861. "[W]e was cherd all a long the way by croud of sitecens. a flag was a waven over most ever house and every winder crouded with ladys and the sides of the road linde with them throwing appels and boquets of flowers in the cars."[44] War made the man; woman was the ostensible reason and indispensable witness.

If white women figured mostly symbolically in southern politics before the war, then that soon changed. Rejecting the passive role scripted for them, white women—yeoman and poor white ones especially—attempted to secure the substance of protection. In petitions and correspondence to state governors, to the Confederate Secretary of War, and to Jefferson Davis, they placed themselves on the political agenda, empowered, as they often put it, as "women [whose] husbands and sons are now in service or has died."[45]

Most adopted the appropriate posture of women and petitioners while calling clearly on the state to live up to its promise to protect them. So "we the unsined Ladys" of Berrien County, Georgia petitioned "Goviner Brown for a little assistance if you pleas sir." Requesting the detailing of a shoemaker to their neighborhood they drew a pathetic picture of their circumstances. "We live in a flat low siction of the country and we have a grate chance of children in this section and the women and children has the work all to do and the wether is gitting cold." If Brown sent the shoemaker, they promised, "we will trie to attend to our affairs and let our Husbands trye to help drive back the enemy from off of our soil." Twenty-two women signed, all "Mrs" somebody.[46] One yeoman woman even appealed to Brown as wife to husband, rendering him state patriarch: "I wont you to think how yore wife would be in my situation," she wrote, begging him to "releas my husband fore a sort time."[47]

Others stepped into public policy more aggressively, tapping precisely the class anger so much discussed in histories of the Confederate home front, but expressing its gendered dimensions as well. So one group of "ladies" told Brown to call out "the whole militia at once and give them [speculators] a whipping . . . Just go round about these towns and see them men they don't know the war is going on . . . they can speculate of soldiers wives make fortunes of them. Just look at ther woman and children that are begging bread husband in the war or perhaps dead." Their venting had a political point. "This has been an unholy war from the beginning," they finished, "the rich is all at home makeing great fortunes." Other southern white women shared their rage at the fat cats. "I wish you would have all the big leguslater men and big men about town ordered in to confederate serviz," another wrote Jefferson Davis. "they any no serciz to us at home."[48] For the first time in southern history, perhaps, as "soldiers' wives" non-elite white women felt empowered to make claims on the state for service.

Protecting white womanhood has been a powerful refrain in southern politics, and populists like Joseph Brown were always alert to its possibilities. More than most southern governors Brown stepped into the role, constituting himself quite self-consciously as the protector and provider of soldiers' wives and families. He formulated relief policies in reference specifically to "soldiers' wives," distributing salt, clothing, and food aid, for example. "Salt! Salt! I have a lot of Salt sent to Rome by Governor Brown for distribution to soldiers' wives and destitute widows," ran the bold face advertisement by the salt agent in Rome, Georgia in January 1862. Brown constantly advertised his own commitment to "feed and clothe the suffering wives, and widows, and orphans and soldiers," as when he announced the Georgia Legislature's appropriation for relief in 1864.[49] The incurred debt to soldiers' wives could never be fully redeemed, but its promise of protection framed much of the popular politics of the Confederate South.

Indeed so legitimate was the claim of the "poor soldier's wife," so useful the identity, that white men, including elite ones, attempted to inhabit it. In one request after another, white men offered service to poor soldiers' wives as justification for details, exemptions and discharges, and offered the signatures of "many ladies" to evidence the legitimacy of their requests. Family sacrifice was the measure of entitlement when poor men spoke on their own behalf: "[I] have five sons they all ready lef home wives and children at the commencement of the war when many others able and stout that could go but dislike to face the enemy," one man complained in 1864, trying to escape Brown's "last call" for men under 55. When elite men spoke on their own behalf or on behalf of one another, the measure was service to soldiers' wives in their locality or the protection of the local white women from emboldened slaves. M.A. Brantly tried to get his brother, "a planter in southwestern Georgia," exempted from service in 1864 by explaining that he has "been since the beginning of the war most abundant in patriotic deeds for the benefit of soldiers' families—for a long time giving corn to these persons, as your excellency also has nobly done, for a year past selling it at a mere nominal price—making glad many needy ones who have walked long distances to partake of his bounty." One planter who began his petition for a furlough on the high ground by explaining that he would serve his country better at home "supplying soldiers' needy families" and controlling local "negroes," revealed his real interest in complaints about impressing officers who "are taking advantage of me in my absence from home to rob me of my property." However inauthentically, the claim of the soldier's wife on the state became a powerful card in the petitioner's hand—a dimension of popular politics in the Confederacy missed in the usual emphasis on class conflict.[50]

The soldier's wife had put herself on the political agenda, invited there by promises of protection. As early as 1862 and even late 1861 in some places, southern governors and the Confederate President and Secretary of War were fielding desperate demands from yeoman and poor white women to release their husbands from military service. "[H]e listed against my will or knowledg," and left me "suffering for both victuals and clothes," a Georgia woman told Governor Brown, not alone, apparently, in her belief in the substance of household representation. "What is to become of the women and children if you call out *all* the men?" another pointedly asked the governor of Mississippi. Home and state might be linked in citizen's duties, but to white women one had always been primary. My husband's "devotion to our country caused him to neglect his more sacred duty to his family," one woman wrote the Confederate Secretary of War, begging her husband's discharge.[51] Urged by private pleas more desperate than the traces left in public records, many husbands too had ultimately to choose. The terms of Confederate mobilization deepened the problem of political obligation.

White women's relation to the state had been defined through marriage, the soldier's wife asked to give up her husband and sons to defend the only right to which she was entitled: the right of protection. The assumptions of coverture and the exclusion of women from the full rights of citizens left the state with little, other than an ethic of sacrifice, by which to secure white women's support for a war to which their right quickly fell victim. White women, and especially non-elite ones driven by the starkest need, would continue to make decisions primarily as wives and mothers, private members of a household defined by marriage and their own distance from the state's claims. Coverture exacted its own price in the course of the war. White women had no obligation to the Confederate state: the consent of these "governed" could not be secured.

The old celebratory tale of white women's unwavering loyalty to the cause has now been abandoned by most historians in favor of a newer narrative, more fitting to the politics of our own time, perhaps, about women's role in military defeat. Drew Gilpin Faust has made the most dramatic claims in this regard, arguing in her recent book on Confederate women that "at every level of the social order women were making their particular contributions to Confederate military defeat." Tempting as it is to assert the significance of women's history in such a grand way, such measures of feminist efficacy are neither necessary or, perhaps, wise.[52] One does not have to make dramatic claims about white women's role in military defeat or look, as other historians have done, to the "legacy" of the war in the late nineteenth century southern women's suffrage movement, to see the significance of women and gender in southern political history.[53] Traces of women's presence can be found in the very terms of political debate and struggle.

A specifically political history of women and gender in the Civil War South seems warranted, then, and promising: it might provide ways to overcome the existing divide between rich new social histories and the still-critical military histories of the Confederacy and to reinvigorate the political history of the C.S.A., which has remained largely untouched by recent scholarship on women and slaves. It might help too, in furthering one line of analysis critical in American women's and southern history but largely overlooked in recent feminist treatments of the war and its legacy: the gendered dimensions of the debate over suffrage that erupted in freedmen's conventions, state constitutional conventions and in southern legislatures around the passage of the 15th amendment. The struggle over the enfranchisement of former slaves, but only of men, represented a historical severing of the long-standing and intimate connection between gender and race as linked categories of dependence and disfranchisement and thus between the history of free women and slaves in southern political culture. The history of that rupture in its critical and varied local southern setting has yet to be written, as does its immediate context in the political history of women and slaves in the Confederate States of America.[54]

The politics of protecting white womanhood has a long and troubled history in the American South, one that significantly predates its well-known Jim Crow career.[55] It figured centrally in the "Glorious Cause," where it did much of the dirty work of diverting the public gaze from slavery long enough to mobilize nonslaveholding men to its banner. The protection of white women also clearly continued to frame popular politics in the Confederacy as this brief treatment suggests, not least because of what white women themselves made of the opening. Both in the originating crisis, in the conduct of the war itself, and, surely, in the political debates of a defeated South, the "soldier's wife" was ever in political view.

Securing white women's consent posed problems of political obligation that few even glimpsed at the beginning of the war and that admitted of no resolution. The disfranchised have a political history and they make political history—a point which takes its sharpest form in reference, not to white women, but to the region's other class of doubly "governed" dependents.

The political status of slaves has yet to find its historian.[56] Common antebellum assertions of slaves' utter alienation from the state coexisted with expressions of fear, equally common at moments of sectional crisis, about slaves' political intelligence. Like other aspects of chattel slavery—the nature of slave marriage, or status at law—slaves' political identity shows just how much masters repressed with respect to slave subjectivity and the slave regime. Like other contradictions, too, this one was pried open by the war, allowing us to consider the slave's political standing and, especially, the immediate problem of political obligation it posed to the new government of the C.S.A.

On the face of it the matter was simple: Slaves had no political standing in relation to the state. "Women had no more right to political or economic power than a slave or a child," one man editorialized in the Albany *Patriot* in 1851, grounding the shaky case in the seemingly steady one. As the Presbyterian minister Benjamin Morgan Palmer had explained, the government of the household and the authority of the master constituted the slaves' state, the means by which they were represented and their best interests served. But, of course, slaves' political interest in sectional developments and their extensive channels of political communication, including their own presence at political meetings in the secession crisis, were well known and troubling to whites. The extent and ferocity of vigilante violence against slaves in late 1860 and early 1861 and the calls from all sides throughout the war for actions designed to "awe" the slaves and hold them in "proper subjection," are clear measures of that white recognition and fear.[57]

But if whites attempted to control slaves *as slaves* by intensification of the usual means of coercion—and they did—William Lee's communication of May 1861 points up how quickly that old framework fell apart and slaves' political desires registered. Referring to the common knowledge that "the Negroes are Hiley Hope up that they will soon Be free," Lee cannily anticipated the problem posed by slaves' desire for freedom, and suggested military deployment of "Negroe felers from 17 years oald up" to relieve the burden on the "meny pore men with large famelys to susport [and whose] famelys will sufer . . . if they have to go into the Army."[58]

By 1862 in some parts of the South, slaves' own actions in pursuit of emancipation and in support of the Union army and navy had already forced an open acknowledgment of what white men had long known: that "the Negroes constitute a part of the body politic, in fact," and "should be made to know their duty" to "the government under which they live," as "Citizens of Liberty County", [Georgia] put it in a letter to the Commander of Confederate Forces in their area. Listing, with outrage, the various acts of local slaves and their military value to Union troops, the Liberty County correspondents declared them "Traitors," thus recognizing the political subjectivity and agency of slaves. "The absconding Negroes hold the position of Traitors," he railed, "since they go over to the enemy and afford him aid and comfort, by revealing the condition of the districts and cities from which they come, and aiding him in erecting fortifications and raising provisions for his support: and now," he added, "that the U.S. have allowed their introduction into their Army and Navy, aiding the enemy by enlisting under his banners and increasing his resources in men, for our annoyance and destruction." As "spies," "guides," "pilots" and especially as soldiers in blue, slaves had committed treason against "the government under which they live." The same actions and logic that made slaves "contraband" in the eyes of Union army officials made them "traitors" in southern eyes. Either way they were no longer just slaves. In the service of the "enemy" they should be "treated as the enemy," the Georgia correspondents maintained, and governed, therefore, under martial law. "Negroes," that is to say, should be governed not as slaves but as political individuals, under the authority not of the master but of the military arm of the state.[59]

By 1862 slaves had put themselves significantly on the Confederate political agenda, had forced recognition of the political agency and subjectivity of the whole massive class of disfranchised people, and posed directly for the individual states and central government of the Confederate States of America the problem of political obligation. A "Traitor," after all, was one who would "overthrow the government or impair the well-being of a state to which one owe[d] allegiance."[60] Did the slave owe allegiance to the state? In exchange for what? However unlikely it might seem, securing the allegiance of slaves to "the glorious cause" became an imperative of Confederate discourse and policy, expressed nowhere more directly than in the debate over enlisting slaves.[61]

One fact is past argument, proclaimed an Augusta, Georgia paper in February 1865: "The negro will be the future soldier of the war." "Is it not now time to enlist the negroes?," a private

citizen wrote to Confederate president, Jefferson Davis, the previous September from embattled Macon, Georgia. "In a very
short time every able bodied negro in the abandoned section will
either be a Soldier in the Yankee army or employed in some way
to contribute to our destruction." "The history of this war demonstrates the wonderful fact, that the Confederate states subsists
both of the immense armies engaged in the conflict," the proslavery intellectual J.H. Stringellow noted in 1865, "and actually after
furnishing all the soldiers to our army, contributes about one half
of those making the army of its enemies."[62] The political agency
of slaves and their politics of freedom was long past doubt by
1864, and one white southerner after another openly acknowledged that fact. Slaves had, additionally, made their military
value painfully clear and, in doing so, posed an impossible problem of consent and allegiance for Confederate officials.

One editorialist for the Jackson *Mississippian* put his finger on
the problem in September 1863, alerted to it early by his region's
experience of defeat and occupation. "We must either employ
the negroes ourselves, or the enemy will employ them against
us," he wrote. "They are no longer negative characters, but subjects of volition as other people." A plainer statement of the problem—and its imperatives—could not be found. "He [the
"negroe"] must be taught that this is his country and he must
further be taught that it is his duty, as well as the white man's,
to defend his home with arms, if need be." The *Mississippian*
recognized the problem posed by securing slaves to "the cause,"
and he was ready with the solution: "If the negroes can be made
effective and trustworthy to the Southern cause in no other way,"
he wrote boldly, "we solemnly believe it is the duty of this government to forestall Lincoln and proceed at once to take the steps
for the emancipation or liberation of the negroes itself. Let them
be declared free, placed in the ranks, and told to fight for their
homes and country."[63] As people possessed of political agency
and especially as able-bodied men available for military mobilization, slaves had put themselves in an entirely new relation to the

state and posed an unprecedented problem of political obligation for the government of the C.S.A.: how to secure their consent and allegiance to the Confederate cause; and how to extract from them the highest obligation of the male citizen—military service. As it had for the editor of the *Mississippian*, the matter led inexorably to the question of freedom.

"If slaves will make good soldiers our whole theory of slavery is wrong," Howell Cobb of Georgia proclaimed in January 1865 as the Confederate debate on slave enlistment heated up. Of course the theory was wrong. But more to the point, most politicians and military men agreed with Cobb about the substance of the matter: you could not make soldiers of slaves. "It is said by us that slaves will not make soldiers, and this," J.H. Stringfellow wrote to Jefferson Davis, is correct. But "escaped slaves fight and fight bravely for our enemies, therefore a freed Slave will fight." Patrick Cleburne, the Major General in the Army of Tennessee who was one of the first advocates of enlisting black troops in the Confederate army, explained more clearly than anyone else the necessary relationship between military service and emancipation. "It is a first principle with mankind that he who offers his life in defense of the State should receive from her in return his freedom and his happiness," he declared, "and we believe in acknowledgement of this principle." But the slave had no allegiance to the state; his consent had never been solicited or secured; and, as a result, he had no political obligation to military duty. Political obligation preceded and secured military obligation. "We must bind him to our cause by no doubtful bonds," Cleburne pointed out, and the only bond sufficient was "the hope of freedom." "When we make soldiers of them we must make free men of them beyond all question, and thus enlist their sympathies also," he said clearly. The problem of political obligation was clearly understood—"We say put the slaves in the army," an editorial in a Georgia paper put it, "but when you do it make them freemen at the same time, and give them an interest in the soil they are called upon to defend"—and it could be resolved only with freedom. Only as freemen could the South's slaves be made to take up arms in defense of "home and country."[64]

The argument was at once familiar in its terms and revolutionary in its implication. Hearth and home had to be put at stake for the slave soldier as for the white one—and womanhood too, as Major Cleburne, for one, understood. We must "give the negro not only his own freedom, but that of his wife and child," he insisted. And "to do this we must *immediately* make his marriage and parental relations sacred in the eyes of the law and forbid their sale."[65] Freedom's boon had to be extended to "their" women. As with white men, so with black: manhood (and its prerogatives) would be earned by military service, and women would come by their freedom and political standing second-hand, through their husbands and in relation to marriage. Marriage, manhood, military service: black men possessed of these perogatives would soon move to claim the other customarily secured to southern free men—citizenship.

None of the Confederate debate over political obligation even begins to get at slaves' own understandings of political subjectivity, of the rights and duties of citizens, of claims to membership in the political sphere, or of its appropriately gendered arrangements.[66] Confederate concern with military mobilization, to take but one example, focused the public discourse of slave agency and resistance exclusively around *men*. In doing so, it pushed to the edges local recognitions of slave women's bids for freedom and the problems of discipline and social control such struggles raised in time and place. Slave women were fully empowered political actors within the drama of the Confederacy, in other words, however invisible they might appear in policy debates.[67] Behind the public discourse about protecting white women and controlling slave men lies a much messier and less binary gendered local history.

In the meantime, however, during the Civil War, slaves' own actions in pursuit of freedom posed an inexorable problem of political obligation to the state that wanted access to men's bodies for military service. They all did the numbers: "half of our entire population is of no avail to us, but on the contrary ready at every opportunity to join the ranks of our enemies," J. H. Stringellow put it to Jefferson Davis. The slaveholding states had four million "negroes," 600,000 of whom were "able-bodied men capable of bearing arms," the editor of the *Jackson Mississipian* calculated. None were in our army, he raged, but 50,000 of them were already "in the Federal ranks."[68]

By putting themselves there, the South's slaves—and the debate they brought on—point up clearly the historical relationship between war, military moblization, and emancipations. Taken together with the Confederacy's other huge class of dependent adults—white "soldier's wives"—they point up, too, how the disfranchised make political history, how central gender is to it, and how we might enrich its telling.

Commentary by Tera W. Hunter

Stephanie McCurry has identified the central issue which will redefine the southern political history of the Civil War era. The dominant narrative of southern politics has largely been constructed as the province of the "citizens," those who were invested with the power to make decisions about the war and, to a lesser degree, those who made up the ranks on the front line, literally doing battle from day to day so that the Confederacy might prevail by war's end. Even with a growing body of research on slaves and freedpeople, and white women (elite and yeomen), the dominant narrative for the most part remains the same. McCurry's work, however, makes considerable advances toward incorporating "citizens" and "non-citizens" together into a broad interpretation of the Southern political landscape in the Civil War era.

McCurry does this by analyzing a pivotal issue that confronted the Confederacy, and indeed the Union as well: how to define political obligations so as to unify all white men around "The Cause" and to harness the loyalties of disfranchised white women and slaves as well. McCurry argues that the ways in which political obligation came to be defined were marked by gender and race, as evident in the most oft-repeated homilies about the southern "Cause." She goes beyond the idealism of the rhetoric in which gender is invoked to look at the ways in which actual power relations were affected by gendered and racialized conceptions of political duties and rights. Her analysis begins in 1859 before the war began as secessionists began rallying for support and continues through the ups and downs of the war itself.

What were the racialized and gendered definitions of political obligations that came to be the basis of ongoing struggles during the course of the war? McCurry argues that loyalty to the Confederacy was linked to the southern white home, which became the basis for unifying white men and reconciling class stratification. The argument that white men should rally to protect the right to own slaves would have had limited appeal, given that the majority of men who had to be won over to supporting secession were not slaveholders. Protecting the property of ownership in white women, however, was an obligation and a right whose sanctity all white men could support. Why? Because it was uniquely male and uniquely white to entail such obligations: one must be a citizen, one must own property (slaves or women will do), and one must enjoy the legal status of marriage, which made one the guardian and master of the household. Thus, the political obligation of white men came to be defined as fighting in the Confederacy to protect the honor and purity of white womanhood and the southern household against the invasions of so-called Black Republicans.

McCurry reveals the complexities of this approach. By defining political obligations in this way, Confederate supporters actually promoted unintended consequences which challenged their ultimate aim of recruiting and retaining soldiers. Should one's loyalty be expressed by fighting for the Confederacy or by literally defending one's home turf—often mutually exclusive goals. One could not protect one's home by going off to battle and leaving women and children behind to fend for themselves against invading Unionists and unruly slaves. The petitions of white men for exemption from military duty speak volumes about the conflicting interests that complicated political obligations.

Clearly, to win the war, the Confederates had to be concerned with gaining the cooperation and loyalties of all members of southern society, disfranchised or not. The immediate problem of incorporating women into the rebel effort was the fact that they had no obligations to the Confederate state. Their obligations were to the state of marriage and its rightful authority, the husband.

The very nature of the war transformed women's obligations, however. They assumed new identities as "soldiers' wives," comprising a new constituency with which the Confederacy, not just husbands, would have to contend. Women pressed for the rights of this new identity, making demands on the Confederate state for food and for protection against the many encroachments on their lives. Women pressured, prodded and critiqued Confederate policies and officials when they failed to live up to the promises of protection. This pressure reinforced even further the obligations that individual men felt to stay home and protect their wives—again posing the conundrum of conflicting loyalties.

Slaves presented the greatest challenge to the new state in its attempt to enforce obligations. The inherent contradiction of slaves as human chattel property was magnified during the war. They were property and yet they were people, and as such they were also willful persons, despite the lack of recognition of this in the law. White southerners certainly acknowledged and understood these contradictions and understood that slaves were political beings. The problem of the Confederacy was to encourage slave loyalty without disrupting the conventional limitations on slave personhood or political subjectivity. As slaves pressed for their freedom by joining the ranks of the Union army or otherwise engaging in acts of "treason" to aid the Union cause, the Confederacy pondered the contradiction between slave and soldier, between the slavery of blacks and the freedom of white male citizens.

I want to emphasize what I see as McCurry's central contribution. She offers a considerable revision of southern political history by insisting that "the disfranchised have a political history and they make political history." In the dominant political narrative of the Civil War era, the disfranchised are almost always absent or marginalized at best. Yet as McCurry so perceptibly demonstrates, they wrote themselves into the script by their own actions despite all efforts to keep them subordinate and serving the interests of the master classes (slaveholders and husbands alike).

McCurry's essay takes the recent histories of women and the Confederacy a step further. Though I am not sure that her findings are necessarily in conflict with those of historians like Drew Gilpin Faust, I believe that McCurry's work demonstrates just how integral gender and women were to the very terms of political debate and struggle within the Confederacy in ways not attempted by other historians.

McCurry's essay does for the Civil War era what Elsa Barkley Brown's essay on Richmond has done for Reconstruction. In her recent article, "Negotiating and Transforming the Public Sphere: African American Political Life in the Transition from Slavery to Freedom," Brown insists that we look more closely at the character and definition of southern politics as it was constructed by and acted upon by African Americans, including women. Even as women were disfranchised by the larger political system, disfranchisement did not preclude their self-definitions, as political beings nor their communities' definitions of them as important political thinkers and actors in the postwar South.[1]

I have a few questions I want to address, mainly for the sake of clarity, and a few areas of inquiry to suggest what would be fruitful to explore further. McCurry's argument that deals with rape, race, and the nature of men as sexual predators is dense and complex. She states, "if the reference to Black Republican 'brutes' exploited a deep seated popular belief in the predatory sexual nature of man they also revealed a deep ambivalence about whether slave men specifically were possessed of it." It would be helpful for McCurry to untangle the secessionists' use of fears of rape and to explain more precisely the evidence of racial ambivalence in their conceptions of white men as natural sex predators.

This notion of white men's self-conscious identity as sex brutes is intriguing. Gail Bederman discusses this issue as it relates to northern white men at the turn of the century in *Manliness & Civilization*. It would be interesting to look at this dimension of white Southern men's identity in terms of changing constructions of masculinity and its regional variations.[2]

In addition, I think it would be fruitful to explore how free blacks fit into the ongoing battles to define political obligations during the Civil War. The Confederacy was more concerned with slaves than with blacks who were already free. But the well-known cases of free blacks mustering regiments in preparation to fight for the Confederacy show them acting as eager political agents. Though it never came to fruition, free black men's offers to aid the Confederacy as soldiers demonstrate, among many things, their loyalty to their communities, as Benjamin Quarles argued in *The Negro in the Civil War*. This bears on McCurry's insights about the localism of political obligation.

And lastly, I think that McCurry's treatment of slaves in this work needs to incorporate more thinking about slave women. The emphasis here is on slave men, which reflects the emphases and anxieties of the Confederates. They feared slave men, as potential soldiers, plunderers, and rapists of their women, who would undermine the security of their homes. The most disfranchised group of all, slave women, however, are not depicted as fully willful, political subjects in this essay. Yet slave women ac-

tively engaged in disrupting business as usual in southern households and plantations, aiding the Union cause by helping soldiers, deserting as domestic and agricultural labor, and in many
other ways. Since this paper is part of a larger project, however,
I trust that some of these issues may be taken up as McCurry's
work progresses.

"New Men in Body and Soul": The Civilian Conservation Corps and the Transformation of Male Bodies and the Body Politic

BRYANT SIMON

Think about the shirtless man pictured on the next page. He is a symbol of the Civilian Conversation Corps, the New Deal program that provided unemployed young men with work out in the country. This man is tall and muscular, fair-skinned, broad-shouldered, and powerful. Busy at work, he looks at a bright future in front of him. He is a romantic figure. But of course this man is not real. Rather, he is an invention, a projection of an ideal. What is the ideal? What does this man stand for? Why does he look like he does? What does this man and this body tell us about the politics of the people who invented him?

The CCC was President Franklin D. Roosevelt's "pet project," his favorite New Deal program. Formed in the spring of 1933, following FDR's promise to the nation in his inaugural address of "action now," the "tree army" rapidly assembled. By the first day of summer, 250,000 largely unemployed, mostly white and unmarried young men between the ages of 17 and 25 were working in CCC camps located far from urban centers. By the time Congress pulled the funding on the project nine years later, 2,670,000 men from big cities, small towns, and farm communities all over the country had completed stints, ranging from six months to a year, as "soil soldiers." During this period, the CCC left its mark on the nation's landscape. Enrollees installed 89,000 miles of telephone line, built 126,000 miles of roads and trails,

"The CCC At Work," circa 1934–35, Franklin D. Roosevelt Library, Hyde Park, New York.

constructed millions of erosion control dams, planted 1.3 billion trees, erected 3,470 water towers, and spent over six million hours fighting forest fires.[1]

Administered by the War Department, the Labor Department, the Department of Interior, and the Department of Agriculture, the CCC reached into virtually every corner of the nation.[2] Along the way, it won the praise of politicians and editorial writers, bankers and steel workers, mothers and wives. Local leaders and state officials lauded the CCC for providing much-needed jobs for unemployed young men and putting money into the pockets of financially strapped consumers. Conservationists celebrated the New Deal agency's efforts to protect the environment. So popular was the CCC that even longtime South Carolina Senator Ellison "Cotton Ed" Smith, who opposed virtually everything about the New Deal and whom *Time* magazine once dubbed a "conscientious objector to the Twentieth Century," liked the program.[3]

Yet middle-class promoters of the New Deal agency talked about more than trees and the environment, relief and patronage when they talked about the CCC.[4] Projecting their own fears of social division, radicalism, and emasculation on to the tree corps, they imagined the CCC as a way to restore the nation's flagging manhood and virility. This meant talking about the body. Few discussions of the CCC, in fact, failed to include some mention (or picture) of manhood, masculinity, and the physical body. President Roosevelt himself declared that the agency's most valuable contribution to the nation was its work in turning boys into men.[5] The second of the CCC's two directors, James J. McEntee, wrote a book about the New Deal agency entitled *Now They Are Men*, in which he boasted that the CCC molded "idle boys" into "sturdy young men."[6] Referring to what he called the sociological side of the CCC, an Army Colonel claimed: "it is our aim to send you men home as better citizens . . . men better physically, better mentally for having joined the CCC—men with clear eyes and renewed or new-born confidence in themselves; men with high morale and superb esprit . . . in fact, new men in body and soul."[7]

Focusing on the idea of turning boys into men and recreating manhood "in body and soul," this essay examines how the white, educated, middle-class supporters of the tree corps envisioned, and in a sense sold, the CCC. This, then, is a story about middle-class men and their hopes and fears for the nation. Between the lines of their sales pitches, these supporters revealed their anxieties about chaos, decadence, industrialization, and the cities. Displaying a surprising lack of self-consciousness, they also made plain their views of male bodies as public spaces.

Most New Dealers regarded healthy male bodies, particularly young male bodies, as symbolic of the nation's manhood, virility, and energy.[8] Physically weak men, they believed, weakened the nation. With this connection buried in their minds, reformers seized on the CCC as a way to "beef up" male bodies and strengthen the state. Examining the language and images used to promote the CCC, therefore, lays bare many broadly held middle-class ideas about health and the physical body, reform and the body politic in the first half of the twentieth century.

CCC backers tailored the tree corps to fit their ideas about masculinity and male bodies. As a new bourgeois culture took shape in the nineteenth century, the physical body became less important to ideas about manhood than it had been in aristocratic Europe where men dueled to prove themselves.[9] Crafting its own aesthetic, the emerging middle class emphasized character and self-restraint as the essential characteristics of manhood. Civilized men, they insisted, controlled their impulses. This discipline over their own urges, in turn, gave them the right to dominate others. Yet as the nineteenth century gave way to the twentieth century, and aggressive nationalism, Social Darwinism, and imperialism gripped the public imagination, some middle-class Americans nervously started to talk about being overcivilized. They feared that the "best" men, college men, educated men, had grown too cultured, too genteel, too soft, and too effeminate to lead. Seeking refinement and civilization, young men, some critics further charged, had drifted away from their competitive, brutish, physical natures.[10] Men quite simply had paid too much attention to their minds and allowed their bodies to go to waste. Many wondered how physically weak men—sissies, stuffed shirts, she-men, and molly-coddles, in the vernacular of the early twentieth century—could protect the nation?[11]

Looking to remake their soft arms and tired legs, middle-class men in the early part of the twentieth century, embarked on a loosely coordinated public fitness campaign. Holding up muscle man Charles Atlas as the model of masculinity, they emphasized appearance as well as good character as essential ingredients for manhood. A righteous man was a strong and muscular man. Trading in books for barbells, the classics for football, men dedicated themselves to toning their bodies before their minds. By the end of World War I, the strong muscular man was celebrated in film and advertisements as the ideal man. Yet more than appearance mattered. Viewing the world as an organic whole, middle-class Americans considered outward beauty to be a clear sign of inner righteousness, not self-indulgence. The discipline and dedication needed to sculpt the perfect body was, CCC backers seemed to believed, the same discipline and dedication needed to create the perfect citizen.

Teddy Roosevelt embodied the new vision of manhood and nation. Every schoolboy in America in the first decades of the twentieth-century knew the Rough Rider's story. Raised by a doting mother in a wealthy, civilized household, well-read and well-mannered young Teddy epitomized "genteel culture." But physically, he was pale and skinny and grew up to be a "sickly, delicate" child, who suffered from all kinds of ailments including asthma, nearsightedness, and just plain clumsiness. Riding on a train one day, he met a few not-so-well read or bred boys. As only kids can do, they teased Teddy to the point of torturing him.

But he was too weak to defend himself. The bitter taste of this humiliation pushed Roosevelt down his own personal road to Damascus. He started to go Wood's Gymnasium everyday. Soon the "frail child" filled out. Strong and muscular, he headed out west, rode across the badlands of South Dakota, beat up a few barroom toughs, and led the charge up San Juan Hill. National glory, wide-open spaces, and powerful bodies were now forever linked.[12]

Not only did a nation need strong men like Teddy Roosevelt to prosper and defend itself, it also had to be unified. Middle-class Americans, however, sensed all kinds of troubling divisions swirling around them in the early twentieth century. They were particularly unsettled by immigrants, especially those who they thought of as living crammed into the ghettoes and slums of the nation's industrial cities. Middle-class people heard foreign accents and saw Old World fashions as disconcerting reminders of fractures in the body politic, of people who placed ethnic bonds ahead of national loyalty. In these packed and noisy neighborhoods, they feared that foreign men gathered at late-night meetings to read Marx, coordinate violent strikes, and plot revolution. And everywhere in these neighborhoods they saw darker skins and darker bodies. All these differences—the sounds, shapes, smells, and politics of the city—fueled middle-class anxieties about social divisions and the explosive potential of these divisions to tear the country apart. America, they believed almost without thinking about it, was white, Protestant, and English speaking. Immigrants, at least European ones, could assimilate, but only by becoming like middle-class white people. That meant talking like them, acting like them, dressing like them, and looking like them. Until immigrants remade themselves, they stuck out to middle-class men as a pressing problem, as something that desperately needed attention.

The onslaught of the Great Depression heightened middle-class concerns. With jobs hard to find, they fretted that not-quite-white Poles would fight with not-quite-white Irish or the not-quite-white Italians might go after not-quite-white Jews. Worse yet, those communists, socialists, and militant trade unionists holding clandestine late-night meetings might find new recruits for their nefarious campaigns to destroy white middle-class society. (Strangely—or maybe not so strangely—reformers never said a word about Anglo uprisings.)

Still, not everyone concerned about social division worried about the immediate ruptures of revolution. Some feared that unemployed city kids spent too much time on street corners "bumming around" trying to "pick up girls" rather than attending 4-H or Boys Scout meetings, learning how to cooperate and work with others.[13] Fraternity man Russell A. Beam, for instance, voiced his apprehensions about the nation's future. He worried that the youth of America had become, in his words, "individualists," self-centered people who resisted "seeking to establish relationships with others." Alarmed about what he saw around him, Beam wondered whether a divided nation could rally to meet a military crisis, or any other crisis for that matter.[14]

Beam and others envisioned the CCC as a way to heal the rifts in American society. Under capable leadership—supporters always made this distinction—the CCC would be a citizenship training school teaching lessons of thrift, sobriety, discipline, and respect for private property to the wayward children of immigrants.[15] Once again, CCC supporters never talked about Anglos. Apparently, middle-class reformers thought that these white people already knew, either by birth or training, what citizenship entailed. By bringing Poles, Slavs, Jews, Irish, and Italians together to work for a common cause, the camps, boosters promised, would erase troubling ethnic differences. Backers' racialized conceptions of the world also shaped the CCC. Only white and ethnic European manhood concerned camp officials; these were the only people they wanted to transform into new men "in body and soul." Despite clearly spelled out sanctions against discrimination in the organization's original charter, CCC camps, like other New Deal programs, remained, for the most part, segregated. African Americans found it harder to get into the CCC than whites did and when they did gain entrance, administrators usually assigned them to inferior camps in out-of-the-way places. Obviously CCC officials were not worried about bolstering African American manhood or healing the nation's racial divide. [16]

Despite these racial biases, supporters touted the CCC as a way to mold a new American man—a white man—dedicated to the nation ahead of neighborhood, region, or religious group. Colonel Alva J. Brasted, Chief of Chaplains of the United States Army, predicted that the CCC would "instill the right character" in enrollees. "Christ," he wrote, "mingled with the common people. He talked and ate and lived with them. The man of character fits into his environment in God's way, and both the military service and the C.C.C. provide the chance to affect right relationships with one's fellowman."[17] A CCC veteran from Ohio claimed that the CCC broke down "strong and ardent sectionalism." "Poles, Slovaks, Italians, Hungarians," he added with enthusiasm, "all are discovering the broad basic brotherhood that welds us all together. They are finding a new pride in saying, 'We are *Americans!*'"[18] Yet another CCC veteran remembered, tying together sociability and manhood: "It was a wonderful thing for us. . . . It taught us to get along with one another. It made men out of boys."[19]

One thing that men supposedly did—something that boys did not do—was fight wars. Yet not all men were born soldiers. The CCC, supporters pledged, could help in this area by teaching the nation's youth the virtues of national service. With copies of William James's "The Moral Equivalent of War" stuck in their breast pockets, CCC backers designed the tree corps as a kind of non-military, military training school.[20] Stressing the lessons of cooperation, citizenship, and service, it would prepare young men ready for battle. The CCC's capacity to shape boys into soldiers took on added significance after Hilter's forces pushed their way into Czechoslovakia and later invaded Poland. With war raging across Europe, CCC supporters increasingly described the organization in explicit military terms. One official bragged that it taught young men how to obey orders. A CCC pamphlet, published in 1941 and subtitled "Contributing to the National Defense," declared: "while helping conserve the natural resources of the Nation [CCC enrollees] have received instruction in military training—the thing most difficult to teach a recruit." As always, there was an emphasis on the physical body. Aware of middle-class notions about the body and their fears of disorder, director James McEntee insisted in 1940 that "the Corps" had "toughened" recruits "physically, taught them work skills, improved their morale, and taught them love and respect for their country and government."[21]

With war looming and the economy in the doldrums, gritty and gray industrial cities with their swarms of dark-skinned, possibly radical immigrants stood out to middle-class men as a potent threat to the nation's ability to prepare for war and pave the way to prosperity. Mixed with their fears of ethnic strife and working-class disorder, CCC boosters worried about the insidious influence of urban space on the nation's young men. Along the teeming streets of New York, Philadelphia, and Chicago, young men, they thought, drifted into corruption and decadence. Just about every piece of CCC promotional literature featured a passage or two describing how the tree army snatched kids from the pool rooms and beer parlors of urban ghettoes, reformed them, and turned them into productive citizens and soldiers. Describing what the CCC did, the editors of *The Forestry News Digest* wrote: "Taking the men from city streets, poor food, insufficient clothing and unventilated and unsanitary living quarters and putting them out in the open, the fine pure air of the forest, feeding them plentifully, clothing them comfortably, housing them serviceably, in addition to exercising them with seven hours work a day is making new men physically of these boys."[22] Highlighting the same theme of redemption, Monogram Pictures produced a feature film in 1935 that told the story of "an incipient gangster in the CCC and his reform in this organization."[23]

Telling a similar story to mark the CCC's fiftieth anniversary, Joseph Toltin recalled that in 1936 he was unemployed. Without anything to do, he wasted his time wandering the streets of Cleveland. One afternoon he found a set of keys and used them to sneak into a local grocery store that was closed. A policeman caught and arrested him. A judge gave him the choice of going to reform school for thirty days or joining the CCC for the standard enlistment of six months. Rescued from the streets, Toltin went to the CCC, reenlisted twice, and eventually earned a high school equivalency degree.[24]

Totlin's story was no doubt true, but it was also part of the myth of the CCC.[25] Most CCC boys were not city kids like Toltin, or "incipient gangsters," or in the words of another observer, "sharp-faced products of big cit[y] slums."[26] More than half of all CCC enrollees, in fact, came from small towns and farms, and the organization's recruitment rules generally barred felons from serving in the tree camps. Still, the city and urban space served as meaningful tropes in the packaging of the CCC.[27]

CCC backers looked at the city through overlapping, some-what clouded, lenses.[28] Like others, they marveled at the architectural, artistic, and industrial accomplishments showcased in the nation's urban areas. But the city was also seen as a breeding ground of vice and corruption. Deluged with a steady steam of urban criticism from Lincoln Steffens, Ida Turbell, Jacob Riis, Upton Sinclair, Theodore Dresier, Mark Sullivan, Stephen Crane, and Charles F. Russell, New Dealers saw the city as a diseased and decadent environment that poisoned and weakened young men.[29] Environment, in fact, was a key concept for CCC officials. Like an earlier generation of reformers, New Dealers associated the urban poor with drink, filth, idleness, and radicalism. But Depression-era activists saw these vices as symptoms rather than causes of poverty. The poor were poor, in other words, not because they drank, they drank because they were poor. Barred from well-paying jobs and crammed into stuffy one-room tenements, the poor, the reformers further believed, inevitably would be degraded and seek escape in the cheap amusements offered by bars, pool rooms, street corners, and tacky music halls. Over time the character of these urban denizens would only get worse. Men and women raised in the chaotic environment of city slums would eventually "degenerate" into nonproductive citizens, unworthy soldiers, and possibly even threats to the government. This theory of urban degeneracy undergirded New Dealers' ideas about the CCC.[30]

CCC supporters did not regard degeneracy as a metaphor; they meant it as something that quite literally happened. For them, overexposure to the city was a kind of disease that infected the body. Sophisticated diagnostic equipment was not needed to identify the illness. The proof was in the body. City kids—the hapless byproducts of "urban degeneracy"—were pale, thin, and soft. They had rotten teeth and narrow chests. All of these things were important clues to CCC officials who generally considered physical appearance to be a direct reflection of moral character.[31] The outwardly ugly were inwardly dangerous. They were sly, untrustworthy men who in the politically charged world of the reformers jeopardized the health of the state.[32]

Molding new citizens, therefore, meant inoculating young men against the degenerative diseases of the city. Like most Americans educated in the Teddy Roosevelt school of morality, CCC officials believed that life "lived in close communion with beneficent nature" possessed "a wholesomeness and integrity impossible for the depraved populations of the cities."[33] Not surprisingly, their views of nature, wilderness, and the outdoors were also gendered. CCC backers imagined these places as wholesome, pure sources of male "virility and toughness." With these ideas in mind, CCC leaders deliberately located the tree camps far from urban slums. They wanted to get vulnerable, impressionable young men off beguiling city streets. Let them breathe clean, fresh air. Let them work outside with their hands digging dirt and planting trees.[34] And let them sleep under the stars. The combination of fresh air and exhausting labor, CCC officials boldly predicted, would eradicate the infection of the city. Six months in the wilderness would, New Deal leaders also thought, strengthen teenaged city boys, flush the tenements out of their systems, and transform them from scrawny, unattractive revolutionaries and criminals into proud, dutiful men.[35]

More than just the pernicious affects of urban space frightened CCC supporters. They also worried about the volatile mixture of urban slums and unemployment. Again, when New Dealers thought of unemployment, they also thought about manhood and male bodies. They feared that joblessness not only sapped the strength of the economy and eroded purchasing power, but devastated young men for years to come, maybe even forever. Most American men in the 1930s linked work to masculinity. Quite simply, self-respecting men worked. When they didn't work, they were not men, but lazy and slothful social parasites. Urging Congress to fund the CCC in 1933, President Roosevelt warned of the "threat of enforced idleness to spiritual and moral stability." Several years later, CCC Director McEntee labeled youth unemployment "human erosion."[36] Without work or the hope of ever getting a job, young men, Roosevelt, McEntee, and others believed, lost their self-respect and sense of manhood. Some young men, they feared, had in 1933 already been unemployed so long that they forget what constituted an honest day's work. Many had become angry and sullen. They spent too much time hanging out on street corners, robbing and stealing, or aimlessly riding the rails. Lacking the manly self-respect that came with having a job, the unemployed represented raw recruits for mischievous revolutionaries. Unless something was done, and done quickly, CCC backers warned, unemployed city kids would become "hostile to the economic and social system," and more ominous still, "the type of sans-culottes who are the first gust of the revolutionary storm."[37]

Arriving just in time, the CCC promised to quell the threat of

"Civilian Conservation Corps," circa 1934–35, Franklin D. Roosevelt Library, Hyde Park, New York.

revolution by giving the jobless work, and not just any kind work, but work outside in the wholesome, pure wilderness. "The greatest achievement of the CCC," crowed one camp administrator, "has not been the preservation of material things such as forests, timber-lands, etc., but the preservation of American Man-Hood."[38] Preserving "American ManHood," CCC supporters argued, required not just jobs and fresh country air, but also rebuilding male bodies.

CCC backers repeatedly described the bodies of enrollees before they entered the camps. Chaos, urban decadence, and chronic unemployment, they suggested, attacked male bodies like an some out-of-control contagion leaving muscles "soft and untrained."[39] Chroniclers of camp life started their stories with descriptions of wiry, hollow-chested, and ragged young men standing in line on the first day of service waiting for fatigues. They looked to one commentator like "the threat of tuberculosis hover[ed] over them." Again, appearance mattered to middle-class men. It was a clear window into character. These sickly boys hardly looked like real men.[40] Unmanly men troubled CCC leaders. They glanced at small, thin men with rotting teeth and saw potential threats to the state.[41] In order to eliminate the specter of rebellion, of sans-coulettes swarming through the streets of Washington DC, government officials developed a wide range of programs to transform—deradicalize and tame—young men by transforming their bodies.

"Very few physically weak men," the Skipper from a Pulaski, New York CCC camp asserted, "ever succeed." "It takes a healthy body," he continued, "a clear eye, a strong constitution to stand the strain of managing a big business or runing [sic] a state or nation."[42] With the goal of sculpting young male bodies into the shapes of corporate managers, tough-minded soldiers, and future politicians, CCC administrators initially sent new recruits to conditioning camps for two weeks of hiking and calisthenics.[43] From there, the boys were transferred to rural forest camps where they performed taxing manual labor outdoors for eight hours a day. Thinking of Teddy Roosevelt, CCC leaders wanted the warm sun to bronze the pale skin of Bowery boys, making them look and feel healthier and more handsome. Proud of their new bodies, according to one rather eroticized report, after a few weeks, soil soldiers "bared their backs to the sun and worked without shirts."[44]

Thinking again of Teddy Roosevelt, CCC leaders made the "strenuous life" a central part of the camp routine. National administrators ordered local officials to set up daily exercise programs. Each morning, CCC enrollees spent ten to thirty minutes, outside, stretching, running, and doing jumping jacks and push-ups. Even leisure in the camps was organized around the body and the open air. CCC outfits included a wide range of extracurricular sports and gymnastics programs. Camp leaders encouraged—some even insisted on—broad participation in athletic competitions, especially team sports.[45] Sports, CCC officials believed, would help to mold strong, muscular, virile young men. Camp administrators pushed the enrollees into sports not just to build up their arms and legs, but also because they were convinced that baseball and football fostered "certain militaristic tendencies" needed to succeed in business and war.[46]

Education was another feature of camp life. Enrollees took classes in American history, civics, grammar, letter writing, etiquette, auto mechanics, aviation, map making, and fish culture.[47] CCC schools also included detailed lessons in personal hygiene. Experts came in each week to lecture on the correct ways to cut fingernails, bathe, and brush teeth. "Look around you," one health official instructed campers, "and note the fellow who is neat, hair combed, and whose clothes are clean, and well kept, and there you will find the fellow who has personal pride. . . ."[48]

Finally, CCC outposts fed enrollees "three square meals a day." Calculating how best to fatten up city kids, officials prescribed a daily diet of 4,000 to 4,500 calories—almost twice the daily recommended diet of today. One CCC veteran remembered that camp leaders punished enrollees who left any food, even a bite, on their plates.[49] Food also played a part in the CCC's military preparedness campaign. When New Dealers set up the tree corps, they were, no doubt, thinking of the undernourished bodies of World War I recruits. If another war broke out, CCC leaders vowed to do their part, serving endless meals of meatloaf, mashed potatoes, and gravy to make sure that the nation's young men were physically fit and sturdy enough to fight.

With so much of the program geared toward changing male bodies, CCC supporters measured the success of the agency quite literally by the pound. From California to Florida, camp leaders wrote to the CCC national newspaper, *Happy Days*, boasting about their outfits. They bragged about forest recovery, fire fighting missions, and tree planting campaigns, but mostly they talked about weight gain. Virtually every CCC story included a description of how men filled out in the camps. California CCC leader, Captain R. R. Haley gushed in the fall of 1933, "Co. 857 has gained a ton since enrolling." He continued: "A total of 177 men jumped in aggregate weight in three months from 25,156 pounds to 26,777 pounds." Carl Abbot of Choctaw, Oklahoma was perhaps the camp's greatest success story. Arriving weighing only 125 pounds, he put on 20 pounds in three short months. Bravo, cheered Captain Haley. New England men, another source enthusiastically reported, gained on average seven and one-half pounds during their tours of duty with the CCC. Yet another camp leader recounted that enrollees put on "at least five pounds." "The increases," he argued, "are attributable, partly, to the variety of health-building goods in the mess and the benefits of clear sunshine and invigorating air."[50] Feeling the pressure to get bigger and worried that he was not gaining enough weight, fast enough, one nervous soil soldier wrote his girl friend, "I hope I'm not too thin for you."[51] In a poem entitled "Seconds," a camper lamely rhymed about the virtues of gaining weight:

> O mother dear did you, hear
>> The news that's going 'round
> Another mess-kit's empty
>> And I've gained another pound
>
> They give me all the toughest jobs
>> They work me soon and late,
> I've worn out twenty brush hooks
>> I've hiked through half the state.
>
> I've blistered in the burning sun
>> In rainstorms I've been drowned,
> But when I smelled the cook-tent
>> I gained another pound.
>
> My pants that went twice 'round my waist
>> And met me coming back,
> Are now so tight that when I bend
>> I wait to hear them crack.[52]

Like the poet, national leaders also pointed to bigger bodies as evidence of the New Deal's success. Each year the director of the CCC in his annual report mentioned how much weight the men had gained over the past twelve months.[53] Speaking before a congressional committee deliberating over whether or not to make the CCC a permanent government agency, the CCC's original director, Robert Fechner bragged: "First of all, it gives them good personal habits, and through proper food . . . makes them into fine physical specimens."[54] In his 1959 New Deal tribute, historian Arthur Schlesinger Jr. concluded his glowing appraisal of the CCC by quoting an enrollee, who beamed: "I weighed about 160 pounds when I went there, and when I left I was 190 about. It made a man of me all right."[55]

CCC supporters presented more than statistics about weight

gain to trumpet the organization's contributions to America. They developed, probably out of necessity, a whole iconography to celebrate the CCC. By the 1930s, seeing was believing in America. Statistics were one thing, but to get people to embrace change, to know it was real and recognize its impact, they had to see it. Tuned into this visual culture, CCC officials created a narrative of still frames to tout the organization's accomplishments.[56] Remarkably, these images rarely depicted long rows of new trees or shiny water towers or cleverly conceived dams. Instead, they were almost always portraits of male bodies, and they told a melodramatic before-and-after story.

Usually the drama opened with a picture of a city kid whose body has been devastated by urban vice. Gray and grizzled, the figure is sometimes slumped over; other times leaning up against a street light smoking a cigarette. His eyes are downcast. Dressed in a dark, heavy coat, his body is entirely covered, as if he is afraid or embarrassed to reveal his frail frame and pale skin. Flash to the next scene. After six months of three square meals a day, jumping jacks, football games, and hard work in the fresh country air, a new man takes shape. Looking a lot like Charles Atlas, the hero of the CCC stands erect. Stripped to the waist, he confidently looks out on the future. He is tall and muscular. His broad, contoured shoulders narrow down from his smooth, hairless, powerful chest to a thin waist. He has a chiseled face, perfect teeth, and a strong prominent square jaw. Even swinging an ax in the hot summer sun, the CCC man is unmistakably neat and clean.

For his time and place, the CCC man was the flawless man, a perfect representation of the middle-class ideal of masculinity. "A century ago," the historian T. J. Jackson Lears wrote in 1981, "the stout midriff was a sign of mature success in life." Yet by the 1930s, society no longer celebrated portly models of conspicuous wealth and gaudy excess. Nor did it praise the cultured and civilized man who neglected his body. By the New Deal era, the ideal male was defined by his physicality. He was younger, not older; his body was powerful and strong, yet still lean and sinewy.[57]

To middle-class promoters of the CCC, the appearance and form of this body, its positioning, stance, and posture, resolved all the tensions that they detected around them. Viewing the world as an organic whole, they believed that the outward beauty of the male figure conveyed his inner righteousness. The determination needed to sculpt the perfect body was, CCC backers believed, the same determination needed to create the perfect citizen-soldier. By the 1930s, the image of man, including the CCC man, took on its perhaps inevitable military dimensions. Given what reformers thought about healthy bodies and a healthy society, they instructed men to hone their bodies not simply for display, but for the higher calling of flag and country. Committed to sacrifice and heroism, the perfect man put the soldierly values of the nation ahead of his individual or group desires.

This well-toned, muscular young man was clearly not overcivilized or incapable of manly action. His bulky arms, solid legs, and barrel-shaped chest paid tribute to the harmony between body and soul, but also to the masculine capacity for brutality. The CCC man's taut body suggested his potential as a warrior and soldier capable of well-channeled fury.

The CCC pictures and posters also celebrated manly labor.[58] Framed clutching an ax or shovel, the shirtless man was always busy at work. This active image addressed yet another middle-class fear. Depression-era narratives are filled with stories, told from a patriarchal perspective, of men who lost their land or job. Displaced as the breadwinner, these beaten men idly stand by as women take over households and turn traditional gender roles upside down.[59] If the private world of the home was in turmoil, then middle-class Americans were certain, the public world of the state would be in trouble. The mythical CCC man, however, was virile, powerful, and in control. Clearly, he had put a stop to "human erosion," fought off the degenerative diseases of the city and unemployment, and learned the value of labor. And just as clearly, he was not emasculated by the devastating economic forces of the depression. To the contrary, the pictures show a handsome, brawny man simultaneously subduing and coexisting with nature.

Of course, there are empty spaces and gaps in the pictures. Most strikingly women are nowhere to be seen in the CCC visual narratives. In part, these images reflect the fact that women were generally blocked from participating in the CCC.[60] Yet their absence also figuratively suggests that the tree soldiers—perhaps all men—could be independent from women, and still be complete men. In this male homosocial setting, men live in a world where women cannot control them, humiliate them, or disgrace them. It is a fantasy world where men apparently do not need women.[61]

Again by saying nothing, CCC imagery also dealt with middle-class fears of the debilitating effects of unemployment and industrialization on male bodies. In other settings, middle-class commentators blamed the nation's growing dependence on machines for making men weak. A cartoon, for instance, in University of Chicago sociologist William F. Ogburn's influential 1935 book *You and Machines* pictures a man propping himself up with what are labeled "machine age crutches." He needs the support, because, writes Ogburn, "[his] LEGS ATROPHIED BY MACHINE AGE!"[62] Convinced, just as the Skipper from Pulaski was, that feeble men rarely prosper, CCC supporters once again looked to the redemptive powers of nature and work. Cool, fresh air without a factory chimney in sight would cure young men of the ruinous effects of dependence on machines. Getting boys out of crowded cities and away from assembly lines and into the woods would, moreover, build up their arms and legs. Strong men would, in turn, strengthen the nation. Each CCC picture portrays a mighty young man working outside in the fresh air. Far from the factories and the constant supervision of management, he is working at his own pace, to his own rhythm. Like the strong men depicted in other forms of New Deal public art, the figure of the manly CCC worker embodied, in historian Barbara Melosh's words, "the nostalgia for an imagined past of individual dignity lost in the world of rationalized work and impersonal bureaucracy."[63]

While honoring manly individualism, the CCC images simultaneously held up the ideal of a single, collective national identity.[64] When pictured together, the "soil soldiers" are harmoniously working toward a common goal. Neither their bodies nor their faces reveal a hint of uneasiness, friction, or division. That's because all of the bodies look exactly alike. Conveying a unified vision of American masculinity, the CCC pictures visually attempt to wipe away ethnic, regional, racial, and class divisions. They venerate a single Anglo ideal. Because all the images are virtually the same, they further suggest a consensus—maybe a forced consensus—on the masculine ideal, one that visually resolves the ethnic and class conflicts that so deeply disturbed middle-class white Americans in the 1930s. The pictures reassured these jittery men that American manhood had been saved. America had been saved.

Obviously, the male bodies displayed by the CCC in the 1930s bear a striking resemblance to the male bodies displayed in Nazi Germany, Stalinist Russia, and other industrial nations at the same time. To note the similarity among these images is not to say, however, that the New Deal was a quasi-fascist or proto-Stalinist movement. Rather, they suggest that all these societies celebrated the same image of man—the muscular, tanned, shirtless, strong-jawed man. Yet each grafted its own social and political ideals on to this strikingly similar man. The image, to put it another way, was the same, but the politics were quite different.

Still, there is one conspicuous similarity between the linkage of politics and masculinity in the United States, Germany, the Soviet Union, and other European nations in the 1930s. Blurring, perhaps even obliterating, the lines between the public and the private, politicians in all of these countries, to quote George

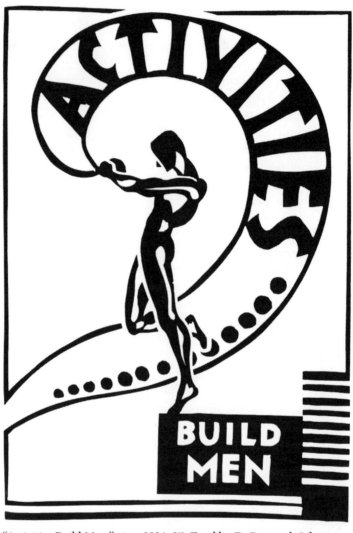

"Activities Build Men," circa 1934–35, Franklin D. Roosevelt Library, Hyde Park, New York.

Mosse, "idealized masculinity as the foundation of the nation and society."[65] What's more, in each of these nations, masculinity was thought to be conveyed through the body. Healthy men were the foundation of a strong state. With these crucial concepts in mind, policy makers saw male bodies quite naturally, that is without really thinking about it, as legitimate, indeed vital, sites of state action.[66]

Bodies were, in other words, public property. As such, they fell under the realm of the state. In fact, in a largely unexamined aspect of twentieth-century reform, social engineers repeatedly contended that maintaining social order required not only tinkering with the economy or bolstering patriarchy or introducing welfare reforms, but also remaking male bodies. Only by transforming the shape and size of men, they believed, could they create stability, and this was the fundamental goal of all state actors everywhere in the first half of the twentieth century. State actors also wanted to make sure the nation was prepared to fight. Healthy bodies, like those featured on posters in the United States, Germany, and the Soviet Union in the 1930s, stood for the strength and determination a nation needed to wage war. And war was on the minds of everyone in those tense years.

The image of the CCC man, however, is not just a vision from the past. He still lives. Just look at a Calvin Klein advertisement, or an episode of *Beverly Hills 90210*. There is the CCC man, the hero of the tree camps. He is still shirtless and in jeans, strong and muscular, clean-cut and square-jawed. He is still here, but there are key differences between the image of man in the 1930s and today. Gone are the ax and shovel, the sweat and the earth. The new model man in magazines and on television is not working, nor is he looking out to a promising future. Rather, he is staring at you with a wry smile, daring you, calling on you, begging you to gaze back at him. No longer the property of the state, he is the product of Madison Avenue, and he sells himself as a private fantasy rather than the public icon of a healthy nation. That's what makes the new shirtless man so different from the older shirtless man. Now he stands in the service of consumption, not politics.

Commentary by Louise M. Newman

> Boys do not become men just by growing up, but by acquiring a variety of manly qualities and manly competencies as part of a conscious process which has no close parallel in the traditional experience of young women (trying adapting "Be a Man!" for use by the other sex.)
> —John Tosh, "What Should Historians Do With Masculinity?" (1994)

In the last fifteen years or so, historical studies of masculinity have proliferated, focusing on the never-ending debates about "manliness," "manhood," "real men," etc., that continue to dominate our cultural landscape. Even a cursory review of this literature reveals that throughout U.S. history, masculinity has always been in question if not in crisis.[1] American men have never been able to take masculinity—their own or others'—for granted. Indeed, simple biological maturation, as historian John Tosh points out, is rarely deemed a sufficient mechanism in the transformation of boys into men.[2] Leave a boy alone, and he all too often will remain a boy. From the days of the Revolution to the present, making boys into men has been considered an arduous and uncertain social process, requiring unremitting cultural work.

Bryant Simon helps us understand just how centrally involved the U.S. government was in this cultural work in the 1930s, and his contribution to the historiography on masculinity is to be applauded on several grounds: first, for reminding us, in the words of cultural historian Gail Bederman, that "gender, whether manhood or womanhood is a *historical, ideological process,*"—not "an intrinsic essence or a collection of traits, attributes, or sex roles."[3] As Simon realizes, the process of making boys into men (as well as distinguishing men from women) is always *in process*—not simply because the meanings attributed to sexual differences change, which they do, but because throughout the history of the United States, gender has encoded power relations and created social hierarchies. Second, Simon's work reminds us that gender is part of a larger discursive system that goes beyond ideologies of sexual difference (how men differ from women) to encompass and cut across other categories of difference as well: race, class, sexuality, etc. In other words, masculinity not only demarcates the boundary *between* women and men (determining cultural norms for male and female behavior), it also establishes social hierarchies *among* men, explaining why, for example, white men are held as superior to black men; middle-class to working-class men; heterosexual to bisexual/homosexual men, and so forth. Third, and most significantly, Simon's work demonstrates how gender is a constituent of other forms of social power—how gender is both implicated within and central to projects of nation-building and identity-formation.

Even so, Simon's article (along with the other contributions in this volume) reminds us that ideals of masculinity have been remarkably stable over time. For several centuries, at least, notions of manhood have included at least three elements: 1) men as providers (the breadwinner role); 2) men as protectors of dependents (although there has been great debate about who should count as a dependent: children, certainly, but what about wives, slaves and domestic servants?) and 3) men as patriotic citizen-soldiers. These three elements of masculinity—provision, protection, and patriotism—accrue different meanings at different moments for different groups, but they always seem to appear in some configuration in prevailing discourses of masculinity.

In addition to these key insights, Simon's work raises several important sets of questions. The first set has to do with the historicity of masculinity. Given that American manhood historically draws from this mix of provision, protection and patriotism, what then is distinctive about the particular discourse of masculinity that was espoused by the directors, supporters and participants of the CCC in the 1930s? How does the CCC's ideology differ from other preceding, prevailing, or competing ideologies of masculinity?

A second set of questions emerges from Simon's claim that the CCC emphasized the physicality of the male body in its redefinition of masculinity. Why did the directors, supporters and participants in the CCC's program desire to remake boys' bodies in this way? Why such emphasis on the physical strength and muscularity of the male body?

A third set of questions probes the larger social and political ramifications of this particular ideological formation. What does the CCC's redefinition of masculinity signify in a broader cultural sense? Why was physical bodily transformation of "weak" boys into "strong" men made the foundation of male citizenship and adult male identity? What might this discourse tell us about other systems of oppression—racial domination, class division, international conflict, and so forth? In other words, what can we discern about the ways in which discourses of masculinity helped remake not just physical bodies, but political bodies as well?

Although in this forum I can venture only sketchy and tentative answers to these questions, let me begin with the first set: What preexisting discourses might the CCC have drawn from in formulating its own ideology of masculinity? How did its ideology differ from other preceding and prevailing ideologies? It may help to remind ourselves, as Bederman has argued, that "masculinity" signals a particular understanding of manhood, which emerged among the middle classes in the late nineteenth century, in challenge to (and eventually as a replacement for) an earlier discourse of "manliness." As Bederman explains, masculinity differed from manliness in several key ways. Manliness invoked moral and psychological (not physical) qualities, notably honor, high-mindedness, independence and self-restraint—qualities that had proved useful to white middle-class men of an earlier period (1820–1860) in their struggle to achieve "independence" and "autonomy" within a certain type of small-scale capitalist economy.[4] Moreover, manliness—purported to be the product of white civilization—was deemed unavailable to those men (Africans, Indians, Chinese, among others) who were still supposedly lodged at a primitive stage in the hierarchy of cultures. As Bederman states, "Manliness was the achievement of the perfect man, just as civilization was the achievement of a perfect race."[5]

By the 1890s, severe depression and large-scale corporate entities threatened the existence of small-scale competitive capitalism, and "Victorian codes of manly self-restraint began to seem less relevant."[6] White middle-class men found their economic opportunities and political power diminished as immigrant men began gaining control over city governments, and white middle-class women began going to college, entering the professions of the law, clergy and medicine, and becoming politically active. In Bederman's words, the cultural visibility of the "new woman" served to undermine "the assumption that education, professional status and political power required a male body."[7] Moreover, the success of the woman's movement in expanding woman's sphere; not only helped to blur the boundary between man's and woman's spheres; it also threatened cultural understandings of femaleness and maleness, as sexual identity was not yet thought of as a stable biological entity. In evolutionary notions of manhood and womanhood that dominated the late nineteenth century, sex differences were easily mutable, the product of culture (social activity) as well as biology. A man could become less masculine, a woman less feminine if the individual in question performed activities deemed inappropriate to his or her sex. To put it most simply, the emergence of the so-called "new woman" required the invention of a new man.

Hence white middle-class men, fearful of physical weakness ("neurasthenia") resulting from "over-civilization," and envious of the virility and vitality seemingly possessed by working-class and immigrant men, began to focus their attention on the physicality of the male body, finding new ways to celebrate their own bodies as healthy, muscular and powerful (through Theodore Roosevelt's ideal of the strenuous life, hunting, bodybuilding, football and of course, war). Terms such as "masculine" and "masculinity" were increasingly invoked to refer to the attributes that white, civilized men seemingly shared with primitive men as part of a universal sexual biology. Whereas manliness had been an explicitly racialized prescription of the best of civilized mankind, masculinity developed as a universalized description of the qualities potentially available to all men (and, equally significant, unavailable to all women). By the 1930s, therefore, masculinity—connoting aggressiveness, physicality and physical force—had overtaken "manliness" as the primary signifier of manhood, dominating the culture's lexicon. The CCC already had an existing discourse from which to draw in its reconstruction of a male body politic. These older notions of a masculinity rooted in the male body which was potentially inclusive of both white and nonwhite groups of men proved useful to the government attempting to create a more inclusive and expansive male citizenry.

As many scholars have noted, the Great Depression represented the most severe challenge (to date) to white men's sense of manhood: their feeling of entitlement to economic opportunity and political power (as a natural birthright) was thrown into question; their traditional roles as economic providers for and protectors of women were no longer assumed. Indeed, the threat to masculinity signified by the "new woman" had not receded; the extension of the franchise to women in 1920, the emergence of the "companionate ideal" in marriage, and white middle-class women's continuing access to "male" professions demonstrated the growing political and personal independence of women from men. Once again, therefore, white middle-class men grew concerned with reformulating ideals of masculinity. New formulations of masculinity were clearly necessary; already existing discourses of masculinity, which stressed the uniqueness of male physiology (the one thing clearly unattainable by women), were conveniently available.

One way to contextualize the CCC's ideology, then, is to argue that in response to the economic crisis of the Great Depression and the shifting gender relations of the 1920s and 1930s, white middle-class men reemphasized the one constituent element of masculinity that women could not appropriate—male bodies—and that this reemphasis on physicality was made that much easier in a realm where women were excluded. As Simon writes: "In this male homosocial setting, men live in a world where women cannot control them, humiliate them, or disgrace them. It is a world where men apparently do not need women." In addition, it might be noted, the CCC sent home a monthly check to contribute to the support of each recruit's family, thereby obviating the need for any individual to provide for and protect family dependents. Thus did the CCC temporarily assume the traditional values in its recruits. Furthermore, the one as-yet-unassailed social function of masculinity was men's role as citizen-soldiers (women were still excluded from military service)—hence the CCC's adoption of a military model for peacetime use.

Perhaps the greatest irony in this reconfiguration of masculinity and citizenship was the unconsciousness of the fact that the discourse of masculinity from which it drew originally held up nonwhite or primitive man as the model of masculine strength. For the CCC, it was the puny, poor, working-class boy (not a rich neurasthenic) who had to be made into a virile man. Many of the recruits targeted by the CCC's programs were boys from European immigrant families, who had only for a short time, if at all, considered themselves to be white. These boys identified with the ethnic group or national origin of their parents, whose racial identities were still fluid and multiple. Thus, the CCC transformed these nonwhite boys into acceptable white citizens in the process of making (white) male political subjectivity dependent upon the serviceability of the (white) male body for military duty. In this regard, Simon's work provides an ironic twist to the stories told by other scholars who have begun to analyze how specific manifestations of masculinity have buttressed discourses of white racial supremacy. The physicality of the male body—its size and strength—helped create a national consensus on masculinity in which regional cultural differences were minimized, even as inter-class tensions were eased. In its reappropriation of a preexisting discourse of white middle-class masculinity, the government successfully took a polygot mass of nonwhite citizens and fashioned a new white body politic.

Redesigning Dixie with Affirmative Action: Race, Gender and the Desegregation of the Southern Textile Mill World

NANCY MACLEAN

> We know too well that winning a front seat on a bus is meaningless if that bus takes us to our job as a maid or a porter, since the basic, fundamental reality of human dignity is a decent job.
>
> —Gerald Reed, Atlanta SCLC
> Employment Committee, 1963[1]

> The best thing that has ever happened to black women in the South in my lifetime is a chance to become full citizens. And that comes from their work. You can't even pretend to be free without money.
>
> —Corine Lytle Cannon,
> Cannon Mills worker, born 1919[2]

Something happened at a southern textile mill in 1975 that would have been unthinkable twenty years before. Daisy Crawford, a black weaver with ten years' seniority at Cannon Mills in Kannapolis, North Carolina, slapped a white loom fixer named Johnny High across the face. Crawford had been showing some wedding photos of her daughter to two white coworkers, women friends who worked on adjacent looms, when Johnny High intruded. Known for his hostility to blacks, High made a crack about not being able to tell who was in the photo because "all of you look alike." High—who had a documented history of groping, pinch-

161

ing, and propositioning women in the mill—then purposely el-
bowed Daisy Crawford in the breast as he walked by. That's
when she slapped him. Suspending High for only five days, Cannon Mills fired and blacklisted Crawford without even asking for
her version of the events. But the story didn't end there.

After being discharged, Crawford turned to two resources that
wouldn't have existed for her two decades before: the federal
government's Equal Employment Opportunities Commission
(EEOC) and the once-Jim Crow Textile Workers Union of
America (TWUA). A longtime NAACP activist and the most vocal
union member in the plant, Crawford had first filed charges of
racial discrimination against Cannon Mills back in 1969 for repeatedly refusing to train her as a weaver while taking on white
women with less seniority, and for renting company housing to
white female household heads while refusing it to their black
counterparts. After the Johnny High incident and ensuing discharge, Crawford took her case to the EEOC and, through the
union, to the National Labor Relations Board. Relying on white
and black coworkers who attested to her good work and "ladylike" comportment, and who buttressed her charges of racial discrimination, retaliation against union activists, and sexual harassment of women workers, Crawford boxed Cannon Mills into a
legal corner. Ultimately, the company found itself held in contempt for failure to obey the terms of an earlier Title VII-based
consent decree.[3]

Here, then, was a black woman holding a skilled job in what
had only recently been a virtually all-white industry. Right
through the 1950s the only work that African Americans could
get in textile mills was janitorial or warehouse jobs, nearly all of
which went to black men. The industry locked black men and
women out of actual production work from operative positions
on up.[4] Yet Crawford now worked side-by-side with white
women and men and—if the post-wedding chat that preceded
the incident with High is any indicator—she was friends with
some. At the very least, she had the respect of several white co-

workers, as was shown by their willingness to swear out affidavits in her support. More importantly, Crawford had access to significant sources of power such as the union, the EEOC, and the federal courts, which could offset the extreme vulnerability that had been black women's lot in the South for so long. And she was not alone; other African Americans, women and men, were waging similar workplace-based antidiscrimination struggles throughout the textile South. "All these daggone possible suits," complained one North Carolina textile executive. Since "this equality thing came along," he said, "we've gotten to the point now, where every time an employer hires anybody, he's subject to a lawsuit."[5] That the actions of a small number of black wage-earners could so agitate the heads of the region's most powerful industry suggests that meaningful changes were underway.

These changes show how southern black working people were able to make use of the reforms won by the civil rights movement, a topic that has so far received little attention from historians, who have concentrated more on struggles than their outcomes. The case of the textile industry demonstrates how those reforms opened up space for effective new forms of grassroots activism, and as such it furthers recent efforts to recover working-class dimensions of the modern black freedom struggle.[6] In particular, Title VII of the Civil Rights Act and new federal pressure for affirmative action by government contractors provided novel tools for black workers such as Crawford who were seeking racial justice. Grasping hold of them, these workers and their allies helped make the late 1960s and early 1970s a moment of exciting new possibility in the South. If deeper change was ultimately aborted by the shift to the right in the federal government, a shift encouraged by textile manufacturers and their representatives in Washington, D.C., that ought not to obscure headway made while this moment lasted.[7]

The events described here remind us that affirmative action was not an abstraction concocted by federal bureaucrats in Washington, D.C., as recent writing insinuates, but instead a multiplic-

ity of public and private responses to widely scattered popular
struggles in workplaces and communities around the country.[8]
State action, itself the outcome of grassroots pressure, had created a new context in the southern textile industry: black workers
had access to once-unheard-of levers of power, which in turn lent
permission for new kinds of challenges to white supremacy. But
for that state action, Daisy Crawford would never even have encountered Johnny High. Similarly, the passage of Title VII transformed the way that textile unions related to black workers.
Afraid right through the 1950s of losing white members and
largely uninterested in racial equality, by the mid-sixties TWUA
officials began to see greater danger in running afoul of either
the federal government or the newly employed black workers
who would soon prove labor's most reliable supporters in the
mills.[9] Contrary to what one might expect, then, textiles proved
a relatively favorable laboratory for affirmative action. Black
workers found themselves suddenly able by the early 1960s to
move ahead in an industry that faced both a labor shortage and a
need to curry favor with the federal government, and that relied
on a largely unskilled, heavily female labor force. The situation
made for, if not equality and interracial harmony, at least significant gains for black workers and functional integration on the job.

Yet, the process of change had its limits. The shift in state policy transformed the legal and institutional context in which black
workers sought to advance their interests. Recasting the terrain
on which individual black and white workers would interact, it
also made way for some novel encounters that helped rewrite
the rules of engagement. But it did not wipe out most whites'
commitment to racial hierarchy. On the contrary, this story dra-
matizes the case made by Michael Omi and Howard Winant that
"racial dynamics must be understood as determinants of class
relationships and indeed class identities, not as mere consequences of these relationships."[10] Whereas in theory white textile
workers might have exchanged a commitment to white privilege
for a sense of common class purpose with black newcomers, in

practice the racial divide usually remained sturdy, if more porous than before. In order to see *how* it persisted in a situation of formal equal opportunity, however, we need to shift our focus from movement struggles and state policy to how white workers, particularly white women, performed on the shop floor in the new circumstances. I will argue that attention to gender is in fact vital to make sense of why white behavior was so different in textiles from what it was in the construction industry. Understanding that the desegregation of their workplaces was a *fait accompli* they lacked the power to challenge, white mill women—especially older women—worked to ensure that integration would not spread beyond the workplace by redoubling their patrols of other spaces and relationships. This much can be gleaned from the oral history sources available, which are quite rich for the lives and thought of white textile workers, but pitifully thin regarding their black counterparts.[11] Using the extant sources, which provide greater insight to white experience than to black, this article examines the process of integration in the southern textile industry.

Not a simple tale of progress, this is the story of entry into an occupation that many longtime veterans longed to flee. One of the poorest-paying manufacturing industries in the country, textile mills were also the least unionized. And they were places that tormented the senses. The looms roaring so loudly that talk was futile and hearing trouble epidemic, the air swarming dank and hot to keep threads pliant, the hum of heavy machinery vibrating bones and joints, the cotton dust fouling the air and lungs, the machines speeded up and jobs stretched out by the 1960s almost beyond human endurance—all these things exacted a toll from workers in exchange for their paychecks. "Hard," said one woman: "That's the best description of my job that I know. Hard."[12] Looked down upon by better-off townspeople—often even by other working people—as "lintheads" or "poor white trash," textile workers almost universally wished their children would escape the mills. "I thought that they should find something better to do," explained Eva Hopkins, of Charlotte, North Carolina; "it was a hard life."[13] This woman's children did, but before the 1960s most couldn't. Poor schooling and a lack of job prospects conspired to reproduce the mill system. As one southern writer observed in 1979, some new competition notwithstanding, "textiles is still *the* industry in the South." One of the largest employers in the country as a whole, it supplied more than half of all manufacturing jobs in the Carolinas and Georgia, where textile production was concentrated. In South Carolina, textiles accounted for two-thirds of all industrial employment.[14]

But if it was nobody's dream, to southern working-class African Americans, the industry looked much better in the 1960s than what most of them had. In 1967, the average wage paid by a North Carolina textile mill was more than twice the annual income of half of the state's nonwhite families. A 1966 report on Union County, North Carolina found "the median income of Negro families to be $55.00 per week where both man and wife worked, $40.00 where only the man worked, and $15.00 where the woman was head of household." Nearly all the women worked as domestics, "working 10 hours a day, 6 days per week."[15] As one woman recalled, "before the mills opened up for black women, all they had was washing and ironing and cooking for white people." That was true even for many young women who had attended college.[16] Indeed, while only three percent of black workers in the South had obtained clerical jobs, a research report found in the early 1960s, they "have almost all of the household jobs and nearly half the laborer jobs, both on and off the farm." Explaining to interviewers in 1961 why black college graduates were fleeing the South, many North Carolina A & T students specifically mentioned Cone Mills and its policies. "Why," reasoned one, "bang your head up against a brick wall?"[17]

Not surprisingly, then, many black women were elated when the news came that the mills might start hiring Negroes. Corine Lytle Cannon, who was then working part-time in a chicken processing plant, recalled how the word spread and what collective excitement it produced when Cannon Mills first started hiring black operatives in 1962:

> I heard that black people were going to be allowed to go to sign up for work in the mill. I had gone to get my hair done and they were talking about it at the beauty shop and they were whispering [about people being urged to apply] . . . So I went back to work that Monday and told everybody. So when we got off work we all went over to the mill and we all walked in . . . We all signed up. All women. . . . We whispered it, you know, they was some things that you just didn't talk about. It was just a new area that was opening up for blacks and you just didn't talk about it.

In her description, applying for mill jobs almost takes on the character of a social movement, one nurtured in a women's institution, spurred by women's communication networks, and emboldened by the numbers of women involved.[18] Moreover, unlike some manufacturing work, mill jobs required little education or prior industrial experience: most textile jobs needed only on-the-job training. This opened the industry to the South's black working-class population as it was, often weakly schooled and experienced only in farm labor, janitorial work, or domestic service due to decades of Jim Crow.[19]

Among scholars, economists have given the most attention to this change. The growth of the postwar southern economy, they have shown, contributed to the breakdown of occupational segregation. As higher-wage manufacturing jobs came to the region, large numbers of white men and some white women left the textile industry for the better wages and more promising work now available elsewhere. Their exit created a labor shortage in established, low-wage industries such as textiles. In this tighter labor market, employers were more likely to consider hiring black workers. Some economists have also demonstrated beyond doubt how federal antidiscrimination policy induced employers to make that decision and so helped secure an improved position for black workers.[20] Yet few economists have recognized the grassroots pressures pushing *both* government and corporate hands. Working with mathematical models more than archival evidence, they tend to miss the ongoing *process* that was affirmative action.[21]

Southern blacks and some white liberals began pushing for access to better jobs in scattered efforts early in the postwar period. By the dawn of the 1960s, those demands had spread in scope and confidence. "We the Negroes of this city," Mrs. Margie Joyce of Charlotte, North Carolina, informed the newly appointed state advisory committee of the Civil Rights Commission in 1959, "need better job opportunities." Her area was home to numerous factories and mills, she said, "but no Negroes are allowed to work in them." A Mrs. Johnson reported a similar situation in Edgecombe County, where even incoming "new firms . . . are staffed with 98 percent white employees." "So you see," Johnson patiently explained to a white committee member, "just sending questionnaires to firms isn't quite enough." She urged tougher action to ensure that "the integration will accomplish something worthwhile." "We can do the jobs that the white women can do," concurred Mrs. Helen Clinton of Gastonia, "but because we are colored they won't give us a chance."[22]

Soon after, the North Carolina State Conference of NAACP branches spoke out on the problem, condemning "a rigid pattern of job discrimination based on separate lines of progression, the limiting of all Negroes, however well qualified, to menial job classifications, and the denial of equal seniority rights." These activists called on the federal government to take responsibility for the situation, and use its power of contract to change it.[23] Led by Sarah Herbin, who would later direct the state's equal employment program, the American Friends Service Committee interviewed over six hundred employers in Greensboro and urged them—along with vocational training centers and state employment offices—to cease preferring whites for jobs and give blacks a chance.[24] Local organizations such as the Durham Committee

on Negro Affairs also pushed for fair employment, albeit with
more savvy about the propects. "We know that many private
white employers in this State," the Durham group informed the
Governor in 1961, "will drop their prejudices only when economic boycotts or other coercions force them to."[25]

In other parts of the South, too, civil rights workers were organizing for jobs in the early 1960s, broadening and deepening
the black freedom agenda. In the Atlanta area, Martin Luther
King, Jr. and the Southern Christian Leadership Conference
founded Operation Breadbasket in 1962 to tackle employment
discrimination by companies that relied on black customers.
"The realm of employment," King and Ralph Abernathy told supporters, was "the next step" for the movement: "We must get
better jobs in order to help our children to better education and
housing, and in order to enjoy some of the entertainment and
eating facilities that are now open to us."[26] These efforts, in turn,
revived a tradition of "Don't Buy Where You Can't Work" campaigns going back to the 1930s. In theory if not in practice, the
fairness of the demand for equal employment opportunity became harder and harder for whites to deny. Acknowledging this,
North Carolina's Governor Terry Sanford announced in January
of 1963 a five-point program to open new job opportunities to
African Americans. Its voluntary nature notwithstanding, its very
existence and its relatively favorable reception were signs of the
changing times.[27]

As these regional efforts moved ahead, new tools to rectify employment discrimination became available from the federal government. By far the most important was President John F. Kennedy's Executive Order No. 10925, which mandated "affirmative
action" for equal opportunity in firms operating with federal government in order to overcome the long white monopoly of good
jobs. The widespread assumption today that affirmative action
developed only in the late 1960s—reinforced by a historiography
hostile to *both* affirmative action *and* the late sixties—has misled
scholars seeking to make sense of the integration of the southern

textile industry, by causing them to focus on the second half of the decade and miss the origins of the changes they chart. Mill managers first felt pressure from federal government agencies to recruit, hire and promote blacks—pressures for affirmative action—as early as 1961. The pressure mounted as the decade progressed. If it was never remotely adequate to the task, it was more than ever before.[28] By 1963, one North Carolina fair employment activist, who had worked for ten years with local employers, "stated categorically" to an interviewer that the opening up of new positions to blacks "was due directly to the 'Compliance' provision of Federal government contracts."[29] Indeed, 1963 was the year many black workers themselves cited as the turning point for black hiring in textiles, the year that opened the way to the mass entry that followed the passage of Title VII of the Civil Rights Act and the creation of the EEOC.[30] Enemies of the change could at least agree on its source. Said one southern white small business owner in a textile town in 1969, angry over the way he perceived "everybody . . . bending over backwards for the Negro": "it's the Government contracts, pure and simple."[31]

That mill managers felt government pressure is clear from the sources. Two features of their industry made them unusually susceptible to it: their reliance on Vietnam-era Defense Department contracts for fabric to clothe and cover soldiers, and their desire for federally imposed import quotas to shield their troubled industry from foreign competition.[32] One thing is plain: it was not enthusiasm for equal opportunity, much less racial equality, that produced the shift in their personnel policies. When the AFSC sought to interview Greensboro employers in 1958 about fair employment, half of the textile and garment companies refused even to meet.[33] Why should they? Many looked for a lead to the boldly retrograde National Association of Manufacturers (NAM). NAM proclaimed in its 1963 "Minority Program," a nationwide series of public forums to head off civil rights legislation, that "compared to Caucasians, the time elapsed between savagery and the present stage of development of the Negro is amazingly short and demonstrates the quickness of growth in a relatively free society." Fuming against "big government" in the same year, the textile management journal *Fibre and Fabric* decried "the pampering of one minority group after another."[34] Yet, however they felt about the matter, by the mid-1960s most mill managers understood that open defiance might be costly.

In this understanding, they were helped along by steadily building pressure from southern black workers and their allies. In September of 1965, the labor secretary of the NAACP called on the newly established EEOC to investigate "the entire southern textile manufacturing industry." In fact, in the first eighteen months of the EEOC's existence, it received more complaints from North Carolina than from any other state: some 869 blacks turned to the new agency for justice, and another 250 from South Carolina.[35] Their action prompted the EEOC to hold major public hearings on the textile industry in January of 1967, which in turn spurred more change. Denounced by an industry journal as "a government-financed 'Turkey-Shoot,' " these hearings were public performances, tribunals in which once all-powerful men were challenged and held accountable for their acts. They were humbled by investigators representing the supreme authority of the national government, while the long-silenced were heeded and their experiences honored by entry in the public record. Not surprisingly, the hearings emboldened even more black workers to become, as one contemporary interviewer put it, "conscious and vocal about the inequalities they observe."[36] By late 1967, an EEOC publicity campaign urged southern blacks, especially women, to apply for textile jobs, to seek training for advancement, to try for promotion—and to contact the EEOC if they encountered problems.[37]

Later, several groups, among them the Southern Regional Council, the NAACP Legal Defense Fund, and the Civil Rights Department of the AFL-CIO, joined to set up TEAM (Textile Employment and Advancement), an organization that worked with the industry, government, and communities to encourage "affirmative action" for blacks. Prodding employers to change voluntarily, TEAM acted as the carrot; in the role of the stick were Legal Defense Fund-backed class action suits by black workers, such as that filed by Daisy Crawford and her coworkers.[38] Some mill officials grumbled to their representatives in Washington, D.C. about "the junk we have to put up with," and others complained of "being singled out" for "persecution." One even harangued against what the EEOC and its "Jew" head was doing to "Dixie Textile plants": "forcing these manufacturers to go out in special search of negroes [*sic*] to place on the best possible jobs in their plants" all because of the "Jews" who had the President's ear.[39] But more striking than the dissent in the archival record is the surrounding silence indicating tacit, if still grudging, compliance with pressure to hire African Americans.[40]

Described by the economist Richard Rowan as "a virtual revolution" and by black workers who lived through it as "the change," the swerve in hiring policy was dramatic.[41] By 1970 blacks made up approximately fifteen percent of the textile labor force in the Carolinas. Almost half of those hired were women, and they found employment "in nearly every aspect of manufacturing" in the plants. All facilities—lunchrooms, washrooms, and drinking fountains included—had been integrated, training programs had been opened, and half of the firms notified the EEOC that they had promoted at least one African American into skilled positions as weavers, loom fixers, or supervisors.[42] By the 1980s, blacks made up an average of twenty percent of southern textile workers. The proportion of the mill work force made up by black women grew four times over from 1966 to 1987; in South Carolina, over the decade 1960–1970, it grew 4,750 percent.[43] Manufacturing employment such as this, moreover, contributed substantially to the improved *overall* economic status of blacks in the South after 1960. While media commentators focused on the rising black middle class, the much larger black working class pulled up the income averages.[44]

Notwithstanding how much had changed, however, textile

companies did not treat these black workers equally with whites. Struggles would go on for years over how to turn access into justice. In particular, blacks had to fight hard for positions above entry-level operative. Content to integrate blue-collar jobs because it became in their own interest to do so, mill managers kept better jobs a white folks' preserve for perhaps the same reason. By the end of the 1960s, few blacks had reached skilled or supervisory positions, and almost none had been hired as clerical workers, salespeople, managers, or professionals. In one EEOC-contracted study, almost one in four black textile workers reported that they personally had experienced discrimination in the mills, and nearly half reported that black workers were held back from advancement relative to white workers and kept out of the training programs that could make such mobility possible.[45] Convincing management to adopt even simple changes—such as the posting of skilled job openings where all employees could see them—could require a formal complaint to a government agency and the threat of a lawsuit.[46]

Moreover, for all the potential access to a new industry held, the overall story is as much of failed promises as those fulfilled. This side of the story needs attention, too. At best a fraction of the millions of blacks displaced from southern agriculture in the postwar years found jobs in textiles or elsewhere in manufacturing. "The issue is not whether Negroes have been making progress," explained Vivian Henderson of the Southern Regional Council in the mid-1960s, "but whether it has been rapid enough to enable them to adjust to an economy whose rate of progress is cumulative and intense."[47] As with other industries such as steel in which affirmative action briefly improved the prospects of black workers, many of those gains have since been partly or wholly wiped out by plant closings and automation. Over the years 1970–1985, textiles lost 155,000 jobs, or one in every four.[48] Sadly, this possibility was foreseen all the way back at the time when the EEOC held its first hearings on the industry. The agency's Director of Research feared from the beginning that the focus on textiles "would not be fruitful" because of the prospect of long-term decline. Outside the administration, civil rights activists warned from the late 1950s that automation was changing the labor market in ways that would devastate unskilled and ill-educated contestants over the long term.[49] Above the Mason-Dixon Line, some noted "an irony" of the times: blacks seemed to "be winning the right to get a job at just the time when the job itself is disappearing."[50]

The critical point for the long view taken here, however, is that the wall had been breached in an industry known for its Jim Crow barriers. And that meant a great deal to the black women and men who crossed to the other side. "One of the things that the mill did," Johnny Mae Fields reflected, "was give me an opportunity . . . to give my kids a college education. They couldn't have gone to school if I'd still be working in that cafeteria." Even a woman who loathed mill work, comparing it to "living in slavery without having a master," reported high hopes for her daughter, whose "advantages" and "alternatives" came in part from her mother's having used the mills to escape from the cotton fields.[51] The move out of field labor and personal service was thus part of a larger cross-generational shift in class formation among southern African Americans in these years. Secure industrial jobs for parents opened the prospect of good working-class or "new middle-class" careers for children. That story remains to be written.

Yet in some ways, the most intriguing thing about the events described here, given the history of the industry and what else was going on in the South in these years, is how relatively smooth the transition was compared to efforts to integrate other industries and other areas of life such as housing and schools. After all, this era saw riots against black children entering white schools, mob attacks on peaceful freedom riders, armed resistance to the desegregation of restaurants and polling places, arson to prevent black families from moving into white neighborhoods, and much more. In Natchez, Mississippi, a truck bomb killed Wharlest

Jackson in 1967; black co-workers believed Ku Klux Klan members in his rubber plant had executed him for moving into a "white" job.[52] Nothing like these things seems to have occurred in the mills when black workers entered. Such resistance as white mill people mounted in this era stopped short of violent collective action, even in the Deep South. The very consistency of that pattern offers an intriguing contrast with school integration, where the range of white responses—from the calm of Atlanta to the fury of Little Rock—proved so much wider. "The greatest surprise some of our managers had at first," reported an Erwin Mills official in 1969, "was the acceptance by whites of the Negroes." As early as 1970, one study reported a dramatic break with Jim Crow not only on the shop floor but also in social life inside many mills. The author noted "the appearance of cordial relations between Negroes and whites at break areas and in eating places in the plants. It was a usual situation," he said, "to find blacks and whites talking, eating, and joking together during their lunch or break periods." There was even a report of an integrated softball team at J.P. Stevens, whose white mill women fans "scream and cheer as loudly for black players as for white" and whose middle-aged white male players might be seen raising "the old Black Power salute" in elation over a double play.[53] Nor were such observations simply the hopeful prescriptions of white outsiders.

Blacks, even with the safety of hindsight, also commented on the relative calm of the integration process in the mills. "People accepted us," recalled Corine Cannon, voicing a hint of surprise even twenty years later; "Very few things happened racially." Of course, the lack of violence did not signify a lack of tension; white hostility, whether loud or quiet, took a toll on black workers. "I've always asked God to give me the wisdom to deal with them," said Johnny Mae Fields of her white coworkers. Indeed, managing relations with whites required both creativity and forbearance. "My mother always told me," she said, "'If the white woman want salt in her pie, put salt in her pie.' So that's what I do." Fields described her efforts to soften a cantankerous older white woman who "had never liked black people"; in time, Fields said, "this woman fell in love with me." By the power of her personality and the patience of her efforts, Fields neutralized a potential enemy and enriched her own work life. Sometimes, though, tolerance for the unfairness of whites would run out; in one such instance, other black women intervened to keep Fields from losing her job in anger.[54] Annie Adams, who was among the first blacks to enter the mills and to defy the segregation of bathrooms, mused on "how I survived in the mill": "if you let people know that you're not afraid, it helps a lot." "I felt like we was educating them sometimes," said Cannon, remembering how, after the assassination of Martin Luther King, Jr., some of the white women were crying but were embarrassed to be shedding tears "over a colored person." "That day," she said, "I was ready for 'em."[55] What stands out from the extant oral histories of black textile workers is their ability to navigate this environment so as to achieve at least tolerable comfort in relations with white coworkers.

Still, the more one thinks about it, the more counterintuitive it seems that white mill workers put up so little overt resistance. They had, after all, a reputation for open racism. F. Ray Marshall described them in the mid-1960s as having long opposed racial egalitarianism in the labor movement, even for all the decades that only a handful of blacks worked in the mills. Some, he said, protested labor's cooperation with the NAACP; a minority joined the Ku Klux Klan and other white supremacist organizations. All in all, they appeared to share "the racial views of their communities." Of course, mill owners had long fostered their white employees' racial consciousness, tweaking it when it was to their advantage. Well into the 1970s, some used race-baiting to try to derail union organizing. Even historians more generous to white mill workers and more attuned to the complexities their consciousness have recognized the exclusion of African Americans as a defining feature of mill life. In the words of Allen Tullos, "white social standing rose upon an unacknowledged black history."[56] Not surprisingly given these traditions, twenty years before some white workers had actively, sometimes violently, protested even the temporary hiring of black workers to fill World War II-caused labor shortages.[57] That resistance stemmed from more than irrational prejudice.

White workers had significant advantages at stake in an industry that for years had prided itself on recruiting through what one mill owner flatly called "nepotism." "A job with the Cone organization," reported one of its officials, "was a job for life and a job for your children if they wanted to go to work for you." This was an industry that rarely bothered to recruit or advertise; hiring was done by word of mouth through personal networks or on-the-spot inquiries in what courts later found to be a highly "subjective" manner.[58] More generally, if we understand the performance of work based on a clear racial division of labor as an important arena of what Tom Holt has aptly called "race-making" (describing how the meanings of race are constructed in everyday activities), then working with other whites day after day while the few blacks present were all confined to menial occupations no doubt helped to constitute what it meant to be white for textile workers, and to define who they were in their communities.[59] Many blacks recognized this in the way they spoke about white workers. Willie Mae Winfield, state secretary of branches for the NAACP in North Carolina in the 1950s and 1960s, said of the whites who protested school integration in her community: "all they had was white." "A lot of them, especially the poor ones," she explained not unsympathetically, "white is all they had, and they were fighting for that white."[60] Precious little, it would seem, prepared white textile workers to accept blacks on their once-exclusive terrain.

Given what we know about how gender and sexual concerns can fuel racism, moreover, it would seem that explosions would be most likely in a setting such as the mills. Management awareness of this potential had shaped earlier labor policies: as late as

1962 one union official reported that "on jobs where the [male] workers may rub against [white] women there are no colored people."[61] Two decades before, one authority described the taboo "against mixing Negroes with white women" on the job as "one of the strongest traditions in the textile industry . . . far stronger than the same tradition in the South as a whole outside the mills." One Alabama labor official at the time "defied anybody to prove to him that a white woman would tolerate a Negro man working near her in the mills."[62] These were not just places where cloth was made, after all. As one worker joked, "there is a lot of courtship and lovemaking going on right there in that mill." Its work spaces were sites of sexual banter and romance among women and men who worked side-by-side, day after day. Again and again, mill workers have described to interviewers the flirtations that went on inside mill walls and the relationships that developed among coworkers. Asked how she met her husband, one woman replied, "he worked beside of me in the mill." Even among the already-married, sexual teasing and story-telling— "rough jokes," as one man called the talk—helped to pass the time on otherwise dull jobs. Sex was not simply a source of play, moreover; it often served in crude displays of dominance. Mill bosses had long preyed on women workers with impunity; sometimes even married women found compliance the price of keeping their jobs.[63] In gaining access to mill employment, blacks would presumably be entering these conversations and ultimately the relationships that emerged from them—this in a society whose sharpest taboo had long been intimacy between black men and white women.[64]

Reasoning from prevailing interpretive models that link private lives with public stances, moreover, one would think that white mill workers would be prone to clashes to retain a white hold on this space because their own families and relationships so often seemed full of trouble. At least that was the impression conveyed by a group of Alabama employees of J.P. Stevens interviewed in the 1980s. The film *Norma Rae*, said one, was "exactly what a textile [mill] is like" in its depiction of mill peoples' vexed personal lives. This woman and her two coworkers—white and black—described marrying at sixteen (we "probably figured it was a way out" said one), dropping out of school, early childbearing, unhelpful and sometimes abusive husbands, near-breakdowns, and divorce. "That's basically what textiles is made up of," one said with obvious exaggeration; "mostly divorced women. And men."[65] Yet personal storms notwithstanding, southern white mill workers did not, by and large, militantly act out anxieties about life troubles on black newcomers, and one has to wonder why. If "all they had was white," why would these workers give way without a more active struggle?

At least a few factors can help us to make sense of why the story turned out as it did. The most important, certainly, was the newly exerted power of the national state, as it was felt through the abrupt shift in policy on the part of mill management. After all, mill bosses' sudden interest in hiring African Americans, as one openly acknowledged, was not "just philanthropic." Numerous white workers described their understanding that at this juncture resistance was futile. Was the entry of blacks "a problem right in the beginning?," a worker at Burlington Industries was asked. "No," she said, "we knew we had to accept them."[66] Asked the same question, a woman in another plant responded: "Well, didn't anybody pick on them, because they [the white workers] knew it was coming. There wasn't anything they could do about it."[67] Even where most hostile, white workers grumbled but in the end gave in without a struggle. When her foreman made his rounds one day and said he'd be bringing black workers in soon, Mildred Edmonds recalled, some of her coworkers "said they'd quit." "They wasn't working with no nigger," they declared. When the time came, not one quit: "They didn't like it too much but they didn't say too much."[68] Ten to twenty years later, no white worker expressed to interviewers a sense of outrage or even anger over the change; distaste or irritation were the strongest negative responses. "They didn't like it too good," Eunice

Austin said of her white fellow workers, "but they got used to it."[69] Clearly, however they felt about it, these workers believed themselves powerless to stop the entry of black workers. Even allowing for how they may have moderated their own responses in hindsight in a time when open racism had become less legitimate, their sense of fatalism about formal integration of the mills stands out. After so many generations of blaming Jim Crow payrolls on white workers' racism, mill management finally showed who really had the power all along to bring change. As the director of the Southern Regional Council's labor program, Emory Via, observed in 1969: "You will hear of individual unpleasant experiences and perhaps even of a whole plant whose integration was plagued with difficulty," he said. "But . . . there are few exceptions to this general rule: Wherever management has taken a firm stand that it will hire and promote without discrimination, the employees accept the situation, and sometimes in a surprisingly cooperative way."[70]

The shift in government policy and employer strategies proved decisive, but another variable—harder to get at—may have influenced that surprising degree of cooperation. It is possible that white mill workers were less—or, more precisely, differently— racist than longstanding stereotypes imply: in particular, more willing to acknowledge as legitimate the need of black working people to be able to earn a decent living. At any rate, at least a small minority appears to have accepted black coworkers with empathy and decency. The woman whose coworkers had threatened to quit, herself not coincidentally a Catholic, told the foreman, "Put one right there on half of this machine . . . Don't bother me. They're human beings, too."[71] "I think you can just fall in and accept it," mused another woman, "and just think, 'Well, they want to live, too.'"[72] "I feel they're entitled to work as much as I am," said another mill woman; "they have families to raise as much as I do."[73] "The colored people just took all they wanted to take," explained Lessie Norman, a Burlington mill worker, "and decided they wasn't going to take no more."[74] Wrestling honestly with her own discomfort over integration—"it's just a lot of change," she said—one retired Burlington worker acknowledged that "a true Christian" could not "object to that."[75] Other whites present when blacks joined the mill labor force claimed, nearly universally, that they "never did have no trouble" over it and that the two groups "got along." All that varied in these accounts was the modifier: "fine," "just fine," "mighty good," or "all right."[76] Of course, these reports were subjective and self-interested—and made at a softening remove from the actual events. Interviewers in the late 1960s found that white textile workers rated their relationships with blacks more positively than blacks rated their relationships with whites, in part because so many whites viewed little contact as a good relationship.[77] Yet at least some black workers saw signs of genuine change among their white fellow workers. "You'd be surprised," Corine Cannon told an interviewer:

> I can call up some of those white women I worked with or they call me up and we just talk. See your work, and this goes for white people and black, is what you are. You associate with the same kind of people on the weekends that you work with during the week. . . . The mill is a way of life. When we black women came in there, this was just a new area of life that was opened up for those white women as well as for us. [78]

At the very least, then, an analysis of the situation requires that differences among white workers be recognized; a monolithic group they were not.

But in making sense of the way integration proceeded in the mills, still another factor needs attention—gender, in this case white women's gender, since it is white perspectives that survive in the textile sources now available. Gender seems to have shaped the outcome in several ways—above all, in the white workers' lack of sense of entitlement or ability to block the change, but also in the nature of covert resistance that developed.

Here, it is important to recall that the mill labor force was over-whelmingly unskilled and heavily female, particularly in the operative jobs where almost all blacks started and where most stayed. A contrast with another industry engaged in struggles over race and gender integration in the same years—construction—may help to clarify why the nature of the mill labor force is so significant to the story, and how gender could help make for different outcomes.

A different work force peopled the building trades, in all but race: largely skilled, all-male, and in their relationship to their work almost a distinct class. Construction workers had a strong sense of collective power on the job, and a feeling of individual property ownership over their trades. "These jobs," one contemporary observed, "are handed down like heirlooms from father to son to grandson."[79] Male bonding, physical prowess, and sexual posturing were core elements of construction workers' day-to-day work culture. When black men and later women of all groups attempted to enter the construction industry, these skilled white men balked. Often, they resisted fiercely, and so effectively that the building trades became a kind of waterloo for those fighting employment discrimination. As building trades workers fought to preserve their monopoly, skirmishes that exacted casualties on both sides were not uncommon. To this day, while the textile industry has become more multiracial and female, the construction industry remains remarkably white and male.[80] My point here is not to vilify construction workers, nor to suggest that gender and skill are the only factors that explain the different outcomes of attempts to integrate these industries. It is instead to highlight the specific character of the textile situation through comparison with a very different regional and gender occupational history, while holding whiteness as a constant.

Yet although gender is important to the story, its role can only be discerned if we see that, in Elsa Barkley Brown's arresting phrase, "all women do not have the same gender." [81] However similar their jobs might seem, black and white women workers in textiles would bring to their interactions longstanding conflicts of interest. While it might appear that, as one white woman maintained, "we didn't have nothing, and they didn't have nothing," that sentimentalism masked telling differences. As little as they had, white mill workers frequently earned enough to hire a black woman to work for them while the white woman of the house went out to the mill, or, as they put it, get "a colored woman to come and keep house."[82] Indeed, the same woman who invoked a community of want spoke of having "a colored lady stay with me for, Lord, I don't know how many years" while she herself worked for Burlington Industries. With a room upstairs, the unnamed hired woman washed, ironed, cooked, cleaned and "raised every one of my children."[83] As household servants for white mill families, often living in and having to sleep in hallways or kitchens, black women in the mid-twentieth century typically earned five dollars a week for five and a half or six full days of labor. Of the four to five dollars she paid them a week, Lottie Adam chuckled, the "colored ladies" were "glad to get it." Miserably paid as they were, white mill women earned six or seven times that amount; they surely could have paid more, but they—for the household division of labor put them in charge of this subcontracting—took advantage of black women's desperation instead. "They pay you what they want to," said an older black domestic; "they pay you seventy-five cents if they can." "They would probably pay us for a week what they made in a day, and sometimes less," said another woman; "of course we resented it."[84]

As much as some white mill women might try to romanticize these relationships in hindsight, the exploitation was hard to erase. "Old Aunt Mary Hemphill"—who washed, ironed, cleaned, raised all the children and was "a Jim Dandy cook"— said Ada Mae Wilson, "was just like one of the family." On questioning, however, Wilson admitted that she knew nothing about Hemphill's history or family situation since she "never did ask her any questions." But "I didn't have to worry about anything" then, Wilson concluded; "them was the good old days back then."[85] So while gender may have mitigated some kinds of conflict in the mills, it also made for distinctive tensions between black and white women. "White women mill workers," as the historian Tera Hunter has observed of another era, might "have objected to working next to women whom they felt entitled to hire as their personal servants." Keenly aware of such attitudes, black women no doubt hardly relished white women's company. A few textile manufacturers even claimed that when they began hiring black women, they received calls from "irate housewives, accusing us of 'stealing their help,'" while some mill overseers were also reported to "talk mean to [black women] to make them give up their jobs and go back to domestic work."[86]

In drawing attention to the part played by white workers' gender in the integration of the mills, I am thus not suggesting that women's interracial contacts were somehow better than men's. On the contrary, in the case of domestic service they were more directly exploitative. The key point is that they were different, in ways that likely had broad consequences. Most obviously, as scholars have found in other situations as well, white women were less likely than white men to use violence or engage in direct, open conflict to defend their privileged position. No less hateful than men, they tended to perform that hostility in more insidious ways.[87] "They bunch up and talk to their selves," observed one disapproving white coworker about those who objected to the presence of blacks; "you can hear them very often making remarks after they get out."[88]

To the extent that oral histories are a good guide, it seems that most white women of that first generation adopted a common coping strategy. Accepting blacks' entry into the mills as a *fait accompli*, they redrew racial boundaries around areas they had more power to control: courtship, family, and church life. In this they, like the turn-of-the-century women described by Gwendolyn Mink, advanced "gender-based solutions to what was widely perceived to be a racial problem" and put forward white women as "managers of racial difference."[89] Again and again, women who spoke with equanimity and even warmth of black coworkers would rush to mark limits to their willingness to interact. "This integration thing," Vesta Finley declared, pointing to her own mill and the local school system, has "been good for our country." "Now I don't believe," she clarified right away, "in mixing, marrying and intermingling with them."[90] Echoing her, another female worker announced that working together was fine and economic equality was only fair—but she didn't approve of "mixing and marrying."[91] The blacks she worked with, especially the women, were "nice colored people" who "make good hands," reported glove worker Nell Putnam Sigmon. She then quickly stated her disapproval of such "scandals" as "whites living with blacks" or "them going to church together." "That's just going too far."[92] In this show of erecting a border between public work and private life, these white women acted within a longstanding tradition that made the work of kinship a female responsibility. Upholding that tradition, they now used their management of social ties to guard against the spread of racial "mingling" beyond the workplace.[93]

Indeed, that boundary marking through kinship work may offer some fresh insights into older white mill workers' habit of describing their old communities as having been "like a family." Scholars and activists alike have commented on the prominence of the metaphor of family for the mill community in older white workers' discussions of their past.[94] What they disagree on is how to interpret it—whether the family analogy signifies a communal ethos that might sustain labor organizing, for example, or whether it evokes paternal relationships in which respect for hierarchy was as important as mutuality. But as Stephanie McCurry has pointed out, for all their insights, both interpretations suffer from white solipsism. They neglect the question of "who was embraced within the family circle and who was kept outside" and so fail to come to terms with how "the 'family' was a segregated one, the village a Jim Crow one."[95] Moreover, if as some have argued, racial thinking builds on kinship metaphors and notions of lineage, then perhaps the use of such family metaphors can tell us more about how race was constructed in this setting.[96] At the least, it is striking that white mill workers stopped thinking of their communities as "like a family" at about the time that blacks entered the mills. Certainly the selling off of company-owned mill housing and the subsequent dispersal of coworkers contributed, but it seems reasonable to think that the demise of the mills' racial homogeneity also played a part. This would help make sense of something noted by union organizers: how this notion of family encouraged white workers to identify with their white employers rather than with a class that included nonwhites. Some may "think [it] silly" but "the analogy of the family," said the southern regional director of the TWUA, "happens to be a pretty doggone effective tactic." More than once, it shut unions out of southern mills.[97]

While white women seemed to play a distinctive role in relocating the borders of racial exclusivity, many also exploited their whiteness to maintain a privileged position over their black counterparts on the job. No white woman admits this in the extant sources. But black women remarked on it time and again. Black men, of course, regularly had to struggle against white men to achieve access to skills and promotion, and white men enjoyed more such privileges than any other group in the workplace. There were white men who stood in the way of black women as well; the white women who capitalized on their position had learned from masters. One Alabama mill worker complained in the 1980s that "all the good jobs" still went to whites, that seniority mattered little when black people were next in line, and that one man who got a job she wanted had no credentials, "he was just white."[98] And sex discrimination blocked white women as well as black women. Explaining the way all female workers were blocked from skilled jobs in her J.P. Stevens plant, a black union leader said "the company . . . want[s] to keep a woman down to where she cannot be independent and can't have any power."[99]

Yet in part stemming from this very sexual division of labor, there was something peculiar to the barriers black women confronted that derived from how their white counterparts benefited from—and sometimes actively exploited—white southern gender codes. Having long had access that black women did not in the textile industry, it seemed many white women were bent on perpetuating that advantage—with the collusion of supervisors.[100] Johnny Mae Fields, a mill worker with seventeen years experience, offered the clearest statement of the problem: "Sometimes they don't know the meaning of fair." "If there are two jobs and one is just a little bit better the white woman will get the better job. No matter how qualified the black woman is, that's just the way it is." She believed her own "boss man" to be a good and fair person, "but somehow they feel like they just got to favor these white women," even the lazy or incompetent ones. "The black woman don't have nobody to look after her in the mill" as a result, Fields said. "Seem like the white men in the mill look after the white women, and the black men look after the white women, and seem like the black women ain't got nobody to look after them but theyselves."[101]

Looking after themselves, some black women came to look well beyond themselves. Daisy Crawford was doing the former when she slapped Johnny High; she moved to the latter when she charged her employer with racial discrimination. In this, she was joined by thousands of other African Americans in these years. We tend to forget today what the labor secretary of the NAACP reminded branches in the summer of 1965: "Title VII is not self-enforcing."[102] To make good on its abstract promises, countless individuals across the country, most of them working-class, had to file charges of employment discrimination with the EEOC and, if necessary, enlist the federal courts. This might entail not only years of commitment, but also a gamble of lean resources; workers whose complaints failed to convince the courts might find themselves having to pay their opponent's legal costs.[103] And there were worse, more immediate dangers: the threat of job loss from vengeful employers, the specter of industry blacklists, intimidation from other members of the white power structure, and—in some communities—the ominous presence of active Ku Klux Klan chapters. The well-grounded fear induced by this arsenal led most workers to stay out of the limelight. Indeed, some feared even to apply for better jobs because they might be fired from the ones they had.[104] The sources are silent on how decisions were made to buck such constraints and file charges, but it is easy to imagine the many late-night discussions around kitchen tables, the consultations with relatives, friends and ministers, and the nights of fitful sleep as workers weighed whether tackling powerful corporations was worth the risks involved.

Among those willing to take these risks were women such as Daisy Crawford, a divorced mother of four who had to struggle for years to get Cannon Mills to train her and then to place her as a weaver. The list included as well Mary Robinson, the daughter of a large Alabama sharecropping family who escaped field labor and domestic work but had to sue and lead a union drive to win fair treatment at J.P. Stevens. Some of these challengers had completed high school, even a bit of college. Other, more typical children of the Jim Crow South struggled along with meager schooling in a hostile job market: "I am an uneducated Black woman," one Opelika, Alabama black mother of four wrote to the TWUA, "but am begging for help."[105] With a seventh-grade education and the ability to read and write, Sallie Pearl Lewis began applying to J.P. Stevens in 1966 when she was thirty-two years old. For the next five years, as many white women were hired, she kept on taking the bus out to the mill and applying over and over again, year after year, to no avail. Rather than surrender, Lewis became the lead plaintiff in class action suits against two different textile companies, heading small brigades of black women out to remake the industry. Most of her co-plaintiffs had similar profiles: little schooled but able to read and write, often thirty-something, with children, and anxious for better jobs than the ones they had as domestics, farm laborers, hospital maids, or nursing home aides.[106] Together, their stories constitute an important yet largely unknown part of the modern black freedom movement, of working-class history, and of the struggle for women's equality. They tackled traditions that had long held down working-class African Americans, and wage-earning white women as well: the white male monopoly of living-wage jobs, the favoritism used as a tool of control, and the sexual harassment from which there had long been no relief save avoidance or flight.[107]

Daisy Crawford's story captures well the promise and limits of this new era of state remedies for employment discrimination, and the questions it leaves open for historians. Her complaints against Cannon Mills span the time from the hopeful days of the mid-sixties, when she and a friend first protested to President Johnson, to the more gloomy year of 1975, by which point the climate had worsened. The suit in which she and her co-complainants charged Cannon Mills with confining black workers to inferior jobs and housing expanded the definition of discrimination and enlisted the federal government in actively monitoring the mills through affirmative action programs. Crawford also named and challenged the racial favoritism practiced by mill management, which she personally experienced over and over again as she sought to be allowed to obtain training as a weaver. Ultimately, she prevailed. Admitted to weaving school, she excelled, and finally won a weaving job at the mill. Those were notable achievements, albeit ones that required constant vigilance.[108]

Yet, for some of the problems Crawford came up against in the mills, the law had no remedy. It didn't even have a category for the specific bias she faced as a black working-class woman.[109] That left her and her counterparts to invent their own solutions—or at least coping strategies. Working among white women, many of whom would not accept the common humanity of blacks, Crawford brought in wedding pictures that drew co-workers into the celebration of her daughter's marriage—with that performance blurring the boundaries many whites worked so hard to maintain. Her claim to "ladylike" comportment under-scored her unwillingness to cede the power of definition to whites, particularly not to those who perpetuated the racist tradi-tion of denying the respectability of black women. Similarly, the specific, racialized form of sexual harassment Crawford encoun-tered from Johnny High was invisible at law. Never mind that he had touched her breasts "on several previous occasions," once calling her "nigger" when he did, and that she had complained to her foreman about this "insulting, degrading" aggression to no avail. In this institutional vacuum, Crawford slapped her abuser and lost her job. Forcing her to choose between labeling the abuse as *either* retaliation against a union activist, *or* racial dis-crimination, *or* sex discrimination, the law failed to see how Johnny High's performance combined all three and how no com-ponent made sense in this case without the others. Such legalism made it nearly impossible to describe the precise harm that had been done Crawford, let alone to win redress for it. Indeed, not seeing the conflict with the company-man Johnny High as pro-tected union activity, the NLRB rejected her claim that she had been fired unjustly. She found herself on a blacklist, looking to a not-yet-recognized union local for help. Fed up with persistent discrimination in every arena of her life, by 1977 Crawford pub-licly proclaimed herself for "socialism where these things won't happen."[110] Thus, while changes in state policy opened up new possibilities, their particular character and their constriction as national politics shifted rightward curbed that initial promise.

Indeed, looking at how blacks entered the textile mills and what happened once they did should put us on guard against the misleading dichotomies that crop up so often in discussions of racial and gender politics, whether those dichotomies proclaim progress while discounting reverses, assert continuity while slighting ruptures, split race from gender, invoke class while ignoring race, or pit struggles from below against the actions of the national state. As black workers sought to secure equal participation and rewards on the job in textiles, they both built and benefitted from affirmative action. In the mills in part because of government pressure, which itself answered years of grassroots organizing, worker activists such as Daisy Crawford claimed the right to define "equal opportunity" their own way, robustly, rather than accepting the gaunt interpretations of their employers and white coworkers. Their efforts remind us that integration is not a thing but a complex and contradictory process, less a noun than a verb open to many modifiers. Turning new laws to their advantage, these black workers made a bid to rewrite the norms of the workplace so as to end practices that menaced their hopes for economic security, family well-being, personal dignity, and fairness. For a brief historical moment, it seemed like their visions might just be realized. Why they got so far should interest us as at least as much as how they were thwarted.

Commentary by Chana Kai Lee

There are two key stories in Nancy MacLean's paper. The central narrative, of course, is about worker struggles in the southern textile industry in the early 1960s. MacLean argues that successful enforcement of affirmative action initiatives happened as a result of workers' everyday battles. Without question, MacLean succeeds at centering workers experiences by taking on the notion of affirmative action as "an abstraction concocted by federal bureaucrats in Washington, D.C." Instead, she points out, affirmative action was defined by a series of popular actions and meaningful struggles by workers—in private and public, in workplaces and other community venues. This, then, is an important accomplishment of the paper: it brings to the surface what MacLean refers to as "the working-class dimensions of the modern black freedom struggle," a good and necessary contribution indeed. The paper also offers a brief history of worker responses to a newly desegregated workplace.

With sensitivity to perspective and condition, MacLean, at the outset, calls attention to black worker attitudes and reactions toward mill work. For most folks, MacLean reminds us that this kind of work was certainly "nobody's dream"—the pay was poor, the work was horrible and monotonous and the workers were generally not unionized. The textile mills, then, were places to leave, not places to end up. Yet MacLean notes that this work was all that southern African Americans had to look forward to since they came from even lower paying jobs in domestic service, farm labor, or other menial service occupations. Relying primarily on recollections from oral history accounts, MacLean concludes that black women welcomed any chance to work in the mills.

Significantly, the industry opened its doors to blacks when workers and activist organizations began using federal anti-discrimination policy to force the hand of employers. MacLean cites specifically the activities of the North Carolina State Conference of NAACP Branches, which demanded that the federal government do something about the Jim Crow labor market as early as the 1950s. Ultimately, the branches pressured employers to stop what, in essence, was affirmative action for white employees. Also involved in pushing for federal intervention was the Durham Committee on Negro Affairs, which dropped the not-so-subtle suggestion that a boycott might help get employers' attention. MacLean also cites SCLC's Operation Breadbasket in Atlanta. Implied here is another important theme, one MacLean might find it useful to develop, the importance of black workers as consumers. After all, the threat of the Durham Committee and Operation Breadbasket drew on the appreciation of workers as consumers and specifically, the black community as a consumer community. Black workers had a fairly large frame of reference for understanding their collective influence and power. Their subjectivity reflected not only the sense of being workers, but also the larger context of injustice.

Eventually, MacLean argues, in theory if not in practice, the "fairness of the demand for equal employment opportunity, became harder and harder for whites to deny." Since MacLean is historicizing the process of integration, I think it certainly makes sense to evaluate employer response. I, however, would take some issue with the idea that white employers conceded the "fairness of the demand" after the passage of time. As MacLean notes later, employer compliance was tied directly to self-interest more than anything. Compliance had little, if anything to do with hearts and minds, which the notion of "fairness" suggests. Rather, it was a good business decision. MacLean's evidence suggests this more than anything, and she herself eventually concedes: "however they felt about the matter, by the mid-1960s most mill managers understood that open defiance might be costly."

Key to winning access for black workers was their use of the Equal Employment Opportunity Commission. Blacks used the EEOC extensively to file complaints, and North Carolina had more than any state. This led to public EEOC hearings on the textile industry in January, 1967.

MacLean notes that these hearings went a long way toward affecting worker awareness: "Not surprisingly, the hearings emboldened even more black workers to become, as one contemporary interviewer put it, 'conscious and vocal about the inequalities they observe.'" While it is likely that most workers were already at that stage of consciousness—why else would they show up at the hearing?— the hearings were certainly a part of the process of mobilizing workers. Given that the mere presence at the hearing was a political act, then, it would be nice to find out about the level of grassroots organizing that took place around these very public occasions, especially where the federal government was involved. How did black workers read federal involvement? And how did white workers perceive this kind of intervention? Did they resent it?

Of the most significant legislation, MacLean singles out John F. Kennedy's Executive Order No. 10925, which required equal opportunity in firms that held federal government contracts. She argues, against much current scholarship, that affirmative action had an earlier impact because of this legislation. Relying on the recollection of black textile workers, MacLean notes that 1963 was a turning point for entry of black workers into the industry. This "flood" followed the passage of Title VII of the 1964 Civil Rights Act. After the bill's passage, black workers continued to use lawsuits, the threat of boycotts, and EEOC complaints to pressure manufacturers.

The result was significant: by 1970, blacks made up 15% of the textile work force in North and South Carolina, and by the 1980s 20% of all southern textile workers were black. Black women's numbers grew most significantly. But, MacLean cautions, access did not equal justice. Black workers still had struggles to face, including relegation to blue-collar jobs and exclusion from skilled or managerial positions. In fact, one might argue that such evidence shows that the transition from an all-white workforce to a racially integrated one was a little rockier and more limited than MacLean claims, even with the absence of violence or stark resistance of the kind that characterized other, earlier, contests around Jim Crow. Here, I question MacLean's use of the term "smooth transition"—a relative description that would have more meaning in the larger context of battles against Jim Crow. It would be helpful to historicize the transition a bit more. To her credit, though, MacLean ultimately concludes that the story is as much about unfulfilled promises as progress.

The incomplete and aborted transitions notwithstanding, MacLean finds meaning and importance in what these jobs meant to black women especially: opportunity and the chance to dream. She observes: "The shift from field labor and personal service was . . . part of a larger cross-generational shift in class formation among southern African Americans."

MacLean notes that the workplace was a site of race-making: ". . . working with other whites day after day while the few blacks present were all confined to menial occupations, no doubt helped to constitute what it meant to be white for textile workers, and to define who they were in their communities." Indeed, this is true. And, I would add, this could have been the case even if there existed a racially homogeneous or exclusive environment. Blacks did not have to be present, in small, large or any numbers in the mills, for class-based race-making to go on. And this is true even when we consider the interdependence of racial identity formation. Race-making activity is a metaprocess that unfolds *across* multiple spheres within a larger social context, and the construction of whiteness happens in various settings—the family, the churches, the schools, all places where black absence was the norm, for the most part. White workers had other sources (beyond the mills) of knowing that whiteness was a kind of property.

Throughout her paper, MacLean continues her search for answers about the seeming easy acceptance of integration by white mill workers. In trying to make sense of this relatively "smooth transition," which might also be framed as an absence of white violent resistance, MacLean makes an interesting point. She notes that in the context of troubled personal lives, the workplace would probably have taken on a more valued position—thus making workers more disposed to protecting the workplace from intrusion by the racial other. Intrigued about why white workers did not act out these anxieties on "black newcomers," MacLean finds answers in the power of the state; workers opted not to resist, she says, because to do so would have been futile. And she includes some persuasive examples of such sentiment. MacLean also notes, however, that 10 to 20 years later, no white workers expressed outrage or anger. Well, here is where we might need to be a little critical of the source, knowing what we know about the tendency of folks to read history backwards, especially after a certain sentiment or way of life is no longer popular or acceptable. Such rewriting may be going on in this case. After all, one black woman worker, Eunice Austin noted, "They didn't like it too good, but they got used to it"—a comment that one senses may have been an understatement. A little later, MacLean herself notes that "Interviewers in the late 1960s [found] that white textile workers rated their relationships with blacks more positively than blacks rated their relationships with whites, in part because so many whites viewed little contact as a good relationship." There were unpleasant experiences, indeed; the transition was not really "smooth." Here is where it might be good to recognize the small day-to-day acts of white resistance. MacLean notes that white workers were not monolithic, and the same can be argued for the experience or process of integration.

The other key story that emerges from MacLean's paper, in fact, is the role of the interplay of race and gender in shaping white responses to integration. She is especially aware of the dangerous mixture of sex and race for this work context: "Given what we know about how gender and sexual concerns can fuel racism, moreover, it would seem that explosions would be most likely in a setting such as the mills." Yes, this is true, and it makes sense to raise this issue. But MacLean fails to fully explore the place of black maleness in this equation. If they entered at all, black males were certainly not entering as mill bosses, especially if patterns of black male employment established in the 1950s held firm. The kind of mixture that MacLean refers to is most deadly around a particular configuration of race and sex: black male, white woman. (This is certainly not to ignore the eruptions—more psychic than social—that resulted from a configuration involving white men and black women.) I am very curious if this deadly mixture was possible in the textile industry, and under what particular conditions, given the gender and racial makeup of the work force.

MacLean sees gender as an influential factor in affecting the transition to integration: "Gender seems to have played into the

outcome in several ways—above all, in the white workers' lack of
sense of entitlement or ability to block the change, but also in the
nature of covert resistance that developed." Here, MacLean finds
it useful to contrast the race and sex makeup of the textile mills
with that of the construction industry, where there was "fierce
resistance" to the entry of black males and all women.

MacLean goes on to note that "while gender may have mitigated some conflicts in the mills, it also made for distinctive tensions between black and white women." Her larger point seems
to be that the experience of integration was defined by gender,
interracially and intraracially. White women "erect[ed] a border
between public work and private life," which, MacLean notes,
was actually a traditional female function. What was new was that
they now used that role to "guard against the spread" of "racial
'mingling' " beyond the workplace.

Here I find it profitable to resituate black women mill workers
in this story, for their experiences also tell us something useful
about gender and white responses to integration. Acceptance was
certainly a two-way street. It may seem odd to problematize acceptance for black women since their initiatives and the initiatives of others in the black community aimed at opening up the
mills in the first place, but we cannot assume that their response
to integration (that is, being among white women) was unprob-
lematic for them. We must, therefore, bring back into clearer
focus their life-long, sometimes seemingly unwinnable struggle
for economic well-being. Black women wanted and needed to be
in the mills to change their material conditions. Moreover they
had lunch and mingled with white coworkers, as some of Mac-
Lean's evidence shows us. But I wonder what else might have
been going on for them (internally and socially) during the process. Such insights would probably require more imaginative ways
of rereading their oral histories. The issue of acceptance brings
me back around to gender.

MacLean starts this paper with the compelling story of Daisy
Crawford, a black woman who used virtually every means at her

disposal to end racial discrimination and sexual harassment. I
want to suggest an additional reading of Crawford's experiences,
particularly the sexual harassment she faced. Perhaps we should
read sexual harassment (specifically, the persistent violation of
historically vulnerable and devalued black women workers) more
explicitly as resistance in this context, as noncompliance—
indeed, as nonacceptance of integration. It is telling that a coworker, in coming to Crawford's defense, commented on Crawford's "ladylike" behavior. This indicates that stereotypical
notions of black womanhood were certainly operative in the
workplace. Yes, race and gender definitely affected the transition
to integration in the mills. But the historical question centers not
just around what we know and appreciate about white womanhood, race and work, but also around this mixture of race, sex
and work for black women. This, too, is part of the history of
integration for the mills.

In the final analysis, MacLean's paper is clearly an important
piece of work on which others will certainly build. As a historian
who has had a strong interest in reshaping our understanding of
the modern freedom struggle, I am heartened and excited to be
exposed to soundly researched work that rereads this history as a
struggle for economic justice and well-being. In addition, as
someone fully taken by the quest to locate historical meaning
and significance in the fundamental issues of work and gender,
I appreciate the serious attention that MacLean has given this
topic.

Notes

Notes to INTRODUCTION
by Nancy Bercaw

1. Nina Silber, *The Romance of Reunion: Northerners and the South, 1865–1900* (Chapel Hill, 1993), 29–38.

2. Lynn Hunt, *The Family Romance of the French Revolution* (Berkeley, 1992). Recent works on gender and political history outside the field of southern history include Leonore Davidoff and Catherine Hall, *Family Fortunes: Men and Women of the English Middle Class* (Chicago, 1980); Elizabeth Fox-Genovese, "Property and Patriarchy in Classical Bourgeois Political Theory," *Radical History Review* 4 (1977): 36–59; Nancy Fraser, *Unruly Practices: Power, Discourse and Gender in Contemporary Social Theory* (Minneapolis, 1989); Catherine Hall, *White, Male, and Middle Class: Explorations in Feminism and History* (New York: 1992); Linda Kerber, *Women of the Republic: Intellect and Ideology in Revolutionary America* (Chapel Hill, 1980); Kerber, "The Paradox of Women's Citizenship in the Early Republic: The Case of *Martin vs. Massachusetts*, 1805," *The American Historical Review* 97 (1992): 349–78; Joan B. Landes, *Women in the Public Sphere in the Age of the French Revolution* (Ithaca, N.Y., 1988); Linda Nicholson, ed., *Feminism/Postmodernism* (New York, 1990); Carole Pateman, *The Sexual Contract* (Stanford, 1988); Joan Wallach Scott, *Gender and the Politics of History* (New York, 1988); and Amy Dru Stanley *From Bondage to Contract: Wage Labor, Marriage, and the Market in the Age of Slave Emancipation* (Cambridge, 1998).

3. Scott, "Gender: A Useful Category of Historical Analysis," in *Gender and the Politics of History*. These books include Kathleen Brown, *Good Wives, Nasty Wenches, and Anxious Patriarchs: Gender, Race, and Power in Colonial Virginia* (Chapel Hill, 1996); Stephanie McCurry, *Masters of Small Worlds: Yeoman Households, Gender Relations, and the Political Culture of the Antebellum South Carolina Low Country* (New York, 1995); Drew Gilpin Faust, *Mothers of Invention: Women of the Slaveholding South in the American Civil War* (Chapel Hill, 1996); LeeAnn Whites, *The Civil War as a Crisis in Gender: Augusta, Georgia 1860–1890* (Athens, Ga., 1995); Noralee Frankel *Freedom's Women: African-American Women in Mississippi, 1860–1870* (Bloomington, Ind., 1999); Elsa Barkley Brown, "Negotiating and Transforming the Public Sphere: African American Political Life in the Transition from Slavery to Freedom," *Public Culture* 7 (1994): 107–146; Leslie Schwalm, *A Hard Fight For We: Women's Transition From Slavery to Freedom in South Carolina* (Urbana, Ill., 1997); Peter W. Bardaglio, *Reconstructing the Household: Families, Sex and The Law in the Nineteenth-Century South* (Chapel Hill, 1995); Laura F. Edwards, *Gendered Strife and Confusion: The Political Culture of Reconstruction* (Urbana, Ill., 1997); Tera W. Hunter, *To 'Joy My Freedom: Black Women's Lives and Labors after the Civil War* (Cambridge, Mass., 1997); Glenda Elizabeth Gilmore, *Gender and Jim Crow: Women and the Politics of White Supremacy in North Carolina, 1896–1920* (Chapel Hill, 1996); Nancy MacLean, *Behind the Mask of Chivalry: The Making of the Second Ku Klux Klan* (New York, 1994); Bryant Simon, *A Fabric of Defeat: The Politics of South Carolina Millhands 1910–1948* (Chapel Hill, 1998).

4. These works include Christopher Clark, *The Roots of Rural Capitalism: Western Massachusetts, 1780–1860* (Ithaca, N.Y., 1990); Fox-Genovese, "Antebellum Southern Households: A New Perspective on a Familiar Question," *Review* 7 (1983): 215–53; Steven Hahn, *The Roots of Southern Populism: Yeoman Farmers and the Transformation of the Georgia Upcountry, 1850–1890* (New York, 1983); James Henretta, "Families and Farms: Mentalite in Preindustrial America," *William and Mary Quarterly* 35 (1978): 3–32; and Michael Merrill, "Cash is Good to Eat: Self-Sufficiency and Exchange in the Rural Economy of the United States," *Radical History Review* 4 (1977): 42–71.

5. Brown, *Good Wives, Nasty Wenches, and Anxious Patriarchs*; Fox-Genovese, *Within the Plantation Household: Black and White Women of the Old South* (Chapel Hill, 1988); MacLean, *Behind the Mask of Chivalry*; and McCurry, *Masters of Small Worlds*.

6. Elsa Barkley Brown, "Negotiating and Transforming the Public Sphere"; Brown, "Uncle Ned's Children: Negotiating Community and Freedom in Post-emancipation Richmond, Virginia" (Ph.D. Diss, Kent State University, 1994); Hunter, *To 'Joy My Freedom*; Robin D. G. Kelley, *Race Rebels: Culture, Politics, and the Black Working Class* (New York, 1994); and Kelley, *Yo' Mama's Disfunktional!: Fighting the Culture Wars in Urban America* (Boston, 1997).

Notes to "YOU MUST REMEMBER THIS": AUTOBIOGRAPHY AS SOCIAL CRITIQUE
by Jacquelyn Dowd Hall

I am indebted to a long list of readers: W. Fitzhugh Brundage, Jane Danielewicz, Laura Edwards, Drew Faust, Peter Filene, Glenda Gilmore, Nancy Hewitt, Robert Korstad, Spencie Love, Louise Newman, David Nord, Jennifer Ritterhouse; the members of my fall 1997 gender and writing seminar; and the members of my writing group, Della Pollock, Joy Kasson, and Carol Mavor. Thanks to Dr. and Mrs. William Glenn, Robert Lumpkin, and Joe Lumpkin for providing photographs and manuscript materials from private family collections. For research assistance, I am grateful to David Anderson, Laura Moore, and Michael Trotti.

1. Michael S. Roth, *The Ironist's Cage: Memory, Trauma, and the Construction of History* (New York, 1995), 11–12; Benedict Anderson argues that the modern nation-state depends on the oscillation between remembering the stories that secure national identity and burying beneath the surface of consciousness the injustices that secure the nation's imagined borders. Benedict Anderson, *Imagined Communities: Reflections on the Origin and Spread of Nationalism* (London, 1991), 187–206. For the suggestion that the fragmentation of postmodernism has produced an obsession with memory and a veritable memory industry, see Andreas Huyssen, *Twilight Memories: Marking Time in a Culture of Amnesia* (New York, 1995); and David Lowenthal, *Possessed by the Past: The Heritage Crusade and the Spoils of History* (New York, 1996).

2. Roth, *Ironist's Cage*, 9–17, 201–11; Marita Sturken, *Tangled Memories: The Vietnam War, the AIDS Epidemic, and the Politics of Remembering* (Berkeley, 1997), 1–12; and Sigmund Freud, "Screen Memories" (1899), in *The Standard Edition of the Complete Psychological Works of Sigmund Freud*, trans. and ed. James Strachey (24 vols., London, 1953–1974), 3:301-22. Popular understandings

of Sigmund Freud tend to visualize memory as a reservoir of imprinted experiences waiting to emerge. But as Marita Sturken points out, Freud offered compelling images of the constructedness, as well as the endurance, of memory. Sturken, *Tangled Memories*, 3–4. His concept of "screen memories," for example, refers both to seemingly trivial memories from childhood that turn out to be associated with repressed experiences and to later fantasies that are translated into memories of childhood. Such "secondary revisions" underscore memory's changeability, suggesting we are always unmoored from a "true" past, always constructing our histories retrospectively. "Our childhood memories," Freud writes, "show us our earliest years not as they were but as they appeared at the later periods when the memories were aroused. In these periods of arousal, the childhood memories did not, as people are accustomed to say, *emerge*; they were *formed* . . . a number of motives, with no concern for historical accuracy, had a part in forming them." Freud, "Screen Memories," 322. Freud emphasized the personal and subjective nature of this process. Maurice Halbwachs and other theorists of collective memory see memory as filtered through social frames. Personal memories tend to disappear unless they are rekindled through repetition, and we repeat what is considered significant by the groups with which we identify. In that sense even personal memory is never merely personal. See Maurice Halbwachs, *The Collective Memory*, trans. Francis J. Ditter Jr. and Vida Yazdi Ditter (New York, 1980). For a critique of Halbwachs's conflation of individual and collective memory, see James Fentress and Chris Wickham, *Social Memory: New Perspectives on the Past* (Cambridge, Mass., 1992), ix–xii, 1–8. For an example of how oral history provides access to the process by which memories are created in dialogue with others, see Samuel Schrager, "What Is Social in Oral History?" *International Journal of Oral History* 4 (June 1983): 76–98.

3. Paul Connerton, *How Societies Remember* (New York, 1989), 1–40, esp. 6; David Thelen, "Memory and American History," *Journal of American History* 75 (March 1989): 1117–29. On the notion that "life consists of retellings," that we experience the present only by taking account of the past, see Edward M. Bruner, "Experience and Its Expressions," in *The Anthropology of Experience*, ed. Victor W. Turner and Edward M. Bruner (Urbana, 1986), 3–30, esp. 12. See also Joan W. Scott, "The Evidence of Experience," *Critical Inquiry* 17 (Summer 1991): 773–97. For the devaluation of memory that can be traced to the rise of print culture and the professionalization of history at the end of the nineteenth century, see Paul Thompson, *The Voice of the Past: Oral History* (New York, 1988), 22–71. For a defense of memory, see Fentress and Wickham, *Social Memory*, xi–xii, 8–11, 14–15.

4. See Pierre Nora, "Between Memory and History: *Les Lieux de Mémoire*," *Representations* 26 (Spring 1989): 7–25, esp. 8–9. Nora mourns the postmodern erosion of organic memory and deprecates the critical-rational operations of history, yet he still believes that the historian, "half priest, half soldier," has a responsibility for preserving the "worked over" memories that now constitute our only link with the past. For the ambiguities in Nora's position, see Steven Englund, "The Ghost of Nation Past," *Journal of Modern History* 64 (June 1992): 299–320. On the contrast between traditional societies, which are "suffused with memory," and postmodern cultures, where all past moments are "equidistant from the present, equally available and remote," see Natalie Zemon Davis and Randolph Starn, "Introduction," *Representations* 26 (Spring 1989): 1–6, esp. 3. For the intertwining

of memory and history, see Raphael Samuel, *Theatres of Memory: Past and Present Contemporary Culture* vol. 1 (New York, 1994).

5. William Cronon, "A Place for Stories: Nature, History, and Narrative," *Journal of American History* 78 (March 1992): 1347–76; Davis and Starn, "Introduction; Susan A. Crane, "Writing the Individual back into Collective Memory," *American Historical Review* 102 (Dec. 1997): 1381–85; Shannon Jackson, "Performance at Hull House: Museum, Microfiche, and Historiography" in *Exceptional Spaces: Essays in Performance and History*, ed. Della Pollock (Chapel Hill, 1998), 261–93. For "body memory," see Connerton, *How Societies Remember*, 25–36, 72–104. For women's studies as countermemory, see the special issue "Women and Memory," ed. Margaret A. Lourie, Donna C. Stanton, and Martha Vicinus, *Michigan Quarterly Review* 26 (Winter 1987), esp. 1–3.

6. Thomas McLaughlin, "Figurative Language," in *Critical Terms for Literary Study*, ed. Frank Lentricchia and Thomas McLaughlin (Chicago, 1990), 80. "Poetic" derives from the Greek word for "making, creative; relating to artistic creation." *Oxford English Dictionary*, s.v. "poetic." In literary theory, poetics usually refers to the study of the conventions that inform given texts, but I am using the term more generally to evoke the realm of memory, creativity, and imagination.

7. My study of the Lumpkin sisters is tentatively entitled *Writing Memory: Katharine Du Pre Lumpkin and the Refashioning of Southern Identity*. Katharine Du Pre Lumpkin, *The Making of a Southerner* (New York, 1946); Grace Lumpkin, *To Make My Bread* (1932; Urbana, 1995). For a sketch of Grace's life, see Suzanne Sowinska, "Introduction," *ibid.*, vii–xliii.

8. I am arguing for fluidity between these phenomena rather than for rigid distinctions. For example, when personal memories are organized into narratives that contrast the "there and then" with the "here and now," they can be seen as informal histories, with their own modes of evidence and analysis. For my understanding of what I call "social memory" (but that others call collective, cultural, or public memory), I am drawing on the works cited above and on Patrick H. Hutton, *History as an Art of Memory* (Hanover, 1993); Daniel Gordon, review of *History as an Art of Memory* by Patrick H. Hutton, *History and Theory* 34 (1995): 340–54; and Sarah Maza, "Stories in History: Cultural Narratives in Recent Works in European History," *American Historical Review* 101 (Dec. 1996): 1493–1515. Maza's historical analysis of stories that occur within a particular historical setting is pertinent to memory studies. See her discussion of the turn away from viewing cultural narratives as straightforwardly ideological or as mere superstructural effects of material change. I have been influenced by involvement with oral history, whose practitioners cannot avoid grappling with issues of memory.

9. Lumpkin, *Making of a Southerner*, 10–11, 99–108; *Columbia State*, 14 March 1910, p. 1; Katharine Du Pre Lumpkin, *The Emancipation of Angelina Grimké* (Chapel Hill, 1974), 10.

10. Lumpkin, *Making of a Southerner*, 49, 72–73. For the name change, see Bryan A. Lumpkin, "Lumpkin," [Dec. 1936], typescript genealogy, Katharine Du Pre Lumpkin Papers (Southern Historical Collection, University of North Carolina, Chapel Hill); Manuscript Population Schedules, Greene County, Georgia, Eighth Census of the United States, 1860, p. 527 (microfilm) (Davis Library, *ibid.*), Manuscript Population Schedules, Greene County, Georgia, Tenth Census of the United States, 1880, vol. II: Supervisors District 2, Enumeration District 34, p. 2

(microfilm), *ibid.* On the "mad carnival," see George C. Rable, *Civil Wars: Women and the Crisis of Southern Nationalism* (Urbana, 1989), 172.

11. Jennifer Fleischner *Mastering Slavery: Memory, Family, and Identity in Women's Slave Narratives* (New York, 1996), 1.

12. Lumpkin, *Making of a Southerner*, 86–99, esp. 86–87, 139; Elizabeth Lumpkin Glenn to K. Dear (Katharine Lumpkin), n.d., Lumpkin Papers.

13. Lumpkin, *Making of a Southerner*, 99, 121; Katharine Du Pre Lumpkin, "Lecture to Prof. Harlow's Class," Spring 1947, p. 8, Lumpkin Papers; Grace Lumpkin, *The Wedding* (New York, 1939), 18–19; Grace Lumpkin, "A Miserable Offender," *Virginia Quarterly Review* 11 (1935): 281–88. For the notion of a magic circle of belonging, see Hollinger F. Barnard, ed., *Outside the Magic Circle: The Autobiography of Virginia Foster Durr* (University, Ala., 1985).

14. On the Lost Cause, see Rollin Osterweis, *The Myth of the Lost Cause, 1865–1900* (Hamden, 1973); Gaines M. Foster, *Ghosts of the Confederacy: Defeat, the Lost Cause, and the Emergence of the New South, 1865 to 1913* (New York, 1987); Charles Reagan Wilson, *Baptized in Blood: The Religion of the Lost Cause, 1865–1920* (Athens, Ga., 1980); Fred Arthur Bailey, "The Textbooks of the Lost Cause: Censorship and the Creation of Southern State Histories," *Georgia Historical Quarterly* 75 (Fall 1991): 507–33; and Catherine W. Bisher, "Landmarks of Power: Building a Southern Past, 1885–1915," *Southern Cultures* (Inaugural Issue 1993): 5–45. On the role of women and gender in the construction of the Lost Cause and the South's early-twentieth century historical awakening, see, more generally, Nina Silber, *The Romance of Reunion: Northerners and the South, 1865–1900* (Chapel Hill, 1993); Anastatia Sims, *The Power of Femininity in the New South: Women's Organizations and Politics in North Carolina, 1880–1930* (Columbia, S.C., 1997); W. Fitzhugh Brundage, "White Women and the Politics of Historical Memory in the New South, 1880–1920" paper, 1998 (in W. Fitzhugh Brundage's possession); Karen Lynne Cox, "Women, the Lost Cause, and the New South: The United Daughters of the Confederacy and the Transmission of Confederate Culture, 1894–1919" (Ph.D. diss., University of Southern Mississippi, 1997); Drew Gilpin Faust, *Mothers of Invention: Women of the Slaveholding South in the American Civil War* (Chapel Hill, 1996); Grace Elizabeth Hale, *Making Whiteness: The Culture of Segregation in the South, 1890–1940* (New York, 1998); Rebecca Montgomery, "Lost Cause Mythology in New South Reform: Gender, Race, Class, and the Politics of Patriotic Citizenship in Postbellum Georgia," paper delivered at the Fourth Southern Conference on Women's History, Charleston, S.C., June 1997 (in Rebecca Montgomery's possession); LeeAnn Whites, *The Civil War as a Crisis in Gender: Augusta, Ga., 1860–1890* (Athens, Ga, 1995); and Cheryl Thurber, "The Development of the Mammy Image and Mythology," in *Southern Women: Histories and Identities*, ed. Virginia Bernhard et al. (Columbia, Mo., 1992), 87–108.

15. Lumpkin, *Making of a Southerner*, 127–30, esp. 128–29.

16. I am drawing here on Sims, *Power of Femininity in the New South*, 33–40, esp. 33, 34, 38, 39; Glenda Elizabeth Gilmore, *Gender and Jim Crow: Women and the Politics of White Supremacy in North Carolina, 1896–1920* (Chapel Hill, 1996), 61–118; C. Vann Woodward, *Origins of the New South, 1877–1913* (Baton Rouge, 1951), 235–63, 321–49; James L. Leloudis, *Schooling the New South: Pedagogy, Self, and Society in North Carolina, 1880–1920* (Chapel Hill, 1996), 133–41; and J. Morgan Kousser, *The Shaping of Southern Politics: Suffrage Restriction and the Establishment of the One-Party South, 1880–1910* (New Haven, 1974). For the

devastating loss of the historical memory of interracial Populism, see Lawrence C. Goodwyn, "Populist Dreams and Negro Rights: East Texas as a Case Study," *American Historical Review* 76 (1971): 1435–56; and Jonathan M. Bryant, *How Curious a Land: Conflict and Change in Greene County, Georgia, 1850–1885* (Chapel Hill, 1996), 184.

17. Bisher, "Landmarks of Power"; Nora, "Between Memory and History." Advocates of the New South creed in the 1870s and 1880s also contributed to the movement, but their interest in the past was strictly utilitarian. It was the later generation that turned its wholehearted attention to history. Thanks to W. Fitzhugh Brundage for helping me clarify this point. See Paul M. Gaston, *The New South Creed: A Study in Southern Myth-Making* (Baton Rouge, 1970).

18. For the trauma of war, see Eric T. Dean Jr., *Shook over Hell: Post-Traumatic Stress, Vietnam, and the Civil War* (Cambridge, Mass., 1997). Dean points out that very few of the fifty thousand plus books on the Civil War have focused on the horror of battle or the turmoil that followed the soldiers' return home. *Ibid.*, 232–35. The postwar travails of Confederate soldiers, moreover, left little trace in contemporary records in part because so many Confederate records were lost and destroyed and because Confederate veterans were not eligible for federal pensions, the records of which constitute Dean's major source for the postwar problems of Union soldiers. In the literature of the Lost Cause, Dean could find nothing of substance pointing to the symptoms of post-traumatic stress disorder, which, he contends, are readily apparent in northern pension records. *Ibid.*, 233. Some historians have suggested that the Lost Cause helped reintegrate veterans into southern society. But it can as well be seen as a collective "screen memory" that overlay less acceptable memories, memories that required tremendous energy to "forget." See also Reid Mitchell, *Civil War Soldiers* (New York, 1988).

19. Edward L. Ayers, *The Promise of the New South: Life after Reconstruction* (New York, 1992), 334; Bisher, "Landmarks of Power," 7. See also Michael Kammen, *Mystic Chords of Memory: The Transformation of Tradition in American Culture* (New York, 1991), 101–31.

20. Sims, *Power of Femininity in the New South*, 40; Jacquelyn Dowd Hall, *Revolt against Chivalry: Jessie Daniel Ames and the Women's Campaign against Lynching* (New York, 1993), 149–57; Jacquelyn Dowd Hall, " 'The Mind That Burns in Each Body': Women, Rape, and Racial Violence," in *Powers of Desire: The Politics of Sexuality*, ed. Ann Snitow, Christine Stansell, and Sharon Thompson (New York, 1983), 328–49; Elizabeth Waring McMaster, *The Girls of the Sixties* (Columbia, S.C., 1937), 105. See also Cox, "Women, the Lost Cause, and the New South."

21. Brundage, "White Women and the Politics of Historical Memory in the New South"; Sims, *Power of Femininity in the New South*, 128–54; Cox, "Women, the Lost Cause, and the New South."

22. *Columbia State*, 20 Aug. 1905, p. 3; *ibid.*, 25 Sept. 1904, p. 11; *ibid.*, 1 Nov. 1905, p. 3.

23. Foster, *Ghosts of the Confederacy*, 97, 136–37; photocopy of letter fragment from Elizabeth Lumpkin Glenn, n.d. (in Jacquelyn Hall's possession); *Columbia State*, 20 Aug. 1905, p. 3. For the adulation of Winnie Davis and the sharp contrast between her image and her life, see Nina Silber, "Intemperate Men, Spiteful Women, and Jefferson Davis," in *Divided Houses: Gender and the Civil War*, ed. Catherine Clinton and Nina Silber (New York, 1992), 283–305; and Florence Elliott Cook, "Growing Up White, Genteel, and Female in a Changing

South, 1865 to 1915" (Ph.D. diss., University of California at Berkeley, 1992), 267–73.

24. *Confederate Veteran*, 12 (Feb. 1904): 69, 70; *ibid*. 13, (July 1905): 298; *Columbia State*, 25 Sept. 1904 p. 11; newsclip, 13 Nov. 1906, pp. 8, 10 (in Hall's possession); *Columbia State*, 14 Nov. 1906, p. 1; Foster, *Ghosts of the Confederacy*, 136. See also *Columbia State*, 19 May 1911, p. 8; *ibid*., 24 June 1909, p. 3. For Grace Lumpkin's account of her experience, see Lumpkin, *To Make My Bread*, 189.

25. Hall, *Revolt against Chivalry*, 150; Sims, *Power of Femininity in the New South*, 135; Walter Hines Page, *The Southerner, a Novel: Being the Autobiography of Nicholas Worth* (New York, 1909), 160.

26. On Elizabeth's career, see Annual Departmental Reports, 1903–1905, box 2 (Winthrop College Archives, Rock Hill, S.C.); Katharine Du Pre Lumpkin to My Dear Sister (Elizabeth Lumpkin), 3 Jan. 1904, Lumpkin Papers; and *Columbia State*, 25 Sept. 1904, p. 11.

27. Elizabeth Lumpkin Glenn, "Bitterroot," [1950] (in Dr. and Mrs. William Glenn's possession); Annette Lumpkin to Sister, 19 Feb. 1924 (in Joe Lumpkin's possession); *Confederate Veteran*, 14 (1906): 494–96, esp. 495, 496; newsclip, *Asheville Citizen*, 15 Feb. 1963 (in Hall's possession).

28. See Sims, *Power of Femininity in the New South*, 135–37; and Montgomery, "Lost Cause Mythology in New South Reform."

29. Wilson, *Baptized in Blood*, 149; Lumpkin, *Making of a Southerner*, 126–27; Bailey, "Textbooks of the 'Lost Cause' "; Fred Arthur Bailey, "Free Speech and the 'Lost Cause' in Texas: A Study of Social Control in the New South," *Southwestern Historical Quarterly* 97 (1994): 453–77. On the best-known of the amateur historians, see Grace Elizabeth Hale, " 'Some Women Have Never Been Reconstructed': Mildred L. Rutherford, Lucy M. Stanton, and the Racial Politics of White Southern Womanhood, 1900–1930," in *Georgia in Black and White: Explorations in the Race Relations of a Southern State, 1865–1950*, ed. John C. Inscoe (Athens, Ga., 1994), 173–201. But textbooks published in the North and written from a New England point of view continued to be widely used in southern public schools. See Kammen, *Mystic Chords of Memory*, 382–83. For the commitment of the United Daughters of the Confederacy (UDC) to women's education, see Mary B. Poppenheim et al., *The History of the United Daughters of the Confederacy, 1894–1955* (Raleigh, 1956), 95–127. For education as the chief panacea of southern reformers, see Leloudis, *Schooling the New South*; A. D. Mayo, *Southern Women in the Recent Educational Movement in the South* (1892; Baton Rouge, 1978); and esp. Dan T. Carter and Amy Friedlander, "Introduction," *ibid*., xi–xxiii.

30. On the professionalization of southern history and the marginalization of women, see W. Fitzhugh Brundage, "Historical Memory in the Modern South, 1865 to the Present," typescript of book in progress (in Brundage's possession); and Brundage, "White Women and the Politics of Historical Memory." See also Bonnie G. Smith, "Gender and the Practice of Scientific History: The Seminar and Archival Research in the Nineteenth Century," *American Historical Review* 100 (Oct. 1995): 1150–76. On the professionalization of history and the careers of William A. Dunning and Ulrich B. Phillips, see Peter Novick, *That Noble Dream: The "Objectivity Question" and the American Historical Profession* (New York, 1988), 1–85, 229, esp. 77. On the impersonal voice, see Frances FitzGerald, *America Revised: History Schoolbooks in the Twentieth Century* (Boston, 1979), 51–52.

31. See Jennifer Fleischner's brilliant study of such "escapes from childhood" in slave autobiographies: Fleischner, *Mastering Slavery*, 1.

32. Sidonie Smith, *A Poetics of Women's Autobiography: Marginality and the Fictions of Self-Representation* (Bloomington, 1987), 17; Lumpkin, *Making of a Southerner*, 128; Katharine Du Pre Lumpkin, "Lecture to a General Audience" 1947, p. 2, Lumpkin Papers. On the utopian and performative aspects of feminist criticism, which aims at "seizing authority from men at the same time that it seeks to redefine traditional models . . . of authority, power, and hierarchy," see Tania Modleski, *Feminism without Women: Culture and Criticism in a "Postfeminist" Age* (New York, 1991), 41–58, esp. 48, 53. On the dialogue between authors and readers see Norine Voss, " 'Saying the Unsayable': An Introduction to Women's Autobiography," in *Gender Studies: New Directions in Feminist Criticism*, ed. Judith Spector (Bowling Green, 1986), 224. Voss argues that the late nineteenth century—a time of constriction for men—was for women a time of "escape toward freedom." Such escape is also the abiding theme of black autobiography.

33. Lumpkin, *Making of a Southerner*, 111–47, esp. 130.

34. *Ibid.*, 115; Katharine Du Pre Lumpkin, "Plans for Work" [1943–1944], Lumpkin Papers; Katharine Du Pre Lumpkin interview by Jacquelyn Hall, Aug. 4, 1974, transcript, p. 66, Southern Oral History Program Collection (Southern Historical Collection). For local newspaper coverage of the reunion, which Katharine consulted in researching her autobiography, see *Columbia State*, 18 March 1903, p. 4; *ibid.*, 3 April 1903, p. 8; *ibid.*, 12 April 1903, p. 10; *ibid.*, 10 May 1903, p. 16; *ibid.*, 11 May 1903, p. 1; *ibid.*, 12 May 1903, p. 9; *ibid.*, 13 May 1903, pp. 1, 5–6, 8; *ibid.*, 14 May 1903, pp. 1–6; *ibid.*, 15 May 1903, pp. 1, 3; *ibid.*, 16 May 1903, p. 4.

35. Lumpkin, *Making of a Southerner*, 117–20.

36. *Ibid.*, 121. See also newsclip, 13 Nov. 1906, pp. 8, 10 (in Hall's possession).

37. Lumpkin, *Making of a Southerner*, 122–24, 184.

38. *Ibid.*, 124–25, 136–37.

39. *Ibid.*, 126.

40. *Ibid.*, 185; Glenn, "Bitterroot"; Grace Lumpkin, "Annette Caroline Morris [Lumpkin]," in Lumpkin, "Lumpkin." For the "mirror stage" in a child's development and the suggestion that alienation from a historically imposed image of self can motivate the creation of an alternative autobiography self, see Shari Benstock, *The Private Self: Theory and Practice of Women's Autobiographical Writings* (Chapel Hill, 1988), 12.

41. Lumpkin, *Making of a Southerner*, 123, 185–86.

42. *Ibid.*, 127–28.

43. For contrasting views of the relationship between commemoration and critical inquiry, see Hutton, *History as an Art of Memory*; and Gordon, review of *History as an Art of Memory* by Hutton. Katharine's insistence on the contingent, social nature of her transformation had the political purpose of persuading white southerners that change was integral to southern history, not imposed from without. She was also adopting a trope of (white) women's autobiography: the attribution of success or personal transformation to "providential circumstance." See Sandra M. Gilbert and Susan Gubar, *No Man's Land: The Place of the Woman Writer in the Twentieth Century*, vol. 1: *The War of the Words* (New Haven, 1988), 66–67. Space does not allow a full explication of Katharine's autobiographical strategies. Suffice it to say that I do not see her stress on contingency and context as a symptom of women's inability to see themselves as the authors of their own lives.

For this problem in women's autobiography, see Patricia Meyer Spacks, "Selves in Hiding," in *Women's Autobiography: Essays in Criticism*, ed. Estelle C. Jelinek (Bloomington, 1980), 112–32; and Jill Conway, "Women Reformers and American Culture, 1870–1930" *Journal of Social History* 5 (Winter 1971–1972): 164–77. Katharine Du Pre Lumpkin, "Lecture to a General Audience," p. 3. See also Lumpkin, *Making of a Southerner*, 233–39.

44. Lumpkin, undated, handwritten note left in her personal copy of The *Making of a Southerner* (thanks to Joe Lumpkin for sharing this with me); Lumpkin, *Making of a Southerner*, 131–32, 151· 73, 180–86; Lumpkin, *Emancipation of Angelina Grimké*, 3–5, 14–16, esp. 5; "Testimony of Angelina Grimké Weld" in *American Slavery As It Is, Testimony of a Thousand Witnesses*, ed. Theodore Dwight Weld (1839; New York, 1969), 52–57; Lumpkin interview, 7. In The *Making of a Southerner*, Katharine referred to the cook's abuser as "the white master of the house." Like Angelina, who, Katharine noted, wrote about her brother's rages anonymously, Katharine could not bring herself to name her father directly.

45. Lumpkin, *Making of a Southerner*, 151–186, esp. 182.

46. Lumpkin interview, 24; Lumpkin, *Making of a Southerner*, 203; Carol Stack, *Call to Home: African Americans Reclaim the Rural South* (New York, 1996). On the significance of this relationship with Dorothy Wolff Douglas, see Jacquelyn Dowd Hall, "Open Secrets: Memory, Imagination, and the Refashioning of Southern Identity," *American Quarterly* 50 (1998): 110–24.

47. For Katharine's denial that racial mores were immutable see Lumpkin, *Making of a Southerner*, 203–4. For how assumptions of agency enable memoir, see Connerton, *How Societies Remember*, 19. For some of Katharine's early works, see Katharine Du Pre Lumpkin, "Factors in the Commitment of Correctional School Girls in Wisconsin," *American Journal of Sociology* 37 (1931): 222–30; Katharine Du Pre Lumpkin, "Parental Conditions of Wisconsin Girl Delinquents" *ibid.* 38 (1932): 232–39; and Katharine Du Pre Lumpkin, *The Family: A Study of Member Roles* (Chapel Hill, 1933). For her turn to social history, see Katharine Du Pre Lumpkin, *Shutdowns in the Connecticut Valley: A Study of Worker Displacement In the Small Industrial Community* (Northampton, 1934). For the beginnings of a more passionate, political approach, see Katharine Du Pre Lumpkin and Dorothy Wolff Douglas, *Child Workers in America* (New York, 1937).

48. Franklin D. Roosevelt characterized the South in these terms; see David L. Carlton and Peter A. Coclanis, eds., *Confronting Southern Poverty In the Great Depression: "The Report on Economic Conditions of the South" with Related Documents* (Boston, 1996), 42. Katharine Du Pre Lumpkin, *The South in Progress* (New York, 1940).

49. Lumpkin, "Lecture to a General Audience," p. 3; Lumpkin, "Lecture to Prof. Harlow's Class," p. 13; Myra Page, review of *The Making of a Southerner*, by Katharine Du Pre Lumpkin and *The Way of the South* by Howard Odum, *Science and Society* 12 (1948): 276–78, esp. 276.

50. Lumpkin, *Making of a Southerner*, 235–36, 239; Modleski, *Feminism without Women*, 46.

51. Studs Terkel, *Hard Times: An Oral History of the Great Depression* (New York, 1970), 17. For the imperative, and impossibility, of keeping faith with the past, see Roth, *Ironist's Cage*, 201–13.

52. The metaphor of the "master's tools" appears in Audre Lorde, "Age, Race, Class, and Sex: Women Redefining Difference," in *Words of Fire: An Anthology*

of African-American Feminist Thought, ed. Beverly Guy-Sheftall (New York, 1995), 291.

53. For contributions by feminist historians to the surge of first-person writing, see Carol Ascher, Louise DeSalvo, and Sara Ruddick, eds., *Between Women: Biographers, Novelists, Critics, Teachers and Artists Write about Their Work on Women* (Boston, 1984); and Sara Alpern et al., eds., *The Challenge of Feminist Biography: Writing the Lives of Modern American Women* (Urbana, 1992). For works of historians who have placed their own memories in the histories they write, by speaking in the first-person singular or by making readers aware of their struggles with evidence and interpretation, see, for example, Robert A. Rosenstone, *Mirror in the Shrine: American Encounters with Meiji Japan* (Cambridge, Mass., 1988); Laurel Thatcher Ulrich, *A Midwife's Tale: The Life of Martha Ballard Based on Her Diary, 1786–1812* (New York, 1990); William S. McFeely, *Sapelo's People: A Long Walk into Freedom* (New York, 1994); Nell Irvin Painter, *Sojourner Truth: A Life, A Symbol* (New York, 1996); Simon Schama, *Landscape and Memory* (New York, 1995); and Luisa Passerini, *Autobiography of a Generation: Italy, 1968,* trans. Lisa Erdberg (Hanover, 1996). On the debates over the *I* in the text, see Robert Rosenstone, Bryant Simon, and Moshe Sluhovsky, "Experiments in Narrating Histories: A Workshop" *Perspectives* 32 (Sept. 1994): 7–10.

54. On African American countermemories and histories, see Genevieve Fabre and Robert O'Meally, eds., *History and Memory in African-American Culture* (New York, 1994); David W. Blight, "'For Something beyond the Battlefield': Frederick Douglass and the Memory of the Civil War" *Journal of American History* 75 (1989): 1156–78; Spencie Love, *One Blood: The Death and Resurrection of Charles R. Drew* (Chapel Hill, 1996); and August Meier, *Black History and the Historical Profession, 1915–80* (Urbana, 1986).

55. See Alon Confino, "Collective Memory and Cultural History: Problems of Method," *American Historical Review* 102 (1997): 1386–1403.

56. "Robert Penn Warren," *Vanity Fair,* April 1985, 45; Love, *One Blood,* 8. I thank Glenda Gilmore and Laura Edwards for helping me clarify this point.

Notes to NATHANIEL BACON AND THE DILEMMA OF COLONIAL MASCULINITY
by Kathleen M. Brown

1. Colonial Office Records [hereafter C.O.], 1/36, fols. 86, 140; 1/37, fol. 14; Stephen Saunders Webb, *1676: The End of American Independence* (Cambridge, Mass., 1984), 50–51, 152–153, 202–203. See also Annie Lash Jester and Martha Woodroof Hiden, eds., *Adventurers of Purse and Person: Virginia, 1607–1625* (Richmond, 1964), 95–100.

2. C.O. 1/31, fol. 179; 1/36, fols. 86, 140; H. McIlwaine, ed., *Minutes of the Council and General Court,* 399. See also Edmund S. Morgan, *American Slavery, American Freedom: The Ordeal of Colonial Virginia* (New York, 1975), 255; Webb, *1676,* 50–51; Warren Martin Billings, "'Virginias Deploured Condition,' 1660–1676: The Coming of Bacon's Rebellion" (Ph.D. diss., Northern Illinois University, 1968), 90–91. For a version of the story featuring the other Ludwell brother see Philip Alexander Bruce, *Institutional History of Virginia in the Seventeenth Century,* 2 vols. (1910; Gloucester, Mass., 1964) 2:449.

3. McIlwaine, ed., *Minutes of the Council and General Court*, 399, 423; C.O. 1/35, fol. 245.

4. Examples of this scholarship include Drew Gilpin Faust, "Altars of Sacrifice: Confederate Women and Narratives of War," *Journal of American History* 76 (1991):1200–1228. Stephanie McCurry, *Masters of Small Worlds: Yeoman Households, Gender Relations, and Political Culture of the Antebellum South Carolina Low Country* (New York, 1995); Nancy MacLean, *Behind the Mask of Chivalry: The Making of the Second Ku Klux Klan* (New York, 1994). By "masculinity," I mean the cultural ideals of manhood as well as the daily performances that gave meaning to male social roles. I understand masculinity to be a historical formation that shifts in meaning as men's legal privileges, economic and military responsibilities, and life risks change over time.

5. Winthrop Jordan, *White Over Black: American Attitudes Toward the Negro, 1550–1812* (Chapel Hill, 1968), 79.

6. Thomas Wertenbaker's portrait of the rebel Nathaniel Bacon *Torchbearer of the Revolution: The Story of Bacon's Rebellion and Its Leader* (Princeton, 1941), emphasized his political and military leadership and depicted the rebellion as a precocious strike for democracy. Wilcomb Washburn's rejoinder to Wertenbaker, *The Governor and the Rebel: A History of Bacon's Rebellion in Virginia* (Chapel Hill, 1957), focused on the racial component of Bacon's attacks upon Indians and condemned the rebels for their vigilantism, but did not expand the definition of politics from that used by Wertenbaker. In *1676*, Stephen Webb teased the reader with vignettes about women's participation in the rebellion, but ultimately remained firmly within the imperial school of interpretation, where the political intrigues of the Restoration court and London's coffeehouses were ultimately of greater significance than the concern of the colony's frontier dwellers for their households.

7. Julia Cherry Spruill, *Women's Life and Work in the Southern Colonies* (1938; New York, 1972), 233–236; Lois Green Carr and Lorena S. Walsh, "The Planter's Wife: The Experience of White Women in Seventeenth-Century Maryland," *William and Mary Quarterly*, 3d ser., 34 (1977): 542–571; Susan Westbury, "Women in Bacon's Rebellion," in Virginia Bernhard, et al., eds., *Southern Women: Histories and Identities* (Columbia, Mo., 1992), 30–46.

8. E. M. W. Tillyard, *The Elizabethan World Picture* (New York, 1944); Gordon J. Schochet, *Patriarchalism in Political Thought: The Authoritarian Family and Political Speculation and Attitudes, Especially in Seventeenth-Century England* (New York, 1975); Keith Wrightson, *English Society, 1580–1680* (New Brunswick, N.J., 1982); Susan Dwyer Amussen, *An Ordered Society: Gender and Class in Early Modern England* (New York, 1988).

9. Anthony Fitzherbert, *The Boke of Husbandry* (London, 1525); Gervase Markham, *Countrey Contentments: or, The English Huswife* (London, 1623); William Gouge, *Of Domesticall Duties* (London, 1622); Richard Brathwait, *The English Gentleman* (London, 1630).

10. In Norfolk County, runaway servants grew in number from an average of .5 per year to 2.3 per year between 1649 and 1670. In Lancaster County, those numbers increased from 1.0 to 3.5 between 1659 and 1670. In York, servants running away jumped from 1.3 to 2.0 between the 1640s and 1650, where the average remained into the 1670s.

11. See Kathleen M. Brown, *Good Wives, Nasty Wenches, and Anxious Patriarchs: Gender, Race and Power in Colonial Virginia* (Chapel Hill, 1996), 140–154.

12. York Deeds, Orders and Wills 3, Jan. 25, 1662, 149.

13. William Waller Hening, ed., *Statutes At Large*, 3 Oct.1670, 2 (Charlottesville, Va., 1969), 280. See also Russell Menard, "From Servant to Freeholder," *William and Mary Quarterly*, 3d ser., 30 (1973): 37–64; Morgan, *American Slavery, American Freedom*, 204, 221, 228–229, 289; Paul G.E. Clemens, *The Atlantic Economy and Colonial Maryland's Eastern Shore: From Tobacco to Grain* (Ithaca, N.Y., 1980), 99, 169; Gloria L. Main, *Tobacco Colony: Life in Early Maryland, 1650–1720* (Princeton, 1982), 59, 78–79; Billings, " 'Virginias Deploured Condition', 1660–1676: The Coming of Bacon's Rebellion" (Ph.D. diss., Northern Illinois University, 1968), 13, 38, 40, 87, 149, 153, 219; Billings, "Causes of Bacon's Rebellion: Some Suggestions," *Virginia Magazine of History and Biography*, 78 (1970): 409–435; Billings, "The Growth of Political Institutions in Virginia, 1634–1676," *William and Mary Quarterly*, 3d ser., 31 (1974): 225–242; Jon Kukla, ed., "Some Acts Not in Hening's *Statutes*," *Virginia Magazine of History and Biography*, 83 (1975): 95; Billings, ed., *The Old Dominion in the Seventeenth Century: A Documentary History of Virginia, 1606–1689* (Chapel Hill, 1975), 263–267; Bruce, *Institutional History*, 2: 442, 491–492; Webb, *1676*, 19; Warren M. Billings, John E. Selby, and Thad W. Tate, *Colonial Virginia: A History* (White Plains, N.Y., 1986), 58.

14. C.O. 1/36, fol. 139; 1/37, fols. 29–30.

15. Hening, ed., *Statutes at Large*, Jan. 6, 1640, I, 227. I am indebted to Michael Jarvis for sharing his research on gun ownership in York County between 1660 and 1676. See Jarvis, " 'The Price of One's Labor': Patterns in Indentured Servant and Slave Ownership in Seventeenth-Century York County," unpublished paper. For the arming of the Virginia countryside, see William L. Shea, *The Virginia Militia in the Seventeenth Century* (Baton Rouge, 1983), 92–93. See also Carole Shammas, *The Pre-Industrial Consumer in England and America* (Oxford, 1990), 206–208; Alan Macfarlane, *The Justice and the Mare's Ale: Law and Disorder in Seventeenth-Century England* (New York, 1981), 191–193; Morgan, *American Slavery, American Freedom*, 239–240; Billings, "The Transfer of English Law to Virginia," in K.R. Andrews, N.P. Canny, and P.E.H. Hair, eds., *The Westward Enterprise: English Activities in Ireland, the Atlantic, and America, 1480–1650* (Detroit, 1979), 241–242; Washburn, *Governor and the Rebel*, 20; Billings, Selby and Tate, *Colonial Virginia*, 97–108. See also Michael A. Bellesiles, "The Origins of Gun Culture in the United States, 1760–1865," *Journal of American History* 83 (1996), 425–455, for his claim that present-day patterns of gun ownership in the United States derive not from the conditions of frontier life, but from the nineteenth-century gun industry and the Civil War. Bellesiles's study, which begins in the middle of the eighteenth century and is based on Pennsylvania and New England inventories, minimizes the regional differences in gun ownership that his own research uncovers. When colonial Virginia is compared to seventeenth-century England rather than to the present day, gun ownership by colonial propertyholders occurs at unprecedented rates.

16. C.O. 1/36, fols. 137, 211–212; 1/37, fol. 2; Lois Green Carr and Russell R. Menard, "Immigration and Opportunity," in Thad W.Tate and David L. Ammerman, eds., *The Chesapeake in the Seventeenth Century: Essays on Anglo-American Society* (Chapel Hill, 1979), 206–242.

17. "Nathaniel Bacon Esqr His Manifesto Concerning the Present Troubles in Virginia," C.O. 1/37, fols. 178–179.

18. Billings, ed., *Old Dominion*, 271.

19. Berkeley to Ludwell, July 1, 1676, quoted in Webb, *1676*, 16.

20. "The Declaration of the People against Sr William Berkeley, and Present Governors of Virginia," VHS; C.O. 1/37, fols. 130–131; Billings, ed., *Old Dominion*, 277–279; Charles M. Andrews, ed., *Narratives of the Insurrections* (New York, 1915), 122; C.O. 1/39, fol. 54; C.O. fols., 130–131, 133.

21. "Bacon's Manifesto," in Billings, ed., *Old Dominion*, 278–279.

22. "Charles City County Grievances 1676," *Virginia Magazine of History and Biography*, 3 (1895): 13; C.O. 1/39, fols. 220–221.

23. Westbury, "Women in Bacon's Rebellion," 45–46.

24. C.O. 1/37, fols. 29–30.

25. C.O. 1/36, fols. 111–112.

Notes to LAW, DOMESTIC VIOLENCE, AND THE LIMITS OF
PATRIARCHAL AUTHORITY IN THE ANTEBELLUM SOUTH
by Laura F. Edwards

1. A revised version of this piece appeared in the *Journal of Southern History* 65 (November 1999). No complete record exists of the testimony against George and Mary Meadows. The trial transcripts only contain a summary of the case and testimony relating to those issues that were central to the two appeals. But these fragments suggest how tenuous the evidence against George and Mary Meadows was. *State v. George and Mary Meadows*, 1847, Criminal Actions Concerning Slaves and Free Persons of Color, Granville County; *State v. George*, 1847, #4188 and *State v. George*, 1848, #4230, Supreme Court Original Cases; *State v. George*, 3 March 1847, 4 March 1847, 8 September 1847, 9 September 1847, Superior Court Minutes, Granville County; *State v. George*, Fall Term 1847, Spring Term 1848, Person County; *State v. Mary Meadows*, 7 March 1849, 9 March 1849, 5 September 1849, 7 September 1849, Superior Court Minutes, Granville County; all in North Carolina Division of Archives and History (NCDAH). For a discussion of this case, see also Victoria Bynum, *Unruly Women: The Politics of Social and Sexual Control in the Old South* (Chapel Hill, 1992), 85–87.

2. Although I do not refer directly to gender in this analysis, it is embedded within the basic conceptual approach and I am drawing on work that uses gender to rethink the nature of race, class, and politics. See Peter Bardaglio, *Reconstructing the Household: Families, Sex, and the Law in the Nineteenth-Century South* (Chapel Hill, 1995); Nancy Bercaw, "The Politics of Household: Domestic Battlegrounds in the Transition from Slavery to Freedom in the Yazoo-Mississippi Delta, 1850–1860," (Ph.D. diss. University of Pennsylvania, 1996); Kathleen M. Brown, *Good Wives, Nasty Wenches, and Anxious Patriarchs: Gender, Race, and Power in Colonial Virginia* (Chapel Hill, 1996); Bynum, *Unruly Women*; Catherine Clinton, "Bloody Terrain: Freedwomen, Sexuality, and Violence During Reconstruction," *The Georgia Historical Quarterly* 76 (Summer 1992): 310–332; Catherine Clinton and Nina Silber, eds., *Divided Houses: Gender and the Civil War* (New York, 1992); Catherine Clinton and Michele Gillespie, eds., *The Devil's Lane: Sex and Race in the Early South* (New York, 1997); Jane Dailey, "Before Jim Crow: The Politics of Race in Post-Emancipation Virginia,." manuscript in progress; Laura F. Edwards, *Gendered Strife and Confusion: The Political Culture of Reconstruction* (Urbana, Ill., 1997); Drew Gilpin Faust, *Mothers of Invention: Women of the Slaveholding South in the American Civil War* (Chapel Hill, 1996); Kirsten Fischer,

Bodies of Evidence: The Racial Politics of Illicit Sex in Colonial North Carolina, (Ithaca, forthcoming); Noralee Frankel, *Freedom's Women: African-American Women in Mississippi, 1860–1870* (Bloomington, Ind., 1999); Elizabeth Fox-Geno-vese, *Within the Plantation Household: Women in the Old South* (Chapel Hill, 1988); Glenda Elizabeth Gilmore, *Gender and Jim Crow: Women and the Politics of White Supremacy in North Carolina, 1896–1920* (Chapel Hill, 1996); Grace Elizabeth Hale, *Making Whiteness: The Culture of Segregation in the South, 1890–1940* (New York, 1998); Jacquelyn Dowd Hall, " 'The Mind That Burns in Each Body': Women, Rape, and Racial Violence," in *Powers of Desire: The Politics of Sexuality,* eds. Ann Snitow, Christine Stansell, and Sharon Thompson (New York, 1983), 328–49, and "Private Eyes, Public Women: Images of Class and Sex in the Urban South, Atlanta, Georgia, 1913–1915," in *Work Engendered: Toward a New History of American Labor,* ed. Ava Baron (Ithaca, N.Y., 1991), 243–72; Nancy A. Hewitt and Suzanne Lebsock, eds., *Visible Women: New Essays on American Activism* (Urbana, Ill., 1993); Martha Hodes, *White Women, Black Men: Illicit Sex in the Nineteenth Century South* (New Haven, 1997); Tera Hunter, *To 'Joy My Freedom: Southern Black Women's Lives and Labors after the Civil War* (Cambridge, Mass., 1997); Steve Kantrowitz, *Ben Tillman and the Reconstruction of White Supremacy* (Chapel Hill, forthcoming); Stephanie McCurry, *Masters of Small Worlds: Yeoman Households, Gender Relations, and the Political Culture of the Antebellum South Carolina Low Country* (New York, 1995); Nancy MacLean, *Behind the Mask of Chivalry: The Making of the Second Ku Klux Klan* (New York, 1994); Nell Irvin Painter, " 'Social Equality,' Miscegenation, and the Maintenance of Power," in *The Evolution of Southern Culture,* ed. Numan B. Bartley (Athens, Ga., 1988), 47–67, and "Of *Lily,* Linda Brent, and Freud: A Non-Exceptionalist Approach to Race, Class, and Gender in the Slaveholding South," *Georgia Historical Quarterly* 76 (Summer 1992): 241–259; Leslie A. Schwalm, *A Hard Fight for We: Women's Transition from Slavery to Freedom in South Carolina* (Urbana, Ill., 1997); Diane Miller Sommerville, "The Rape Myth in the Old South Reconsidered," *Journal of Southern History* 61 (August 1995): 481–518; Bryant Simon, "The Appeal of Cole Blease of South Carolina: Race, Class, and Sex in the New South," *Journal of Southern History* 62 (February 1996): 57–86; Brenda Stevenson, *Life in Black and White: Family and Community in the Slave South* (New York, 1996); LeeAnn Whites, *The Civil War as a Crisis in Gender: Augusta, Georgia, 1860–1890* (Athens, Ga., 1995).

    3. For this literature, see note 9, below.

    4. The classic statement of the law's hegemonic role in southern society is Eugene D. Genovese, *Roll, Jordan, Roll: The World the Slaves Made* (New York, 1976), 25–49. Southern historians have generated a voluminous literature debating the implications of Genovese's concept of hegemony. But they have tended to accept the conception of the law as a hegemonic force more uncritically than legal historians. As a result, many southern historians have embedded the notion of legal hegemony within their own work without sufficient attention to its theoretical implications. I am suggesting a more complicated view of the law than the one in Genovese's model, based on recent work in oppositional movements and legal history. First, I am arguing that the planter class's hegemony was never as complete as Genovese implied. See, for instance, T. J. Jackson Lears, "The Concept of Cultural Hegemony: Problems and Possibilities," *American Historical Review* 90 (June 1985): 567–593; Robin D. G. Kelley, *Race Rebels: Culture, Politics, and the Black Working Class* (New York, 1994); James C. Scott, *Weapons of the Weak:*

Everyday Forms of Peasant Resistance (New Haven, 1985) and *Domination and the Arts of Resistance: Hidden Transcripts* (New Haven, 1990). Rather than arguing, as Genovese himself did, that conflicts were shaped by but were nonetheless contained within planter hegemony, I am suggesting that conflict often took place outside the parameters set by planters. Indeed, the work on Reconstruction suggests how fragile the planters class's control over the hearts and minds of poor white and black southerners really was. Southern law contained such conflicts within its own arena by creating the legal fiction of a private sphere and then isolating there the problematic issues raised in these conflicts. These claims, in other words, were only hidden in the legal arena. Outside, they were there for everyone to see.

Second, I do not see the law as a tool that can be completely captured by one class, but as a complicated ideology, deeply rooted in the past, with its own logic and universalizing principles that can alter and impede as well as facilitate the interests of those who try to use it. For a discussion and application of this point, see Michael Grossberg, *A Judgment for Solomon: The d'Hauteville Case and Legal Experience in Antebellum America* (New York, 1996). Also see Mary Dudziak, "Josephine Baker, Racial Protest, and the Cold War," *Journal of American History* 81 (September 1994): 543–70; Sarah Barringer Gordon, " 'The Liberty of Self-Degradation': Polygamy, Woman Suffrage, and Consent in Nineteenth-Century America," *Journal of American History* 83 (December 1996): 815–847; Ariela Gross, "Pandora's Box: Slave Character on Trial in the Antebellum Deep South," in *Slavery and the Law*, ed. Paul Finkelman (Madison, 1997), and "Litigating Whiteness: Trial of Racial Determination in the Nineteenth-Century South," *Yale Law Journal* 108 (October 1998): 109–88; Hendrik Hartog, "Pigs and Positivism," *Wisconsin Law Review* 4 (July 1985): 899–935, "The Constitution of Aspiration: The Rights that Belong to All of Us," *Journal of American History* 74 (December 1987), "Marital Exits and Marital Expectations in Nineteenth Century America," *Georgetown Law Journal* 80 (October 1991): 95–129, and "Lawyering, Husbands' Rights, and 'the Unwritten Law' in Nineteenth-Century America," *Journal of American History* 84 (June 1997): 67–96; Barbara Y. Welke, "When All the Women Were White, and All the Blacks Were Men: Gender, Class, Race, and the Road to *Plessy*, 1855–1914," *Law and History Review* 13 (Fall 1995): 261–316, and "Unreasonable Women: Gender and the Law of Accidental Injury, 1870–1920," *Law and Social Inquiry* 19 (1994): 369–402.

5. For the Meadows's social marginality and their connection to free blacks and slaves, see Bynum, *Unruly Women*, 90–92. For court cases involving the Meadowses, see: *State v. James Philpott and John Whitlow*, 1819; *State v. David Adcock and Joseph Briant*, 1821; *State v. Samuel Jackson*, 1845. Jesse Meadows, the father of James Meadows, was just as raucous: see *State v. Jesse Meadows Sr. and David H. Hayes*, 1847. All in Criminal Action Papers, Granville County, NCDAH. For the South's biracial subculture generally, see Charles C. Bolton, *Poor Whites of the Antebellum South: Tenants and Laborers in Central North Carolina and Northeast Mississippi* (Durham, N.C., 1994); Bynum, *Unruly Women*; Scott P. Culclasure, " 'I Have Killed a Damned Dog': Murder by a Poor White in the Antebellum South," *North Carolina Historical Review* 70 (January 1993): 13–39; Bolton and Culclasure, eds., *The Confessions of Edward Isham* (Athens, Ga., 1998).

6. Given the historiography, the predominance of such cases in the local courts is surprising. Nineteenth-century southern historians have tended to treat

violent acts as extralegal matters outside the institutional structures of governance, political only in the sense of displaying individual men's honor and authority. In fact, some historians see violence as a premodern remnant, opposed to such "modern" developments as the rule of law, that lingered in the South because of the region's backwardness. Recent work, however, has emphasized southerners' respect for the law and the law's power in shaping southern society. As the sheer volume of cases in local courts indicates, that respect and power extended to violence. Not only did southerners expect the law to play some role in mediating violent acts, but the law itself structured the public treatment of physical violence.

Although my emphasis is not on honor, I am dealing with violent acts usually seen as manifestations of male honor and engaging the work on honor. The classic statement is Bertram Wyatt-Brown, *Southern Honor: Ethics and Behavior in the Old South* (New York, 1982). See also Bardaglio, *Reconstructing the Household*; Kenneth Greenberg, *Masters and Statesmen: The Political Culture of American Slavery* (Baltimore, 1985) and *Honor and Slavery: Lies Duels, Noses, Masks, Dressing as a Woman, Gifts, Strangers, Humanitarianism, Death, Slave Rebellions, the Proslavery Argument, Baseball, Hunting, and Gambling in the Old South* (Princeton, 1996); Ted Ownby, *Subduing Satan: Religion, Recreation, and Manhood in the Rural South, 1865–1920* (Chapel Hill, 1990); Steven Stowe, *Intimacy and Power in the Old South: Ritual in the Lives of Planters* (Baltimore, 1989). Both Bardaglio and Wyatt-Brown not only ground honor within the antebellum South's social relations, but also link it to the law and other institutions of governance. Building on this juxtaposition of honor and the law, I am arguing that the two not only coexisted, but were fundamentally linked. Honor may have been "premodern," but that did not necessarily imply an incompatibility with law.

7. This paper relies on a range of local court and church records from various places in the two states, although the bulk of the legal material comes from Anderson District in the upcountry of South Carolina, which contained a small slave population and a preponderance of white yeoman households, and Granville County, North Carolina, which contained large plantations and a large slave population in the north and white yeoman households in the south. Rather than doing a survey of records from a number of different counties, I have chosen to look intensively within a few counties. Doing so enables me to piece together the particular social context, including kin and community ties as well as other similar conflicts, that shaped each case—as I have done with the Meadows case. Fleshing out this social context is also central to my argument that the law's abstractions are legal fictions with political implications. Moreover, secondary literature and supporting evidence from other areas in the two states indicates that the broad patterns of criminal prosecution and the kinds of cases in Granville County and Anderson District were not unusual. For Granville County, I relied on the Criminal Actions Concerning Slaves and Free Persons of Color and Criminal Action Papers, NCDAH. Theoretically, there is a strict racial division between the two record groups, with the former including cases involving slaves and free blacks and the latter including cases involving free whites. In practice, however, there is a good deal of overlap between the two, because antebellum North Carolina did not have separate courts for slaves, free blacks, and free whites. By design, moreover, the Criminal Actions Concerning Slaves and Free Persons of Color also include cases of white-on-black violence. For Anderson District, I used the Session Rolls, Court of General Sessions; Trial Papers, Court of Magistrates and Freeholders; Vagrancy Trials, Court of Magistrates and Freeholders; all in the South

Carolina Department of Archives and History (SCDAH). The racial distinction was more closely followed in South Carolina courts, largely because the state continued to try slaves and free blacks in a separate court—the Magistrates and Freeholders Court. Free whites were tried in the Court of General Sessions. The only exception was whites charged with vagrancy, who were tried in the Magistrates and Freeholders Court; most of the vagrancy trials in South Carolina involved free whites, not free blacks. In addition, I also used Trial Records, Court of Magistrates and Freeholders, Spartanburg District; Vagrancy Trials, Court of Magistrates and Freeholders, Spartanburg, Laurens, Camden, Kershaw, Pendleton Districts, all in SCDAH.

8. This was not always the case, see Sir William Blackstone, *Commentaries on the Laws of England*, ed. St. George Tucker (Philadelphia, 1803); in Tucker's edition of Blackstone, volume four is devoted to civil matters or "private wrongs" and volume five deals with criminal matters or "public wrongs." I am using "assault" in a broad sense to include all physical violence other than maiming or homicide. In common law, these last two categories of violence, which resulted in the loss of life or limb, were considered more serious than other forms of violence and were thus always categorized as "public" crimes in the colonial period.

9. Most work on slave law has ignored the importance of gender, assuming that only race and class shaped the institution of slavery. See, for instance: Genovese, *Roll, Jordan, Roll*; Thomas D. Morris, *Southern Slavery and the Law, 1619–1860* (Chapel Hill, 1996); James Oakes, *Slavery and Freedom: An Interpretation of the Old South* (New York, 1990); Mark V. Tushnet, *The American Law of Slavery, 1810–1860: Consideration of Humanity and Interest* (Princeton, 1981). As a result, historians of the nineteenth-century South have only begun to examine the connections between slavery and other domestic relations. My work builds on the recent work of scholars who have used the law and legal discourse to illuminate the gendered dimensions of power and the connections among various relations of dominance and subordination in southern society. See Bardaglio, *Reconstructing the Household*; Brown, *Good Wives, Nasty Wenches, and Anxious Patriarchs*; Bynum, *Unruly Women*; Edwards, *Gendered Strife and Confusion*; Fischer, *Bodies of Evidence*; Hodes, *White Women, Black Men*; McCurry, *Masters of Small Worlds*; Mary Beth Norton, *Founding Mothers and Fathers: Gendered Power and the Forming of American Society* (New York, 1996).

For the legal position of slaves as both persons and property as well as the absence of any sense of legal contradiction about that dual status, see Thomas R. R. Cobb, *An Inquiry into the Law of Negro Slavery in the United States of America* (Philadelphia and Savannah, 1858), especially 83. McCurry also emphasizes this point in *Masters of Small Worlds* and "The Two Faces of Republicanism: Gender and Proslavery Politics in Antebellum South Carolina," *Journal of American History* 78 (March 1992): 1245–1264. Standard antebellum legal texts on domestic relations make it abundantly clear that antebellum husbands, fathers, and masters of menial and domestic servants retained property rights in the bodies of their wives, children, and workers. See, for instance, Tapping Reeve, *The Law of Baron and Femme*, 3rd. ed. (1862; New York, 1970); Zephaniah Swift, *A System of Laws of the State of Connecticut* (Windham, Conn., 1795). The idea of husbands' property rights in their wives' bodies did become increasingly repellant over the course of the nineteenth century and began fading from the legal literature in both the North and the South. But, despite the denials and omissions, its traces were still embedded in law and practice. Wife-selling, a customary form of divorce based on the idea that husbands could transfer property rights in their wives to other men, highlights wives' traditional legal status as both persons and property in a particularly dramatic way. This practice continued in the antebellum South, although it was uncommon and discouraged, probably because it pushed free white women too close to the status of slaves for the comfort of many white southerners. For references to wife-selling, see McCurry, *Masters of Small Worlds*, 89; Suzanne Lebsock, *The Free Women of Petersburg: Status and Culture in a Southern Town, 1784–1860* (New York, 1984), 237–38.

10. During the nineteenth century, the legal connections that once bound all domestic dependents together began to deteriorate and a separate body of law began to develop around each one. In decisions regarding the corporal punishment of slaves, even southern jurists usually analogized from the status of free servants or children and omitted wives from their discussions, although the same legal principles applied to them. Legal treatises authored in the North displayed a similar sense of discomfort with the idea of husbands' unlimited legal authority over their wives, particularly on the issue of corporal punishment. In the North, it was the implication that free, adult women were like children that was troubling. Tapping Reeve, for instance, denied a husband's legal right to corporal punishment long before husbands actually ceased exercising that authority in law and even as he supported that right for fathers and the masters of minor servants. See Reeve, *The Law of Baron and Femme*, 141–42, 420–21, 534–35.

11. It applied the same logic to wives in cases of rape. Because husbands had property rights in their wives' sexual services, the law did not acknowledge marital rape. No one could legally rape female slaves, who could neither give or withhold consent to give access to bodies that were not their own. For a discussion of the issues involving wives, see Reeve, *The Law of Baron and Femme*, 49–343. For slaves, see Cobb, *An Inquiry into the Law of Negro Slavery*. North Carolina did acknowledge common law restraints on a master's power in theory, although, by definition, that placed the responsibility for disciplining errant masters with the *community* and not the *state*. See Morris, *Southern Slavery and the Law*, 188–93. South Carolina criminalized a master's abuse of slaves in 1740; see Morris, *Southern Slavery and the Law*, 195. It was applied and upheld in *State v. Bowen* 2 Strob. 574 (S.C., 1849). Georgia acknowledged the rape of slave women as a criminal offense during the Civil War. Also see Bardaglio, "Rape and the Law in the Old South: 'Calculated to excite indignation in every heart,' " *Journal of Southern History* 60 (November 1994): 749–772; and *Reconstructing the Household*, 3–112; Bynum, *Unruly Women*, especially 59–87; McCurry, *Masters of Small Worlds*; Melton McLauren, *Celia, A Slave* (Athens, Ga., 1991); Morris, *Southern Slavery and the Law*, 161–208; Jennifer Wriggins, "Rape, Racism, and the Law," *Harvard Women's Law Journal* 6 (Spring 1983): 103–141; Wyatt-Brown, *Southern Honor*, 281–83. The Puritans had criminalized wife beating in the colonial period as part of their mission to revise the laws, social governance, and to create a harmonious society. But these and other legal measures that limited husbands' authority over wives fell into disuse as religious enthusiasm weakened, the colonies grew, and the courts began to follow English common law more closely. See Cornelia Hughes Dayton, *Women Before the Bar: Gender, Law, and Society in Connecticut, 1639–1789* (Chapel Hill, 1995). Georgia and Tennessee were actually the first states in the nation to criminalize wife beating by statute after the Revolution, although the laws were not widely used. Wife beating usually entered the courts through divorce cases, as jurists, legislators, and local official debated what level

of abuse constituted legal grounds for separation. As in most southern states, the North Carolina State Supreme Court refused to even consider the possibility that wife-beating might be a criminal offense until after emancipation; see *State v. Rhodes*, 61 N.C. 453 (1868). Northern courts and legislatures were also slow to deal with this particular issue, although they did begin intervening in other domestic matters long before southern courts; see Michael Grossberg, *Governing the Hearth: Law and Family in Nineteenth-Century America* (Chapel Hill, 1985). But Tapping Reeve is mistaken in claiming, in *The Law of Baron and Femme*, 141–42, that this principle no longer extended to husbands and wives in the United States. For violence by husbands against wives in the nineteenth century, see Stephanie Cole, " 'Keeping the Peace': Domestic Assault and Private Prosecution in Antebellum Baltimore," in *Over the Threshold: Intimate Violence in Early America*, Christine Daniels and Michael V. Kennedy, eds. (New York, 1999), 148–69; David Peterson del Mar, *What Trouble I have Seen: A History of Violence Against Wives* (Cambridge, Mass., 1996); Laura F. Edwards, "Women and Domestic Violence in Nineteenth-Century North Carolina," in Michael Bellesiles, ed., *Lethal Imaginations: Violence and Brutality in American History* (New York, 1999), 115–36; Linda Gordon, *Heroes of Their Own Lives: The Politics and History of Family Violence* (New York: Viking, 1988); Pamela Haag, "The 'Ill-Use of a Wife': Patterns of Working-Class Violence in Domestic and Public New York City, 1860–1880," *Journal of Social History* 25 (Spring 1992): 447–477; Jerome Nadelhaft, "Wife Torture: A Known Phenomenon in Nineteenth-Century America," *Journal of American Culture* 10 (Fall 1987): 39–59; Elizabeth Pleck, *Domestic Tyranny: The Making of Social Policy Against Family Violence from Colonial Times to the Present* (New York, 1987); Christine Stansell, *City of Women: Sex and Class in New York, 1789–1860* (Urbana, Ill., 1987), 78–83.

12. Reeve, *The Law of Baron and Femme*, 420; for masters and servants, see 535. Morris, *Southern Slavery and the Law*, 161–181. Jurists in both North and South Carolina drew on the same logic as Reeve when they considered masters' violence toward slaves, even using the exact words at times. The opinions of Justice Thomas Ruffin, whose influential cases involving slaves and violence shaped the law in the South as a whole, are representative. Ruffin's decision in *State v. Mann*, 13 N.C. 263 (1829) is often cited by historians as the most extreme interpretation of a master's authority. In it, Ruffin argued that the shooting of a slave by his master (or in this instance the hirer of the slave who temporarily assumed the role of master) could not be assault because the "power of the master must be absolute, to render the submission of the slave perfect." But he refused to intervene for the same reasons that Reeve refused to gainsay the intent of masters and fathers when disciplining their servants and children. "The danger would be great indeed," wrote Ruffin, "if the tribunals of justice should be called on to graduate the punishment appropriate to every temper and every dereliction of menial duty." Ten years later in *State v. Hoover*, 20 N.C. 500 (1839) Ruffin seemed to backtrack from his position in *Mann*, arguing that a master's authority was not absolute to the point where he can take a slave's life at will, and upholding the conviction of a master for the murder of his slave. But the two decisions are both consistent with the logic laid out by Reeve. In *Hoover*, Ruffin gives masters the same kind of latitude with their slaves that Reeve gave to parents and masters of servants. "If death unhappily ensue from the master's chastisement of his slave, inflicted apparently with a good intent, for reformation for example, and with no purpose to take life or to put it in jeopardy," argued Ruffin, "the law would doubt-

less tenderly regard every circumstance which, judging from the conduct generally of masters towards slaves, might reasonably be supposed to have hurried the party into excess." But in this case, Ruffin believed that there was ample proof of *malus animus*, the only evidence that would make a household head's killing of a domestic dependent into murder.

13. The basis of the two states' legal treatment of slavery, however, differed. North Carolina governed slavery through common law precepts. The state's inclusion of slaves within the common law—which tacitly limited the absolute power of masters by acknowledging that slaves were people with basic rights protected by the state—seems to highlight the inherent contradiction of slaves as both people and property. In practice, however, it emphasized slaves' legal similarities to other domestic dependents, who also had only limited rights under the common law. South Carolina, by contrast, insisted common law principles did not apply to slaves, because they were subjects of their masters, not the state. As a result slave law was governed by statute in that state. Yet the outcome was much the same as in North Carolina because South Carolina legislators used the logic of domestic dependency in common law as the basic structure for its statutes.

14. *State v. Warner Taylor*, 1819; *State v. Thomas Huff and Warner Taylor*, 1825; both in Criminal Actions Concerning Slaves and Free Persons of Color, Granville County, NCDAH. Taylor asked for the benefit of clergy, a privilege of free people that waived the death sentence in capital offenses, if granted. Use of the benefit of clergy was increasingly rare during the antebellum period, suggesting that Taylor probably would not have been allowed it if his victim had been free and white. For Taylor, also see Morris, *Southern Slavery and the Law*, 180, 477n95. Many other masters never even appeared in court for such abuse, even when it resulted in a slave's death.

15. The quote is from *State v. Hoover*, 20 N.C. 500 (1839). The courts in North Carolina and South Carolina routinely denounced the idea that masters' absolute authority extended to the slaves' life. It was this limit that allowed third parties to be tried for the murder or manslaughter of slaves; see, for instance, *State v. Reed*, 9 N.C. 454 (1823). But it took a great deal for a master's violence against a slave to be "beyond the pale." In addition to *State v. Hoover* see, for instance: *State v. Weaver*, 3 N.C. 77 (1798); *State v. Walker*, 4 N.C. 662 (1817); *State v. Mann*, 13 N.C. 263 (1829); *State v. Fleming* 2 Strob. 464 (S.C., 1848); *State v. Bowen*, 2 Strob. 574 (1849). Also see Cobb, *Law of Negro Slavery*, 84–96, 98–99. The racial ideology of elite white southerners, some of whom were certain that African Americans' racial makeup kept them from feeling pain in the same way as whites, reinforced legal practice. Elizabeth B. Clark, " 'The Sacred Rights of the Weak': Pain, Sympathy, and the Culture of Individual Rights in Antebellum America," *Journal of American History* 82 (September 1995): 463–493; Kirsten Fischer, "Embodiments of Power: Slavery and Sexualized Violence in Colonial North Carolina" (paper given at the Tenth Berkshire Conference on the History of Women, Chapel Hill, North Carolina, June 1996).

16. *State v. Dicy Jones, Ben Wheeler, Winny Wheeler, John Stem*, 1814, Criminal Action Papers, Granville County, NCDAH. For similar cases, see for instance: *State v. Phillip Roberts*, 1803, *State v. Nimrod Ragsdale, Jones W. Ragsdale, Pleasant Ragsdale, Samuel Peace, Flemming Peace and John Oliver*, 1814; *State v. Richard Arnold*, 1819; *State v. Bridgett Harris*, 1828; *State v. Hansel Guy*, 1828; all in Criminal Action Papers, Granville County, NCDAH. *State v. Edward Hall*, 1829, Fall Term, #12; 1829, *State v. Alexander Gaillard, Chanley Gaillard Jr., Peter C.*

Gaillard, Hobson Pinckney, Shulbrick Pinckney, Oakley Grant, John Huger, and John Gibby, 1829, Spring Term, #3; *State v. Daniel H. Cochran*, 1830, Fall Term, #5; *State v. Daniel H. Cochran, James Crawford, Joshua Reeves, Joshua Crosley, and George Taylor*, 1834, Fall Term, #7; all in Court of General Sessions, Session Rolls, Anderson District, SCDAH. Male household heads also acted for children, mothers, and others under their care. See for instance *State v. Hiram G. Kellers, David Champ, John Adams*, 1834, Spring Term, #22; *State v. Benjamin Dupree*, 1837, Fall Term, #2; *State v. John Low*, 1837, Fall Term, #7; all in Court of General Sessions, Session Rolls, Anderson District, SCDAH. Also see: *State v. John Washington and Woodson Washington*, 1827; *State v. William Hicks and Jacob Hicks*, 1829; in Criminal Action Papers, Granville County, NCDAH. For a discussion of the legal principles that guided these cases, see Reeve, *The Law of Baron and Femme*, 137–41.

17. *State v. Willie Howington*, 1802, Criminal Action Papers, Granville County, NCDAH. *State v. Abington Kimbel*, 1815–1816, Criminal Actions Concerning Slaves and Free Persons of Color, Granville County, NCDAH. See also: *State v. Joseph Crews*, 1818; *State v. Vincent Day*, 1818; *State v. Charles Robertson*, 1825; *State v. John Prewett and John Jenkins*, 1828; *State v. Robert Rolleston*, 1829; all in Criminal Action Papers, Granville County, NCDAH. The case against Susannah Bressie "for killing the bay horse of Ichabod Smith" was similar to those cases where a free person was charged with the assault of a slave; see *State v. Susannah Bressee*, 1817, Criminal Action Papers, Granville County, NCDAH.

18. North Carolina allowed charges of murder and manslaughter to be filed in the cases where slaves were killed. South Carolina allowed only murder. In North Carolina, the common law governed all homicides as well as third-party violence against slaves. In South Carolina, these matters were governed by statute. But the courts in both states explicitly stated that whites were often "justified" in using violence against slaves and, by extension, free blacks. For further discussion of provocation, see note 21. For significant decisions involving third-party violence against slaves see: *State v. Boon*, 1 N.C. 191 (1801); *State v. Hale*, 9 N.C. 582 (1823); *State v. Reed*, 9 N.C. 454 (1823); *State v. Tackett*, 8 N.C. 210 (1820); *State v. Raines*, 3 McC. 315 (S.C., 1826); *State v. Gaffney*, Rice 431 (S.C., 1839); *State v. Motley et al*, 7 Rich. 327 (S.C., 1854). Also see Cobb, *Law of Negro Slavery*, 84–96; Morris, *Southern Slavery and the Law*, 161–208, 262–302. Over time, South Carolina extended its statute prohibiting masters' excessive abuse of slaves to third parties, although the application was limited and still allowed "justified" violence: *State v. Wilson* Cheves (Law, 1839–40), 163 (S.C., 1840); *State v. Boozer*, 5 Strob. 22 (S.C. 1850); *State v. Harlan*, 5 Rich. 471 (S.C. 1852). But South Carolina never recognized the assault of slaves as a criminal offense in common law; see *State v. Maner*, 2 Hill 355 (S.C., 1834). These decisions were an extension of the logic previously applied in civil cases, which allowed masters damages when third parties abused slaves without justification: *White v. Chambers*, 2 Bay 71 (S.C., 1796); *Witsell v. Earnest*, 1 N. and McC. 183 (S.C. 1818); *Richardson v. Dukes*, 4 McC. 93 (S.C. 1827); *Grimké. v. Houseman* 1 McMul. 132 (S.C., 1841); *Caldwell ads. Langford*, 1 McMul. 277 (S.C., 1841). For South Carolina, also see Morris, *Southern Slavery and the Law*, 201–2.

19. *Amelia Parham v. Elizabeth Blackwelder*, 30 N.C. 446 (1848) contains a particularly revealing discussion about how servants and slaves could be at once legally subsumed within private space and yet still able to act with public consequences in practice. So does the South Carolina court's justification of that state's

statute against a master's abuse of slaves: *State v. Bowen* 2 Strob. 574 (S.C., 1849). Also see Morris, *Southern Slavery and the Law*, 249–261, 289–302.

20. *State v. Thomas Wright*, 1821; *State v. Barnett Jones*, 1822; both in Criminal Action Papers, Granville County, NCDAH. For Wright's acquittal, see September Term 1822, Superior Court Minutes, Granville County, NCDAH. Also see Hartog, "Lawyering, Husbands' Rights, and 'the Unwritten Law'." The North Carolina Court affirmed what Hartog identifies as the "unwritten law" that exempted husbands from murder prosecutions if they killed in the "heat of passion" when they found their wives with the seducers and allowed them to use force to regain "possession" of wives who left without permission; see *State v. Craton*, 28 N.C. 165 (1845). Hartog analyzes how three such cases in the North became focal points for larger concerns about the changing roles of men and women.

21. For the issue of provocation and slaves in North Carolina, see *State v. Hale*, 9 N.C. 582 (1823); *State v. Jarrott*, 23 N.C. 76 (1840); *State v. Tackett*, 8 N.C. 210 (1820); *State v. Ceasar*, 31 N.C. 391 (1849). The exception is *State v. Will* 18 N.C. 121 (1834). North Carolina was unusual in allowing the charge against a slave who had killed a free white person to be reduced from murder to manslaughter if the slave killed in self-defense. But that did not deny the free white assailant's right to beat the slave in the first place if "provoked." In South Carolina, the issue of provocation was resolved by statute and assumed "wicked intent" whenever a slave physically harmed a white person; killing was always murder and assault was never justified. See Morris, *Southern Slavery and the Law*, 296. Also see Cobb, *Law of Negro Slavery*, 84–96, 98–99; Morris, *Southern Slavery and the Law*, 262–302. The discussion of provocation among free white men in *State v. Barfield*, 30 N.C. 344 (1848) provides an interesting counterpoint.

22. As the North Carolina court explained in a 1798 murder case: "If a free servant refuses to obey . . . and the master endeavor to exact obedience by force, and the servant offers to resist by force . . and the master kills, it is not murder, nor even manslaughter, but justifiable." While this particular case analogized from the condition of free servants, both North and South Carolina applied the same standard to all household dependents throughout the antebellum period, although making the master's violence "much more . . . justifiable" when directed against slaves. In subsequent cases, most of which dealt with slaves, jurists debated the limits of masters' power and qualified it in particular circumstances, but left the general principle in place. See *State v. Weaver*, 3 N.C. 77 (1798). In both states, manslaughter included killing done in the "heat of passion" and as "undue correction" without necessarily making it clear whether the latter applied only to masters or to any free person. In South Carolina a 1740 statute explicitly included "undue correction" along with "heat of passion" within manslaughter. But a subsequent 1821 statute did not. The South Carolina court interpreted this omission to mean that "undue correction" was no longer a criminal offense; see *State v. Raines*, 3 McC. 315 (S.C., 1826). The results made it nearly impossible to secure a conviction against any white for killing a slave. But the court later reversed itself, arguing that "undue correction" was covered by "heat of passion" in the 1821 statute; *State v. Gaffney*, Rice 431 (S.C., 1839); *State v. Fleming* 2 Strob. 464 (S.C., 1848). See Morris, *Southern Slavery and the Law*, 179.

23. For slaves, see Morris, *Southern Slavery and the Law*, 227–48. For women, see Bardaglio, *Reconstructing the Household*, 74–77; Dayton, *Women Before the Bar*.

24. *State v. Ceasar*, 31 N.C. 391 (1849). Ruffin was actually dissenting from

the majority opinion as stated by Justice Richmond Pearson, but his point was that the "rule" Pearson laid out in this instance was unnecessary because the common law already allowed for the resolution of such cases. The same logic shaped the adjudication of slave violence in South Carolina, although there the rule was by statute; see note 21. For the application of these legal assumptions to wives and free women, see Brown, *Good Wives, Nasty Wenches, and Anxious Patriarchs*; Bynum, *Unruly Women*; Dayton, *Women Before the Bar*; Fischer, *Bodies of Evidence*; Stansell, *City of Women*.

25. For the courts' construction of domestic dependency in the antebellum South, see Bardaglio, *Reconstructing the Household*; Bynum, *Unruly Women*; McCurry, *Masters of Small Worlds*. See also note 9. During this same period northern courts were altering their interpretation of domestic dependency, particularly for wives and servants. In marriage, they moved toward a more companionate, contractual definition that limited husbands' absolute authority over their wives and allowed for the termination of the relationship when the contracting parties did not fulfill its terms. See, for instance, Grossberg, *Governing the Hearth* and *A Judgment for Solomon*. Similarly, as the courts emphasized the contractual nature of labor relations and the concept of labor as a commodity separable from the body, servants became free laborers. See, for instance, Tomlins, *Law, Labor, and Ideology in the Early American Republic* (New York, 1993) and Robert J. Steinfeld, *The Invention of Free Labor: The Employment Relation in English and American Law and Culture, 1350–1870* (Chapel Hill, 1991). But as Tomlins and Grossberg make clear, the hierarchies previously embedded within the domestic relations of husband/wife and master/servant continued to shape marriage and labor relations.

26. *State v. George and Mary Meadows*, 1847, Criminal Actions Concerning Slaves and Free Persons of Color, Granville County, NCDAH. See also Bynum, *Unruly Women*, 85–87.

27. *State v. John Armstrong and Thomas Patrick*, Fall Term, 1833, #1, Court of General Sessions, Session Rolls, Anderson District, SCDAH. For North Carolina, also see *State v. John Morris*, 1800; *State v. John Bumpass and Benjamin Murray*, 1800; *State v. Ephram Fraizer*, 1803; *State v. William Brame and Anderson Brame*, 1808; *State v. Thomas Banner*, 1813; *State v. Ezekiel Banner*, 1815; *State v. John Sack*, 1816; *State v. Andrew Samuel*, 1816; *State v. Simeon Hays*, 1816; *State v. Randall Minor*, 1816; *State v. Smith Cosby*, 1817; *State v. Thomas Graves, Jackson Young, James Falconer, and John Bayley*, 1817; *State v. George Cozens*, 1817; *State v. William Kittrell*, 1817; *State v. Nathan Hawley*, 1817; *State v. Thomas House*, 1818; *State v. John Minor, Jr.*, 1818; *State v. Andrew Samuel*, 1818; *State v. John Minor*, 1818; *State v. William Oakley*, 1819; *State v. John Minor, Jr.*, 1819; *State v. William and James Nuttall*, 1819; *State v. John Robards*, 1819; *State v. Ruth Hudspeth alias Anderson, Dicey Anderson, and Dilly Taborn*, 1820; *State v. Henry Rowland*, 1820; *State v. Shearrod Harris*, 1820; *State v. John Stephenson*, 1820; *State v. William Taborn, Jr.*, 1821; *State v. Jechonias Bledsoe*, 1823; *State v. Evan Ragland*, 1824; *State v. Hanson Guy*, 1824; *State v. Henderson Day*, 1824; *State v. Allan Yancey and Joel Chandler*, 1825; *State v. Pleasant Mitchell*, 1825; *State v. William Weathers*, 1825; *State v. John Leman*, 1826; *State v. Samuel A. Tumbler*, 1826; *State v. John B. Manier*, 1827; *State v. John Wood*, 1827; *State v. John Haley*, 1829; *State v. Benjamin Williams*, 1829; *State v. Thomas Powell*, 1829; *State v. William Ball*, 1829; all in Criminal Action Papers, Granville County, NCDAH. Also, *State v. Jeremiah D. Gee and Evan Richardson*, Fall Term, 1829, #11; *State v. Leroy H. Smith*, Spring Term 1831, #10; *State v. J.W. Buson*,

D. Horton, B. Wilson, J. Barkley, Spring Term 1834, #3; *State v. Barney McCully*, Spring Term 1834, #25; *State v. Sylvanus Prince, Washington Scroggins, Henson Posey, Patsy Dove, and Fanny Davis*, Fall Term 1834, #17A; *State v. James Jolly*, Fall Term 1835, #9; *State v. Tolliver Scott*, Spring Term 1836, #10; *State v. William R. Williams*, Spring Term 1836, #18; Court of General Sessions, Session Rolls, Anderson District, SCDAH.

28. *State v. Mary Hester, Nancy H. Pullam and Rachel Hester*, 1813; *State v. Abigail Guy*, 1818, Criminal Action Papers, Granville County, NCDAH; *State v. Sylvanus Prince, Washington Scroggins, Hansen Poesy, Patsy Dove, and Fanny Davis*, Fall Term 1834, #17A, Court of General Sessions, Session Rolls, Anderson District, SCDAH. Also see *State v. Nancy Hayes*, 1803; *State v. Lucy Roberts*, 1803; *State v. James Carden, Robert Carden, Susannah Carden, and Armstead Carden*, 1809; *State v. Dicy Jones, Ben Wheeler, Winny Wheeler, John Stem*, 1814; *State v. Hezekiah and Elizabeth Hobgood*, 1817; *State v. Abigail Guy, William Guy, Ansil Guy, Clark Guy, Craven Grisham, and Pascal Buckner*, 1819; *State v. Ruth Hudspeth alias Anderson, Dicey Anderson, and Dilly Taborn*, 1820; *State v. Celah Oakley*, 1821; *State v. Moody Fowler, Ellison Parrish and Polly Harris*, 1823; *State v. William Adcock and others*, 1824; *State v. Clara Hobgood*, 1824; *State v. Polly Stewart*, 1826; *State v. Charles Butler, Daniel Butler, Overton Butler, Elizabeth Butler, and Sarah Butler*, 1826; *State v. Betsy Oakley*, 1827; *State v. MaryAnn, Sally, Elizabeth, and Anderson Wall*, 1827; *State v. Elveny Landers*, 1828; *State v. Bridget Harris*, 1828; *State v. John Hutchings, Alexander Hutchings, Frank [or Francis] Hutchings, and Parnelia [or Amelia] Wilkerson*, 1830; Criminal Action Papers, Granville County, NCDAH.

29. *State v. Castle Davis*, 1819, Criminal Action Papers, Granville County, NCDAH. For further discussion and examples of the way poor whites and African Americans defined marital responsibilities and mediated domestic disputes, see Laura F. Edwards, " 'The Marriage Covenant Is at the Foundation of All Our Rights': The Politics of Slave Marriages in North Carolina After Emancipation," *Law and History Review* 14 (Spring 1996): 81–124, and "Women and Domestic Violence in Nineteenth-Century North Carolina."

30. The cases involving violence between slaves and free whites are too numerous to list here. *State v. Joe*, 1841, case #34, 2920, Trial Records, Magistrates and Freeholders Court, Spartanburg District, SCDAH. For similar cases involving masters or overseers and slaves, see *State v. George*, 1851, case #134, 2921; *State v. Eddy*, 1849, case #97, 2920; Trial Records, Magistrates and Freeholders Court, Spartanburg District, SCDAH.

31. *State v. Lease*, 1841, #37, 2920; *State v. Violet*, 1854, case #160, 2921; Trial Records, Magistrates and Freeholders Court, Spartanburg District, SCDAH. The cases of whites filing charges against slaves for assault are too numerous to list here.

32. *Marion Converse v. Augustus L. Converse*, Sumter District Equity Court Records, roll 227, 1854, SCDAH. For the final cash settlement with Augustus Converse, see Agreement, 20 February 1857, Singleton-Deveaux Family Papers, South Caroliniana Library (SCL). Marion's petition in the separation suit reveals how she involved her family during her marriage. See also: Marion Converse to Matt Singleton, 20 December 1853; Marion Converse to Matt Singleton, 25 December 1853, Singleton Family Papers, SCL. For the response of the extended family and friends, see, for instance, Betty Coles to Marion Deveaux, 19 February 1854; Betty Coles to Marion Deveaux, 1 April 1854; Betty Coles to Marion De-

veaux, 11 April 1854; Betty Coles to Marion Deveaux, 16 May 1854; Betty Coles to Marion Deveaux, 31 July 1854; Betty Coles to Marion Deveaux, 15 January 1855; Betty Coles to Marion Deveaux, 5 June 1856; Betty Coles to Marion Deveaux, 28 June 1856; Betty Coles to Marion Deveaux, 17 September 1856; Betty Coles to Marion Deveaux, 11 January 1857; Sally W. Taylor to Marion Converse, 11 March [1850–1855]; Singleton Family Papers, Library of Congress (LC). J. Hamilton to Marion Converse, 22 November 1853; Illegible to Marion Deveaux Converse, Charlottesville, 11 January 1858; Singleton-Deveaux Family Papers, SCL. The rest of the family correspondence, particularly the Singleton-Deveaux Family Papers, SCL and the Singleton Family Papers, LC, indicate that Marion lived as if the marriage had never happened. She dropped the Converse name, her daughters married well, and she lived happily thereafter, consumed in the business and social affairs of her large family.

33. *State v. James Woodruff*, 1834; *State v. Marvel Littlefield*, 1841; Vagrancy Trials, Magistrates and Freeholders Court, Spartanburg District. *State v. Thomas Watkins*, 1819; Vagrancy Trials, Magistrates and Freeholders Court, Laurens District. See also *State v. William Brittain*, 1807; *State v. Stephen Bass*, 1847; Vagrancy Trials, Magistrates and Freeholders Court, Spartanburg District. *State v. William Gray*, 1833; *State v. Jeremiah Timms*, 1849; *State v. David Griffin*, 1851; Vagrancy Trials, Magistrates and Freeholders Court, Anderson District. Also see Edwards, *Gendered Strife and Confusion*, chaps. 1 and 5; and "Women and Domestic Violence." For women in similar social contexts—although very different time periods—mobilizing community ties to protect themselves against violence by their husbands, also see Susan Dwyer Amussen, " 'Being Stirred to Much Unquietness': Violence and Domestic Violence in Early Modern England," *Journal of Women's History* 6 (Summer 1994): 70–89; Shani D'Cruze, *Crimes of Outrage: Sex, Violence and Victorian Working Women* (DeKalb, Ill., 1998); Haag, "The 'Ill-Use of a Wife.' "

34. *State v. Marvel Littlefield*, 1841; Vagrancy Trials, Magistrates and Freeholders Court, Spartanburg District, SCDAH. The account of Westley Rhodes appears in Bill Cecil-Fronsman, *Common Whites: Class and Culture in Antebellum North Carolina* (Lexington, 1992), 133; also see 156–164. For a similar case, see: *State v. Castle Davis*, 1819, Criminal Action Papers, Granville County, NCDAH. Edwards, *Gendered Strife and Confusion*, chap. 5; and "Women and Domestic Violence."

35. See, for instance, *State v. Jim*, 1849, case #109, 2920; *State v. Patsy*, 1854, case #165, 2921; Trial Records, Magistrates and Freeholders Court, Spartanburg District, SCDAH. For other examples of slaves complaining about their own masters' treatment to powerful neighbors, see Christopher Leonard Doyle, "Lord, Master, and Patriot: St. George Tucker and Patriarchy in Republican Virginia, 1772–1851," (Ph.D. diss. University of Connecticut, 1996), 111–113, 151.

36. For the dispute between Brother Johnson and Judy, see Big Creek Baptist Church, Anderson District, SCL, 10 September 1823, 16 September 1823, 17 September 1823, 4 October 1823, 5 January 1827.

37. As James Blalock testified, Mary Meadows told him "about the treatment of her husband Jas. Medows [sic] towards her, and that she said that she intended to have him fixed at . . . court, so that he should not be scandalizing her." See *State v. George and Mary Meadows*, 1847, Criminal Actions Concerning Slaves and Free Persons of Color, Granville County, NCDAH. For peace warrants, see *State v. Patrick O'Briant*, 1800; *State v. William Mitchell*, 1810; *State v. Benjamin*

Fuller, 1811; *State v. Solomon Bobbitt*, 1817; *State v. William Hickman*, 1818; *State v. Jeremiah Rush*, 1819; *State v. Samuel Cauthon*, 1819; *State v. Archibald Husketh*, 1822; *State v. William Hickman*, 1823; *State v. Thomas Chandler*, 1825; *State v. Joel Strong*, 1826; *State v. William Hickman*, 1827; *State v. Wyatt Short*, 1828; *State v. Green Stanton*, 1828. For assault indictments, see: *State v. Evan Ragland*, 1822; *State v. Charles Bearden*, 1823; *State v. Barnett Eakes*, 1824; *State v. Thomas Chandler*, 1825; *State v. William Hickman*, 1828. Barnett Eakes and Evan Ragland apparently disappeared after their indictments; for Ragland's disappearance, see *State v. Evan Ragland*, 1824. Although there is no record that his wife brought the charge, Willie Parham gave bond to answer "the State for a nuisance and great violence committed on his wife"; *State v. Willie Parham*, 1816. All of these men were poor. Most either had been arrested for other offenses before their wives filed charges against them or were arrested for other offenses subsequently. All in Criminal Action Papers, Granville County, NCDAH.

38. *State v. Sam*, 1830, case #50, 2916, Trial Records, Magistrates and Free-holders Court, Anderson District. See also: *State v. Ephraim Irvin*, 1839, case #108, 2916, Trial Records, Magistrates and Freeholders Court, Anderson District. *State v. Redmon*, 1850, case #120, 2920; *State v. Joe*, 1841, case #34, 2920; both in Trial Records, Magistrates and Freeholders Court, Spartanburg District. All in SCDAH. As Bardaglio argues in "Rape and the Law in the Old South" and *Reconstructing the Household*, 64–78, the suspicion of a woman's word often resulted in an emphasis on legal formalism that worked in the slaves' favor in cases where slaves were accused of rape. See also Morris, *Southern Slavery and the Law*, 303–321. But the appearance of "even-handedness" did not necessarily push slave men any closer to legal personhood or indicate the absence of whites' racialized concerns about the unbridled sexuality of black men, as some have recently suggested; see Sommerville, "The Rape Myth in the Old South Reconsidered." The same class concerns apparent in Sam's acquittal also shaped cases involving third-party violence against slaves. In these cases, the courts limited the ability of whites to use violence against slaves they did not own and delivered the occasional denunciation of vengeful and disorderly poor whites who sought to settle scores with their social betters by destroying slave property. In North Carolina, see for instance *State v. Hale*, 9 N.C. 582 (1823); *State v. Hailey*, 28 N.C. 11 (1845). For South Carolina, see *White v. Chambers*, 2 Bay 71 (S.C., 1796); *Witsell v. Earnest*, 1 N. and McC. 183 (S.C. 1818); *Richardson v. Dukes*, 4 McC. 93 (S.C. 1827); *Grimké. v. Houseman* 1 McMul. 132 (S.C., 1841); *Caldwell ads. Langford*, 1 McMul. 277 (S.C., 1841); *State v. Motley et al*, 7 Rich. 327 (S.C., 1854). Also see Morris, *Southern Slavery and the Law*, 196–208.

39. When Brother Beasley's congregation heard unfavorable "repoarts . . . respecting him & his family," they followed standard procedure and dispatched a committee to investigate and to work with Beasley and his wife to resolve their differences. But in this case, both Beasley and his wife were excluded for their recalcitrance and their unwillingness to reconcile. Lower Fork of Lynches Creek (Gum Branch) Baptist Church, Darlington District, SCL, 15 June 1850. See also the troubles between Brother and Sister Delk in the same church, March 1820, 14 April 1820, 15 April 1820, 18 May 1820, 17 June 1820, 19 August 1820. Occasionally, only the husband was excluded; see Bethabara Baptist Church Records, Laurens District, Records, SCL, 17 October 1834 and 15 November 1834; Methodist Church, Waccamaw Circuit and Conwayborough Circuit, Minutes, Horry District, SCL, August 1847.

South Carolina's vagrancy statute was passed in 1787; see Benjamin James, *A Digest of the Laws of South Carolina* (Columbia, 1814), chap. 80. In 1836 several new classes of vagrants were added, but the treatment of vagrants remained essentially the same; the constitutionality of the law was challenged, but upheld by the state supreme court in 1837. See *State v. Maxcy, Arthur, et al*, 1 McMul. 501 (S.C., 1840). Although North Carolina did not prosecute whites for vagrancy, it carried out the same kinds of discussions and accomplished the same results under different guises. The state prosecuted poor men for nonsupport of their families and for maintenance of illegitimate offspring, thereby forcing them to work to pay the imposed fees. The state also forcibly institutionalized paupers in county poorhouses where they were forced to labor for their living. See, for instance: Minutes and Accounts, Wardens of the Poor, 1832–1855, Ashe County; Minutes, Wardens of the Poor, 1838–1851, Bertie County; Minutes of the Wardens of the Poor, 1844–1866, Carteret County; Minutes of the Wardens of the Poor, 1837–1871, Craven County; Minutes of the Wardens of the Poor, 1820–1868, Lincoln County; all in NCDAH. Wardens of the Poor, Records, Person County, Southern Historical Collection, University of North Carolina, Chapel Hill. North Carolina whites did, however, use vagrancy charges against free black husbands in the same way South Carolina whites used them against troublesome poor white husbands. See, for instance, *State v. Martin Taborn*, 1829, Criminal Action Papers, Granville County.

40. John Moore, 1801; Jonathan Bryan, 1827–28; Divorce Petitions, General Assembly, Sessions Records, NCDAH. Although petitioners tried valiantly to fit the facts of their lives into legal categories, they inevitably left loose ends and made statements that betrayed both the particularity of their lives as well as recognized social customs and claims to rights not recognized by law. For petitions that make similar points, see: John Farrow, 1801; James Critcher, 1827–28; Edward Pugh, 1827–28, Divorce Petitions, General Assembly, Sessions Records, NCDAH. In 1832, North Carolina changed its divorce laws, eliminating the need to petition the legislature and giving jurisdiction to the county superior courts. These petitions, however, are similar to those that went to the legislature. Also see: Richard Hembree Hughes, 1818; Curtis Winget, 1830; Divorce Petitions, General Assembly Records, SCDAH. In South Carolina, few husbands and wives bothered to petition for divorce because the legislature flatly denied every request it received. But the few existing petitions as well as other records reveal that South Carolina husbands and wives behaved in much the same way as those just to the north of them. For similar behavior in the nineteenth-century U.S. as a whole, see Hartog, "Marital Exits and Marital Expectations."

41. James W. Mills, 1827–28; John Farrow, 1801; Divorce Petitions, General Assembly, Sessions Records, NCDAH. See also, Alexander Smith, 1802; James Hoffler, 1803; David Blalock, 1808; Stephen Starling, 1808; Micajah Mustgrove, 1808; Willie Kerr, 1808; Richard Brite, 1809; William Lane, 1809; Samuel Murray, 1809; William Wood, 1809; James Cray, 1809; John D. Barber, 1824–25; Lewis Tombereau, 1824–25; William Mooncham, 1824–25; Elijah Pope, 1826–27; William Robards, 1827–28; James Critcher, 1827–28; Edward Pugh, 1827–28; William Holland, 1830–31; Divorce Petitions, General Assembly, Sessions Records, NCDAH. Also see Richard Hembree Hughes, 1818; William Chick, 1821; Curtis Winget, 1830; Thomas Miller, 1841; Wilson Bartlett, 1844; Divorce Petitions, General Assembly Records, SCDAH. Men also separated themselves from their wives in order to "marry" another woman. A good example is Mary Wilson, 1821,

Divorce Petitions, General Assembly Records, SCDAH. Of course, the law shaped the way men and women represented self-divorce in their petitions: in antebellum law, wives could claim divorce on the basis of adultery and abandonment, while husbands could claim divorce on the basis of either adultery or abandonment. But the practice of self-divorce was well established in the antebellum South. Susannah Sharp, for instance, admitted to living with another man in a relationship accepted by the community as a marriage and having four children with him, although she thought that this might undercut her request for a divorce. For further discussion of customary marriage and divorce practices, see Edwards, *Gendered Strife and Confusion*, chap.1 and " 'Marriage is at the Foundation of all Our Rights.' " The better strategy was for wives to claim that their husbands' behavior forced them to leave: Trucy Fannigan, 1808; Betsy Warmouth, 1808; Jane Welborn, 1823–24, Divorce Petitions, General Assembly, Sessions Records, NCDAH.

Mary Southwick was not the only woman who insisted on claiming property that belonged to her husband by law. Susannah Brown's husband alleged that she took a "valuable horse and forty dollars in cash . . . leaving him with four small children" when she went to Tennessee to live with a younger man. After Barbara Dough took up with another man while her husband was at sea, she retained possession of the house her husband had built and the adjoining seventy-six acres of land she had brought into the marriage. Bond V. Brown, 1809; Ambrose Dough, 1809; Divorce Petitions, General Assembly, Sessions Records, NCDAH.

42. *State v. George and Mary Meadows*, 1847, Criminal Actions Concerning Slaves and Free Persons of Color, Granville County. *State v. George*, 1847, #4188; *State v. George*, 1848, #4230; Supreme Court Original Cases. *State v. George*, 3 March 1847, 4 March 1847, 8 September 1847, 9 September 1847, Superior Court Minutes, Granville County. *State v. George*, Fall Term 1847, Spring Term 1848, Superior Court Minutes, Person County. All in NCDAH. For a discussion of self-defense as "natural" see: *State v. Ceasar*, 31 N.C. 391 (1849). *State v. Will* 18 N.C. 121 (1834), although exceptional in many respects, also conforms to the general rule of self-defense as a "natural" reaction.

Notes to COMMENTARY
by Peter Bardaglio

1. I've changed the names here for obvious reasons.

2. Stephanie McCurry, *Masters of Small Worlds: Yeoman Households, Gender Relations, and the Political Culture of the Antebellum South Carolina Low Country* (New York, 1995); Victoria Bynum, *Unruly Women: The Politics of Social and Sexual Control in the Old South* (Chapel Hill, 1992); and Martha Hodes, *White Women, Black Men: Illicit Sex in the Nineteenth-Century South* (New Haven, 1997).

3. Peter W. Bardaglio, *Reconstructing the Household: Families, Sex, and the Law in the Nineteenth-Century South* (Chapel Hill, 1995).

4. (Urbana, Ill., 1997).

5. Eugene D. Genovese, *Roll, Jordan, Roll: The World the Slaves Made* (New York, 1976). For a critique of Genovese's interpretation of plantation society, see Peter W. Bardaglio, "Power and Ideology in the Slave South: Eugene Genovese and His Critics," *Maryland Historian* 12 (Fall 1981): 23–37.

6. Bertram Wyatt-Brown, *Southern Honor: Ethics and Behavior in the Old South* (New York, 1982); and Edward L. Ayers, *Vengeance and Justice: Crime and Punishment in the Nineteenth-Century American South* (Oxford, 1984).

7. Examples of studies that have made good use of southern church records include Jean E. Friedman, *The Enclosed Garden: Women and Community in the Evangelical South, 1830–1900* (Chapel Hill, 1985); and Ted Ownby, *Subduing Satan: Religion, Recreation, and Manhood in the Rural South, 1865–1920* (Chapel Hill, 1990).

8. Jane Turner Censer, " 'Smiling Through Her Tears': Ante-Bellum Southern Women and Divorce," *American Journal of Legal History* 25 (January 1981): 27–29.

9. *Ibid.*, 29.

10. Robert Coles, *The Moral Life of Children: How Children Struggle with Questions of Moral Choice in the United States and Elsewhere* (Boston, 1986) and *The Political Life of Children* (Boston, 1987).

11. Elliot West, *Growing Up with the Country: Childhood on the Far Western Frontier* (Albuquerque, 1989); Wilma King, *Stolen Childhood: Slave Youth in Nineteenth-Century America* (Bloomington, Ind., 1995); and James Marten, "Stern Realities: Children of Chancellorsville and Beyond," in *Chancellorsville: The Battle and Beyond* (Chapel Hill, 1996), 219–43. See also Marten's booklength study, *The Children's Civil War* (Chapel Hill, 1998).

12. Marten, "Stern Realities," p. 228.

13. Ira Berlin, *Slaves without Masters: The Free Negro in the Antebellum South* (New York, 1974) is the classic account of the shifting status of free blacks in the years before the Civil War. Michael P. Johnson and James L. Roark document the attack on the position of free blacks in Charleston during the late antebellum period in *No Chariot Let Down: Charleston's Free People of Color on the Eve of the Civil War* (New York, 1986).

14. Bardaglio, *Reconstructing the Household*, pp. 32–34, 92.

15. For a recent report from the front lines of the culture wars, see Gary B. Nash, Charlotte Crabtree and Ross E. Dunn, *History on Trial: Culture Wars and the Teaching of the Past* (New York, 1997).

16. A session at the 1996 annual meeting of the Southern Historical Association in Little Rock was devoted to domestic violence in early America. I served as a commentator for this panel, and the papers by T. Stephen Whitman, Stephanie Cole, and Bridgett William-Searle have done much to spark my thinking about the issues raised here. See Christine Daniels and Michael V. Kennedy, eds., *Over the Threshold: Intimate Violence in Early America* (New York: Routledge, 1999).

Notes to CITIZENS, SOLDIERS' WIVES, AND "HILEY HOPE UP" SLAVES: THE PROBLEM OF POLITICAL OBLIGATION IN THE CIVIL WAR SOUTH
by Stephanie McCurry

1. William H. Lee to Jefferson Davis, 4 May 1861, in *Freedom: A Documentary History of Emancipation, 1861–1867*, Series II, *The Black Military Experience*, ed. Ira Berlin, Joseph P. Reidy, and Leslie S. Rowland, (Cambridge, 1982), 282.

2. Linda K. Kerber, " 'A Constitutional Right to Be Treated Like American Ladies': Women and the Obligations of Citizenship," in *U.S. History as Women's History: New Feminist Essays*, ed. Linda Kerber, Alice Kessler-Harris, and Kathryn Kish Sklar, (Chapel Hill, 1995), 19-20, 18. One exception is Robert B. Westbrook's " 'I Want a Girl, Just Like the Girl That Married Harry James': American Women and the Problem of Political Obligation in World War Two," *American Quarterly*, 42, (December 1990): 587–614.

3. Milton Barrett to Dear Brother and Sister, 2 August 1861, reprinted in *"The Confederacy Is On Her Way Up the Spout": Letters to South Carolina, 1861—1864*, ed. J. Roderick Heller III and Carolyn Ayres Heller, (Athens, Ga., 1992), 22.

4. Edwin Bass to "Dear Sister," 22 April 1861, reprinted in *"Dear Mother: Don't Grieve About Me. If I Get Killed, I'll Only Be Dead": Letters from Georgia Soldiers in the Civil War*, ed. Mills Lane, (Savannah, 1977), 4; William F. Plane to his wife, 1 June 1861, in "Letters of William F. Plane to his Wife," ed. S. Joseph Lewis Jr., *Georgia Historical Quarterly*, 48 (1964): 217; K.T. Pound to his Parents, 29 September 1861, *"Dear Mother"*, xii; Tulius Rice, 17 February 1863, *"Dear Mother"*, xii.

5. James M. McPherson, *What They Fought For, 1861–1865* (Baton Rouge, 1994), 20 and passim. Historians are still more likely to reiterate the gendered language of "the cause" than to analyze its claims and the power relations it invoked. For another example, see George Rable, *The Confederate Republic: A Revolution Against Politics* (Chapel Hill, 1994), 27.

6. *Charleston Mercury*, 12 November 1860, 5 October 1860, 13 November 1860. I have drawn here from the *Mercury* rather than from the more moderate *Charleston Courier* because it was in radical (or fire-eater) discourse that the federal threat was given earliest and sharpest form.

7. Secessionists' language had popular currency: "Our country is invaded— our homes are in danger—We are deprived of . . . that glorious liberty for which our fathers fought and bled," Ella Gertrude Clanton Thomas wrote in her diary in July 1861. A few months later she noted: "[W]e are engaged in a war which threatens to desolate our firesides. Our men are fighting for liberty and homes." Virginia Ingraham Burr, ed., *The Secret Eye: The Journal of Ella Gertrude Clanton Thomas, 1848–1889* (Chapel Hill, 1990), 184, 195.

8. *Charleston Mercury*, 28 July 1858; D.H. Hamilton to William Porcher Miles, 23 January 1860 and 2 February 1860, William Porcher Miles Papers, Southern Historical Collection, University of North Carolina, Chapel Hill [hereafter SHC].

9. *Charleston Mercury*, 10 May 1860, 25 May 1860.

10. Joseph E. Brown, *The Federal Union*, 11 December 1860 reprinted in *Secession Debated: Georgia's Showdown in 1860*, ed. William W. Freehling and Craig M. Simpson, (New York, 1992), 147, 155, 154, 153. The whiteness literature has not typically traced the gender and sexual dimensions of the claim. For important recent exceptions see Tera Hunter, *To 'Joy My Freedom: Southern Black Women's Lives and Labors After the Civil War* (Cambridge, Mass., 1997); Glenda Elizabeth Gilmore, *Gender and Jim Crow: Women and the Politics of White Supremacy in North Carolina, 1896–1920* (Chapel Hill, 1996).

11. *Charleston Mercury*, 11 November 1859. Robert Barnwell Rhett called John Brown's raid "fact coming to the aid of logic." Rhett quoted in Peter Wallenstein, "Incendiaries All: Southern Politic and the Harpers Ferry Raid," in *His*

Soul Goes Marching On: Responses to John Brown and the Harper's Ferry Raid, ed. Paul Finkelman, (Charlottesville, Va., 1995), 166. The paranoia about "abolition emissaries" in the aftermath of Harper's Ferry and the formation of vigilance committees to root them out was hardly confined to South Carolina. For the response in Virginia, for example, see Wallenstein, "Incendiaries All," 149–73; in Georgia, see Clarence Mohr, *On the Threshold of Freedom: Masters and Slaves in Civil War Georgia* (Athens, Ga., 1986), 3–67.

12. *Charleston Mercury,* 11 November 1859. The reference to Seward's "Rochester speech" was a common one. Until the Republican convention in June 1860, many southerners regarded Seward as the leading candidate and likely next President. See, for example, John Townsend's remarks as late as October 1860 about "the Black Republican wing [of the Republican Party] over which Seward is the master mind." *Charleston Mercury,* 31 October 1860. Well into 1860, then, radical invective usually centered on the person of William Seward, not Lincoln; even in the North, Lincoln was perceived as more of a moderate on the slave question than was Seward.

13. "Black" Republicans were, of course, racially "white," and "black" metaphorically by virtue of their principles, political associations, and "fiendish" designs. Usually fire-eaters used the term "black" to lend the valence of evil to Republican politics, but there were a few notable occasions when principles and bodies were literally conflated: in references to Frederick Douglass—"They [black Republicans] would vote for the negro *Douglass* to be a cabinet minister, rather than Mr. Lincoln's Administration should fall"—and in prurient gossip about Hannibal Hamlin's racial ancestry: "The [Republicans] have put forward as a candidate for the Vice-Presidency, a man asserted to be, and thus far without contradiction, a *mulatto.*" *Charleston Mercury,* 31 October 1860, 2 October 1860.

14. *Charleston Mercury,* 22 December 1859.

15. Nor is this representation of the matter excessive or abstract. Recall that white southern men, like most antebellum white men, had such established legal claim to the sexuality of their wives and daughters—such recognizable rights of property in them—that they could and did successfully sue each other for monetary damages when those rights were infringed and the value of the property thereby diminished. See, for example, the "seduction" cases in Swift Creek Baptist Church, Kershaw District, South Carolina, Records, August 22, 1829 and August 28, 1829; First Columbia Presbyterian Church, Richland District, South Carolina, Session Book, June 25, 1841, both in South Caroliniana Library, University of South Carolina, Columbia, South Carolina. On the matter in southern courts, see Peter Bardaglio, "Rape and the Law in the Old South," *The Journal of Southern History,* (November 1994): 749–772 and Dianne Miller Sommerville, "The Rape Myth in the Old South Reconsidered," *The Journal of Southern History* 61 (August 1995): 481–518.

In the North, the feminist reappropriation of chastity and women's rights of property in their own bodies was underway. See for example, Sarah Grimke, "Letters on the Equality of the Sexes," (1838) in *Sarah Grimke: Letters on the Equality of the Sexes and Other Essays,* ed. Elizabeth Ann Bartlett, (New Haven, 1988); Pamela Susan Haag, "A History of the Private Self: Sexual Freedoms, Sexual Violence and Individual Rights in Modern American Culture" (Ph.D. diss., Yale University, 1995).

16. United States Senate, *Report of the Secretary of War,* Executive Document No. 53, 38th Congress, 1st Session (Washington, D.C., 1864)—American

Freedmen's Inquiry Commission Report, 2, 4, 5. On slave marriage, see Margaret A. Burnham, "An Impossible Marriage: Slave Law and Family Law," *Law and Inequality* 5 (July 1987): 187–225, and Laura F. Edwards, " 'The Marriage Covenant is at the Foundation of All Our Rights': The Politics of Slave Marriages in North Carolina After Emancipation," *Law and History Review* 14 (Spring 1996): 81–124.

17. Thomas Roderick Dew, "On the Characteristic Differences Between the Sexes, and on the Position and Influence of Woman in Society," *Southern Literary Messenger* 1 (May, July, August, 1835), 1 (May 1835): 495–96 and passim. Dew draws equally on Burke and Rousseau in his account; James Henry Hammond, "Hammonds Letters on Slavery," in *The Pro-Slavery Argument as Maintained by the Most Distinguished Writers of the Southern States* (1845; reprint ed., Charleston, 1852), 117–20; Carol Bleser, ed., *Secret and Sacred: The Diaries of James Henry Hammond, a Southern Slaveholder* (New York, 1988), 167–76.

18. Burr, ed., *Secret Eye*, 167–69, 252–54. It is interesting to note in this regard, that it was not until slave men were possessed of men's martial powers that Thomas expressed any fear of sexual violence at their hands. It was not slaves, but ex-slaves, under arms and in Union blue, that she was afraid of; with that exception, the brutal and rapacious men she awaited in horror during the war were white. See Burr, ed, *Secret Eye*, 195–96.

19. Townsend's article began as an oral address to the Edisto Island Vigilant Association in Charleston District, South Carolina but became pamphlet No. 4 of the 1860 Association publications, an organization with explicitly propagandistic purposes. For the original address see *Charleston Mercury*, 31 October 1860, and for the 1860 Association tract see John Townsend, *The Doom of Slavery in the Union: Its Safety Out of It* (Charleston, 1860).

20. *Charleston Mercury*, October 31, 1860.

21. Thomas R. R. Cobb, *Substance of Remarks Made By Thomas R. R. Cobb, Esq., In The Hall Of The House Of Representatives, Monday Evening, November 12, 1860* (Atlanta, 1860), reprinted in Freehling and Simpson, *Secession Debated*, 29, 6, 11.

22. "Abolitionists cannot contend with men combined for the sole purpose of guarding the sovereignty of their state—of defending their families and protecting their home." *Charleston Mercury*, November 23, 1859.

23. Cobb, *Substance of Remarks*, 6.

24. Lynn Hunt, *The Family Romance of the French Revolution* (Berkeley, 1992), 13; *Charleston Mercury*, 28 September 1860.

25. *Charleston Mercury*, 28 September 1860; John Townsend, *The South Alone Should Govern the South and African Slavery Should be Controlled By Those Only Who Are Friendly To It*, 3rd ed., (Charleston, 1860), 40, 9. This was distributed as pamphlet No. 1 of the 1860 Association and sold out in one month after its September publication.

26. On France see Hunt, *Family Romance*; Joan B. Landes, *Women and the Public Sphere in the Age of the French Revolution* (Ithaca, N.Y., 1988); Maurice Agulhon, *Marianne Into Battle* (Cambridge, 1981). On Britain see Susan R. Grayzel, *Women's Identities at War: Gender, Motherhood, and Politics in Britain and France during the First World War* (Chapel Hill, 1999), especially chapter 2. On the late-nineteenth century South, see Jacquelyn Dowd Hall, *Revolt Against Chivalry: Jesse Daniel Ames and the Women's Campaign Against Lynching*, (rev. ed. New York, 1993) and "The Mind That Burns in Each Body': Women, Rape,

and Racial Violence," in *Powers of Desire: The Politics of Sexuality*, ed. Ann Snitow, Christine Stansell, and Sharon Thompson, (New York, 1983), 328–49; and
Glenda E. Gilmore, *Gender and Jim Crow: Women and the Politics of White Supremacy in North Carolina, 1896–1920* (Chapel Hill, 1996).

27. Nancy F. Cott, " 'Giving Character to Our Whole Civil Polity': Marriage
and the Public Order in the Late Nineteenth Century," in Kerber, Kessler-Harris
and Sklar, eds., *U.S. History as Women's History*, 121, 110, 119.

28. For a thoughtful treatment of the "politics of slave marriages," and the
relationship between citizenship and manhood "rights," see Edwards, " 'The Marriage Covenant.' "

29. Westbrook, "I Want a Girl," 589.

30. The long history of this particular construction of the glorious cause
throws considerable doubt on LeeAnn Whites's recent argument that it was in
fact a revisionist production of postbellum southern white women. See LeeAnn
Whites, *The Civil War as a Crisis in Gender, Augusta, Georgia, 1860–1890* (Athens, Ga., 1995), 160–98.

31. Jno R. Allen to Joseph E. Brown, 7 September 1861, Governors Incoming
Correspondence, Joseph E. Brown, RG 1-1-5, Box 22, Georgia Department of
Archives and History [hereafter GDAH]. It is also quite clear that Governor
Brown's own resistance to the authority of the Confederate government embold-
ened white Georgians. One man requesting an exemption from the first Confeder-
ate Conscription Act expessed his views "that the new act is unconstitutional and
entirely agree with the views that you have gave upon the act . . . It is certainly
subversive of state sovereignty." Clay Alexander to Brown, 15 September 1862,
Governor's Incoming Correspondence, Joseph E. Brown, RG 1-1-5, Box 22,
GDAH.

32. Edwin Bass to "Dear Sister," 22 April 1861, in Lane, *"Dear Mother,"* p. 4;
Shephard Pryor to "My Dear Penelope," Travellers' Rest, Virginia, August 17,
1861, reprinted in *"Dear Mother"*, 51; William Stillwell to his wife, Fredericks-
burg, Virginia, August 13, 1861, reprinted in *"Dear Mother"*, 260–61; William
Moore and Others, 2 August 1864, Executive Department, Petitions, RG 1–1, Box
1, GDAH.

33. Jacob Blount to Brown, 12 August 1863, Governors Incoming Correspondence, Joseph E. Brown, RG 1-1-5, Box 24, GDAH.

34. Jefferson Davis, *Gentlemen of the Congress of the Confederate States of
America, Friends and Fellow-Citizens*, February 18, 1861 reprinted in *The Papers
of Jefferson Davis*, ed. Lynda Lasswell Crist and Mary Seaton Dix, (Baton Rouge,
1992), 7:46.

35. Despite the massive revision in understandings of slave emancipation produced by the various productions, documentary and otherwise, of the Freedmen
and Southern Society Project, the political history of the Confederacy continues
to adhere to traditional definitions of political subjects and political history. See,
for example, the recent treatment by George Rable, *The Confederate Republic* in
which he acknowledges that much of the pressure driving Confederate policy
debate and struggle originated in popular politics outside the Confederate Congress but which focuses, nonetheless, almost exclusively on matters internal to
that political body. ["Political pressures (including legitimate concern about civilian morale) greatly influenced strategic and even logistical decisions," he points
out (116), but the concern remains parenthetic.] For an introduction to the work
on slave emancipation see Ira Berlin et al., *Slaves No More: Three Essays on*

Emancipation and the Civil War (New York, 1992); on Confederate "morale" and the ideological necessities of the war, see Drew Gilpin Faust, *The Creation of Confederate Nationalism: Ideology and Identity in the Civil War South* (Baton Rouge, 1988).

36. Kerber, " 'A Constitutional Right to Be Treated Like American Ladies."

37. Benjamin Morgan Palmer, *The Family in its Civil and Churchly Aspects: An Essay in Two Parts* (Richmond, 1876), 69, 49. "Women had no more right to political or economic power than a slave or a child," one southerner editorialized in 1851, "while the husband is vested with a property in her labor and may dispose of it at his plesure, because it is thought the best arrangement for her well being." *Albany Patriot*, 11 July 1851, quoted in Susan E. O'Donovan, "Transforming Work: Slavery, Free Labor, and the Household in Southwest Georgia, 1850-1880," (Ph.D. diss. University of California, San Diego, 1997), 46–47.

38. Cobb, *Substance of Remarks*, 8–9; A. B. Briggs, Sr., et al., 8 August 1863, Executive Department, Petitions, RG 1-1, Box 1, GDAH.

39. Thavolia Glymph, " 'This species of Property': Female Slave Contrabands in the Civil War," in Edward D. D. Campbell, Jr., and Kym S. Rice, *A Woman's War: Southern Women, Civil War, and the Confederate Legacy* (Richmond and Charlottesville, Va., 1996), 55–72; Burnham, "An Impossible Marriage;" Edwards, " 'The Marriage Covenant.' "

40. George Rable notes that after only a few months in the army at the beginning of the war, "Irish soldiers in Dorsey Pender's regiment were already receiving letters from home telling of starving wives and children." George Rable, *Civil Wars: Women and the Crisis of Southern Nationalism* (Urbana, Ill., 1989), 63.

41. *Charleston Mercury*, 15 November 1860, 3 November 1860, 12 November 1860; L.S.M., "To the Editor of the *Charleston Mercury*," *Charleston Mercury*, 23 November 1860. On McCord's gravestone in Columbia, South Carolina is inscribed "Mother of the Gracchi."

42. As late as 1975, Bell Wiley used that construction—what women "gave up" were their husbands and sons—to measure their contribution to the cause. See Bell Irvin Wiley, *Confederate Women* (Westport, Conn., 1975), 154–55. George Rable notes that Confederate men's failure to secure their wives consent to enlist was a common reason women provided in seeking a discharge for male family members. Rable, *Civil Wars*, p. 81.

43. Here note the difference in emphasis from Elizabeth Varon who has recently argued for the centrality of women to partisan politics in antebellum Virginia. Her own evidence, while interesting surely, nonetheless supports the general contention that women were mobilized as wives; her best examples are politicians' wives, a point not entirely acknowledged in her analysis. The desire to gender politics and to intrude women into its narratives is a common project of many feminist historians of the South, but a number of different approaches to the problem have already emerged. See Varon, "Tippacoanoe and the Ladies, Too: White Women and Party Politics in Antebellum Virginia," *The Journal of American History*, 82, (September 1995): 494-521. For a different approach, see my *Masters of Small Worlds: Yeoman Households, Gender Relations, and the Political Culture of the Antebellum South Carolina Low Country* (New York, 1995), 208–304.

44. Milton Barrett to Dear Brother and Sister, 11 August 1861 in Heller and Heller, eds., *The Confederacy is Up the Spout*, 24–26. Barrett belonged to the 16th Regiment, Georgia Volunteers, Company A.

45. M. H. Bray and Others, 26 January 1864, Executive Department, Petitions, RG 1–1, Box 1, GDAH.

46. Mrs. Margaret Tucker and Others, 10 October 1864, Executive Department, Petitions, RG 1–1, Box 1, GDAH. It is interesting to note that even during the war white women used the formal petition more frequently than informal "correspondence" in communications to Governor Brown. I'd like to thank Margaret Storey, a graduate student at Emory University History Department for her research assistance with the Joseph E. Brown Papers. The fullest description and analysis of these sources is in Rable, *Civil Wars*, 50–90.

47. Frances Bolton to Governor Brown, 22 July 1864, Governors Incoming Correspondence, Joseph E. Brown, RG 1-1-5, Box 24, GDAH.

48. Anonymous, From the ladies of Spaulding County, Griffin, Georgia, 15 June 1864, Governors Incoming Correspondence, Joseph E. Brown, RG 1-1-5, Box 22, GDAH; Mrs. L. E. Davis to Jefferson Davis, 22 August 1864, quoted in Rable, *Civil Wars*, 107. More elite women took the opportunity of the war to advance moral crusades against licentious men, complaining to Brown about drinking, horse racing, and fast young men. See, for example, Anonymous to Governor Brown, n.d [1864], Governors Incoming Correspondence, Joseph E. Brown, RG 1-1-5, Box 22, GDAH.

49. *Rome Weekly Courier*, 3 January 1862, 1, quoted in Paul Escott, "Joseph E. Brown, Jefferson Davis and the Problem of Poverty in the Confederacy," *Georgia Historical Quarterly*, 61 (Spring 1977): 64, 69. Brown boasted that he had "labored day and might" to send clothes and food to suffering families when "they could get none from the Confederacy." Escott, "Joseph Brown," 69.

50. Captain John Bragg to Brown, 13 March 1863; Anonymous to Governor J. E. Brown, 5 August 1864; M. A. Brantly to Brown, 5 February 1864; James M. Brantley to Brown, 16 January 1864, all in Governors Incoming Correspondence, Joseph E. Brown, RG 1-1-5, Box 24, GDAH. Paul Escott's article on Joseph Brown is a good example. Escott astutely analyzes Brown's construction of himself as the people's governor—that is, the class appeal—but while documenting his services to "soldiers' wives," fails to consider that gender vehicle of class politics in his analysis. See Escott, "Joseph Brown."

51. Charlott White to Brown, 12 April 1861, Executive Department, Petitions, RG 1–1, Box 1, GDAH; Mrs. L.W. Nicholson to John J. Pettus, 17 December 1862 quoted in Rable, *Civil Wars*, 74; Virginia Thornton to Jefferson Davis, 22 October 1862 quoted in Rable, *Civil Wars*, 74.

52. As late as 1975, the otherwise astute Bell Wiley still adhered to the loyalty narrative. See Wiley, *Confederate Women*, xi. In recent years, however, it has come under serious attack. See Faust, *Mothers of Invention: Women of the Slaveholding South in the American Civil War* (Chapel Hill, 1996), 243. The political direction of the argument was discernible also in Rable, *Civil Wars*, 89. By contrast, LeeAnn Whites still maintains the loyalty claim, although in a different valence entirely than the traditional one of admiration. See Whites, *Civil War as a Crisis in Gender*. For my views on Faust and Whites see my review essay, "Steel Magnolias," in *The Women's Review of Books* 14 (March 1997): 13–14.

53. The tendency to measure the political significance of Confederate women's history in relation to its "legacy" in postbellum issues (notably white supremacy, the Lost Cause, and the southern women's suffrage movement starting in the 1880s and 90s usually) is evident in most recent work. See Faust, *Mothers of Invention*, 248–57; Whites, *Civil War as a Crisis in Gender*; Marjorie Spruill

Wheeler, "Divided Legacy: The Civil War, Tradition, and 'the Woman Question,'" in Campbell and Rice, eds., *A Woman's War*, 165–91. It is interesting to note that no one has yet tried to write the nearer history of southern women's suffrage in the debates of the freedmen's conventions or the state constitutional conventions of the late 1860s. The only treatment of the subject, to my knowledge, is contained in Suzanne Lebsock's piece, "Radical Reconstruction and the Property Rights of Southern Women," *The Journal of Southern History*, 43 (May 1977): 195–216.

54. The most widely cited history of the woman suffrage movement in immediate post-Civil War America is still Ellen DuBois, *Feminism and Suffrage: The Emergence of An Independent Women's Movement in America, 1848–1869* (Ithaca, N.Y., 1978). DuBois takes Kansas as the critical local case. With respect to the South there is one important article by Lebsock, "Radical Reconstruction and the Property Rights of Southern Women." As the title suggests, suffrage was not the author's main concern. More recent work on freedpeople's politics by Elsa Barkley Brown has revived the discussion but interestingly while she is concerned with the gendered definition of the black public sphere in the immediate postwar period in the South, she does not say how the extension of women's suffrage—or of gendered arguments for an exclusively male franchise—played in the debate. See Brown, "Negotiating and Transforming the Public Sphere: African American Political Life in the Transition from Slavery to Freedom," *Public Culture* 7 (1994): 107–46.

55. For an excellent recent treatment of the politics of "home protection" in the Jim Crow South (though one not aware of the antebellum and Civil War prehistory), see Gilmore, *Gender and Jim Crow*, 91–118.

56. For one of the first direct engagements with this subject, see Steven Hahn, *To Build a New Jerusalem: The African-American Political Experience in the Rural South, 1860–1900* (Cambridge, Mass., forthcoming), chapter 1.

57. Albany *Patriot*, 11 July 1851 quoted in O'Donovan, "Transforming Work," 46–47; "When the 'Breckinridge Party' hosted a 'great mass meeting and barbacue' at Albany before the fall election in 1860, 'about 2000 people of all sizes and coloring attended.' " A.J. Swinney Diary, 8 October 1860 quoted in O'Donovan, "Transforming Work," 91. On vigilante organizations in the secession crisis, see McCurry, *Masters of Small Worlds*, 292–302; on "aweing the negroes and . . . rendering them more subservient," see "A Citizen" to Governor Joseph E. Brown, 12 August 1864, Governors Incoming Correspondence, Joseph E. Brown Papers, RG 1-1-5, Box 22, GDAH.

58. William H. Lee to Jefferson Davis, 4 May 1861, in Berlin et al, *Freedom, The Black Military Experience*, 282.

59. Ira Berlin et al., *Free At Last: A Documentary History of Slavery, Freedom, and the Civil War* (New York, 1992), pp. 62, 64, 62–63.

60. "Treason," *The Random House College Dictionary* (New York, 1975), 1399.

61. Drew Gilpin Faust offers the best treatment of the issue of slave consent in the Confederacy. She treats the matter in ideological terms as part of the wartime defense of slavery and is interested more in the way the war changed the "context of legitimation" of slavery itself than in the relevance for political history. Her analysis is extremely suggestive of other lines of investigation and argument, however, and was the seedbed of this inquiry. See Faust, *The Creation of Confederate Nationalism*, 58–81.

62. Augusta *Southern Christian Advocate*, February 1865, quoted in Mohr, *Threshold of Freedom*, 276; F. Kendall to Mr. President, September 16, 1864, in

Berlin et al., *Freedom, The Black Military Experience*, 286–87; J.H. Stringfellow to Jefferson Davis, 8 February 1865, Glenn Ellen, Henrico, Virginia, in Berlin et al., *The Black Military Experience*, 291.

63. *Jackson Mississippian* reprinted in Montgomery, Alabama *Weekly Mail*, 9 September 1863, in Robert F. Durden, *The Grey and the Black: The Confederate Debate on Emancipation* (Baton Rouge, 1972), 29–32.

64. Cobb quoted in Mohr, *Threshold of Freedom*, 278; J.H. Stringfellow to Jefferson Davis, 8 February 1865, in Berlin et al., *Freedom, The Black Military Experience*, 291; Major General Patrick R. Cleburne, 2 January 1864 in Durden, *The Grey and the Black*, 60; *Christian Index*, 23 February 1865 quoted in Mohr, *Threshold of Freedom*, 283.

65. Cleburne, 2 January 1864 in Durden, *The Grey and the Black*, 60–61.

66. Such concerns constitute the focus of recent work by Elsa Barkley Brown, Steven Hahn, and Laura Edwards among others, and they indicate the direction of my ongoing research. See Brown, "Negotiating and Transforming the Public Sphere," Hahn, *To Build A New Jerusalem*, and Laura F. Edwards, *Gendered Strife and Confusion: The Political Culture of Reconstruction* (Urbana, Ill., 1997).

67. On slave women's contributions to the destruction of slavery see Leslie Schwalm, *A Hard Fight For We: Women's Transition From Slavery to Freedom in South Carolina* (Urbana, Ill., 1997), pp. 75–147.

68. Stringfellow to Davis, 8 February 1865, in Berlin et al, *Freedom, The Black Military Experience*, p. 291–96; Jackson *Mississippian* reprinted in Montgomery, Alabama, *Weekly Mail*, 9 September 1863, in Durden, *Grey and the Black*, 30.

Notes to COMMENTARY
by Tera W. Hunter

1. Elsa Barkley Brown, "Negotiating and Transforming the Public Sphere: African American Political Life in the Transition from Slavery to Freedom," *Public Culture* 6 (1994): 107–146.

2. Gail Bederman, *Manliness and Civilization: A Cultural History of Gender and Race in the United States 1880–1917* (Chicago, 1995).

3. Benjamin Quarles, *The Negro in the Civil War* (Boston, 1953).

Notes to "NEW MEN IN BODY AND SOUL": THE CIVILIAN
CONSERVATION CORPS AND THE TRANSFORMATION OF MALE
BODIES AND BODY POLITIC
by Bryant Simon

1. For overviews of the CCC, see "The Civilian Conservation Corps," in *American Conservation*, 2, Printed Material, Vertical File, CCC, Franklin D. Roosevelt Library, Hyde Park, New York, (herein FDRL); T. H. Watkins, *The Great Depression: America in the 1930s* (Boston, 1993), 131; and Robert S. McElvaine, *The Great Depression: America, 1929–1941* (New York, 1984), 154–55.

2. For a succinct, clear explanation of the structure of the CCC and the roles of various agencies in administering the CCC, see Watkins, *The Great Depression*, 130.

3. *Time*, 7 August 1944, 18.

4. For the standard institutional account of the CCC, see John A. Salmond, *The Civilian Conservation Corps, 1933–1942: A New Deal Case Study* (Durham, N.C., 1967).

5. "Message From the President of the United States to the Members of the Civilian Conservation Corps Read Over the National Broadcasting Company Red Network," 17 April 1936, Official File, 268, Folder—March–June 1937, FDRL.

6. James J. McEntee, *Now They Are Men: The Story of the CCC* (Washington, 1940), 58.

7. *Happy Days*, 19 August 1933.

8. For more about masculinity and the body in the larger context, see George L. Mosse, *Fallen Soldiers: Reshaping the Memory of the World Wars* (New York, 1990), esp. 73.

9. For an examination of changing European conceptions of manhood, see Robert A. Nye, *Masculinity and Male Codes of Honor in Modern France* (New York, 1993).

10. On the fears of overcivilization and changing conceptions of manhood see, E. Anthony Rotundo, *American Manhood: Transformations in Masculinity from the Revolution to the Modern Era* (New York, 1993); Gail Bederman, *Manliness and Civilization: A Cultural History of Gender and Race in the United States, 1880–1917* (Chicago, 1995), 10–15; George Chauncey, *Gay New York: Gender, Urban Culture and the Making of the Gay Male World, 1890–1940* (New York, 1994), 111–22.

11. Chauncey, *Gay New York*, 111–14.

12. On TR's transformation, see Theodore Roosevelt, *Theodore Roosevelt: An Autobiography* (New York, 1913). See also, Richard Slotkin, "Nostalgia and Progress: Theodore Roosevelt's Myth of the Frontier," *American Quarterly* 33 (Winter 1981): 608–37; Arnaldo Testi, "The Gender of Reform Politics: Theodore Roosevelt and the Culture of Masculinity," *Journal of American History* 81 (March 1995): 1515–18; Bederman, *Manliness and Civilization*, 170–215; Chauncey, *Gay New York*, 113–14; and J. Anthony Lukas, *Big Trouble* (New York , 1997), 386.

13. See Kenneth Holland and Frank Ernest Hill, *Youth in the CCC* (Washington, 1942), 205.

14. Russell A. Beam, "Counseling for Adjustment and Rehabilitation," *The Phi Delta Kappa* 19 (May 1937): 338—Folder—Education in CCC, Printed Materials, CCC Vertical File, FDRL.

15. Quite explicitly, CCC educational programs attempted to teach students "character and citizenship training." See Holland and Hill, *Youth in the CCC*, 158. For the most insightful account of the CCC as a citizenship training ground, see Eric B. Gorham, *National Service, Citizenship, and Political Education* (Albany, N.Y., 1992), 130–140.

16. Salmond, *The Civilian Conservation Corps*, 88–101; and Harvard Sitkoff, *A New Deal for Blacks: The Emergence of Civil Rights as a National Issue: The Depression Decade* (New York, 1978), 74–75.

17. Col. Alva J. Brasted, Chief of Chaplains, US Army, *Character Building Agencies*, (Fort Leavenworth, Kansas, 1936), Folder—General CCC Pamphlet, Re—Introduction, FDRL.

18. James W. Danner to FDR, September 21, 1936, PPF File, FDRL. Robby Cohen pointed this source out to me.

19. Michael Kernan, "Back to the Land: CCC Alumni Reunite on Skyline Drive," Washington Post, April 6, 1988, Folder—Virginia, Vertical Files, FDRL.

20. On the importance of James's essay to the conception of the CCC, see Leslie A. Lacy, *The Soil Soldiers: The Civilian Conservation Corps in the Great Depression* (Radnor, PA 1976), 17–18. In fact, one CCC camp was named after James. See Jack J. Preiss, *Camp William James* (Norwich, Vt., 1978).

21. In order, these references to the CCC and war come from Robert Fechner's testimony before the United States Congress, House Committee on Labor, "To Make the Civilian Conservation Corps a Permanent Agency," 9, 23, 24 February 1939, (Washington, D.C.), 9; *Civilian Conservation Corps: Contributing to the National Defense*, (1941), Eleanor Roosevelt Papers, Pamphlets, Folder—U.S. Civilian Conservation Corps, FDRL; and James McEntee, *The CCC and National Defense*, (1940), Printed Materials, CCC Vertical File, Folder—American Forestry Association Publications, FDRL. See also, the chapter entitled, "Workers for Defense" in Holland and Hill, *Youth in the CCC*, 182–89.

22. *The Forestry News Digest* (This journal was published by the American Tree Association. This particular issue was labeled a "Special CCC Edition"), July 1933—Folder—American Forestry Association Publications, Vertical Files, FDRL. See also Helen Mabel Walker, *The CCC Through the Eyes of 272 Boys: A Summary of the Reactions of 272 Cleveland Boys to Their Experience in the Civilian Conservation Corps*, (Cleveland, 1938), 12, 22–23, 27–28; and *Happy Days*, 12 August 1933.

23. Guy D. McKinney to William Hassett, 4 June 1937, OF 268, Folder—March–June 1937, FDRL.

24. David Sewab, "CCC Alumni Recall the Hard Times and FDR's Fast, 'Creative' Response," *The Sunday Star-Ledger*, 24 April 1983—Folder—CCC 50th Anniversary Printed Materials, CCC Vertical File, FDRL.

25. According to one survey done in 1937, only 16 percent of CCC recruits were from "large" cities. See Holland and Hill, *Youth in the CCC*, 83. One CCC enrollee addressed this issue in 1935. In an open letter, he wrote: "What about rescinding some of those press notices about the CCC boys ALL being anemic, undernourished bums before they came into the C.C.C. I've never been a bum and I've never been undernourished, but I did need a job—and thanks to FDR I got one and I'm proud of it." Boys of Company 1699 CCC, Richland Center, WI to FDR, 25 May 1935, attached is the *Weekly Journal* 1 (25 May 1934), OF 268, Civilian Conservation Corps, Box 11, Folder—CCC Periodical 1933, FDRL. Again the reality of the situation often contradicted the CCC's self-generated mythology. To cite another example, CCC recruits were usually portrayed as poor, uneducated urbanites rescued from the vices of the city, but according to one survey, more than half of the enrollees, in fact, came from families that owned their own homes and most had completed the tenth grade. Walker, *The CCC Through the Eyes of 272 Boys*, 13, 16.

26. James W. Danner to FDR, 21 September 1936, PPF File, FDRL.

27. Scholars have repeated, almost verbatim, this view of the city and the country in their own accounts of the CCC. For instance, in his recent book on the 1930s, T. H. Watkins writes: ". . . [T]he CCC at its best took some young men out of the urban tangle of hopelessness . . . [and] . . . introduced them to the intricacies and healing joy of the outdoors." Watkins, *The Great Depression*, 131.

28. For FDR's view of the city, see Lacy, *The Soil Soldiers*, 18.

29. Teddy Roosevelt, for example, was influenced by this stream of urban

literature. What's more, he obviously influenced Franklin Roosevelt's thinking. On TR, see George Mowry, *The Era of Theodore Roosevelt, 1900–1912* (New York, 1958), 60–61, 65.

30. On the idea of "urban degeneracy," see Gareth Stedman Jones, *Outcast London: A Study in the Relationship Between Classes in Victorian Society* (New York, 1971), 127–30, 285–87. See also Max Nordau, *Degeneration* (1892; Lincoln, Neb., 1968). On similar ideas about the sources and impact of poverty in the United States, see William F. Ogburn, *You and Machines* (Chicago, 1934), 33. Historians have looked at this connection; see Robert Bremner, *The Discovery of Poverty in the United States* (1956; New York, 1992). See, finally, from the CCC, William L. Talbott, "The New Challenge: Twentieth Century Pioneers," *The Builder* 1 (November 1934), OF 268, Box 12, Folder—CCC Periodicals, 1935, FDRL.

31. See for example, Russell A. Beam, "Counseling for Adjustment and Rehabilitation," *The Phi Delta Kappa* 19 (May 1937): 338—Folder—Education in CCC, Printed Materials, CCC Vertical File, FDR Library.

32. For a broader discussion of this organic conception of the world, which linked physical appearance with the intellectual and emotional health, see George L. Mosse, *The Image of Man: The Creation of Modern Masculinity* (New York, 1996).

33. Richard Hofstadter made this observation about nature in *Age of Reform* (New York, 1955). He is quoted by Salmond, *The Civilian Conservation Corps*, 104.

34. Some people, like Georgia Congressman Robert Ramspeak, assumed that deleterious effects of the city and the redemptive aspects of nature were obvious; so obvious that they required no explanation. See Ramspeak's comments, United States Congress, House Committee on Labor, "To Make the Civilian Conservation Corps a Permanent Agency," February 1939, 34–35.

35. Roderick Nash, *Wilderness and the American Mind* (New Haven, 1967), 145, 153. For more on ideas about nature, see Simon Schama, *Landscape and Memory* (New York, 1995). See also a discussion of Jacob Riis's views of the world in David Leviatin's introduction to Riis, *How the Other Half Lives: Studies Among the Tenements of New York* (Boston, 1996), 20–21. The editorial "City Men Win" talks about how urban boys are transformed in the camps: *Happy Days*, 30 September 1933. See also the comments by a CCC enrollee in Lacy, *Soil Soldiers*, 126. For more on the purifying view of nature in the CCC, see Hoyt, *We Can Take It*, 59; and Salmond, *The Civilian Conservation Corps*, 108.

36. McEntee, *Now They Are Men*, 10, 58. For more on Roosevelt's view, see Donald Day, *Franklin D. Roosevelt's Own Story* (Boston, 1951), 166.

37. Lacy, *Soil Soldiers*, 20; and James Lasswell, "Shovels and Guns: The CCC in Action," (1935) in Printed Material, Vertical Files, Folder—CCC Pamphlets, FDRL.

38. Wm. L. Talbott, "The New Challenge: Twentieth Century Pioneers," *The Builder* 1 (November 1934), OF 268, Box 12, Folder—CCC Periodical 1935, FDRL.

39. Enrollees of Company 1261, T.V.A. Camp 20, Clouds, Tennessee, "The Program of the C. C. C. in the United States," *The Cloud Gazer*, 23 June 1934, 2, OF 268, Box 11, Folder 1933, FDRL; Captain Francis V. Fitz Gerald, "The President Prescribes," *The Quartermaster Review* (July–August 1933): 10, Printed Materials, Vertical Files, CCC, FDRL. See also *Happy Days*, 16 September 1933.

40. Enrollees of Company 1261, T.V.A. Camp 20, Clouds, Tennessee, "The Program of the C. C. C. in the United States," *The Cloud Gazer*, 23 June 1934, 2, OF 268, Box 11, Folder 1933, FDRL; *Happy Days*, 5 August 1933.

41. Similarly, homosexual men, who, of course, many people believed could be identified just by looking at them, were also typically characterized as a threat to the state. Chauncey, *Gay New York*, 8–9.

42. "The Skipper Says," *The Weekly Blabber*, 11 January 1935, 3, OF268, Box 12, Folder—CCC Periodicals, 1935, FDRL.

43. On the conditioning camps, see Jack Irby Hayes Jr., "South Carolina and the New Deal, 1932–1938" (Ph.D. diss., University of South Carolina, 1972), 265.

44. Hoyt, *We Can Take It*, 57.

45. *Happy Days*, 30 September 1933; Salmond, *Civilian Conservation Corps*, 137, 139; Holland and Hill, *Youth in the CCC*, 202–04; and Lacy, *The Soil Soldiers*, 133, 178. For a broader discussion of exercise, see George L. Mosse, *The Image of Man*, 109. There was, however, criticism from some quarters that the sports were reserved for the best athletes, leaving others on the sidelines. See Holland and Hill, *Youth in the CCC*, 204–05; and Walker, *The CCC Through the Eyes of 272 Boys*, 47–48.

46. On the importance of team sports, see Steven A. Riess, "Sport and the Redefinition of American Middle-Class Masculinity, 1840–1900," in Riess, *Major Problems in American Sport History* (Boston, 1997), 197–98; and Harvey Green, *Fit for America: Health, Fitness, Sport, and American Society* (New York, 1986), 233.

47. See a list of the kinds of classes offered in Clarence Riley Aydelott, "Facts Concerning Enrollees, Advisers, and the Educational Program in the CCC Camps of Missouri" (Ph.D. diss., University of Missouri, 1936), 80–83.

48. See for example, Charles C. Bucyzinski, "Your Health: Mouth Hygiene," and article by Lorenzo D. Kiersey, *Northlander* 9 (June 1936): 4, 7, 16, Printed Material, Vertical File, FDR Papers, Folder—Michigan, FDRL. See also the recollections of CCC member in Michael Kernan's "Back to the Land," *Washington Post*, 6 April 1983, Printed Material, CCC Vertical File, Folder—Virginia, FDRL; and Holland and Hill, *Youth in the CCC*, 195–98.

49. Quartermaster Corps Subsistence School, "Subsistence Menus and Recipes for Feeding 100 Men for One Month," CCC Vertical File, Folder—CCC Menu Printed Materials, FDRL; and Holland and Hill, *Youth in the CCC*, 58. See also Hayes, "The New Deal in South Carolina, " 267. Not surprisingly, there was considerable rancor over the food. Several camps, in fact, had food strikes. For more on food protests, see Walker, *The CCC Through the Eyes of 272 Boys*, 29. For the larger context on the American diet, see Harvey Levenstein, *Paradox of Plenty: A Social History of Eating in Modern America* (New York, 1993). The last story was related to me by Jane Barrasso, who had talked to her father who was in the CCC.

50. On weight gain, see *Happy Days*, 30 September 1933; 21 November 1933; and *The Forestry News Digest* (August 1933)—Folder—American Forestry Association Publications, 12, Vertical File, FDRL. See also Walker, *The CCC Through the Eyes of 272 Boys*, 29; Holland and Hill, *Youth in the CCC*, 191; Perry Merill, *Roosevelt's Forest Army: A History of the Civilian Conservation Corps, 1933–1942* (New York, 1981), 73, 102; and Mrs. Ella L. Parent to FDR, 26 August 1933, OF 268, Folder—Misc., Sept.–Oct., 1933, FDRL.

51. Lacy, *The Soil Soldiers*, 33.

52. *Happy Days*, 26 August 1933.

53. Salmond, *Civilian Conservation Corps*, 129.

54. Statement of Robert Fechner to the United States Congress, House Committee on Labor, "To Make the Civilian Conservation Corps a Permanent Agency," 9, 23, 24 February 1939, p. 3.

55. Schlesinger, *The Coming of the New Deal*, 339.

56. Not surprisingly, CCC supporters also developed written narratives to pay tribute to the agency's impact on individual lives. See for instance, Holland and Hill, *Youth in the CCC*, 1–6.

57. Lears, *No Place of Grace: Antimodernism and the Transformation of American Culture, 1880–1920* (New York, 1981), 4. See also Green, *Fit for America*.

58. Interestingly, it is usually the middle class which celebrates work. While certainly recognizing the necessity of work, working class writers and artists rarely celebrate work itself. More often, they talk about time *away* from work. See for instance, the songs of Bruce Springsteen. Jim Cullen, *Born in the U.S.A: Bruce Springsteen and the American Tradition* (New York, 1997), 102–08.

59. For discussions of family relations during the Great Depression, see Ruth Shonle Cavan and Katerine Howland Ranck, *The Family and the Depression: A Study of the Effects of Unemployment Upon the Workers' Social Relations and Practices* (Chicago, 1938); E. Wight Bakke, *Citizens Without Work* (New Haven, 1940); and Mirra Komarovsky, *The Unemployed Man and His Family* (New York, 1940). Think also here of the role of Ma Joad in John Steinbeck, *The Grapes of Wrath* (New York, 1939). See how a CCC chronicler deals with this link between the work of the relief agency and the Depression-era crisis of masculinity in Lacy, *The Soil Soldiers*, 7.

60. The Federal Emergency Relief Administration did set up a few "She-She-She Camps" for women. On this subject, see Joyce L. Kornbluh, "The She-She-She Camps: An Experiment in Living and Learning, 1934–1937," in *Sisterhood and Solidarity: Workers' Education for Women, 1914–1984* ed. Joyce L. Kornbluh and Mary Frederickson (Philadelphia, 1984), 255–83.

61. For some ideas on this fantasy, see Klaus Theweleit, *Male Fantasies: Volume 1: Women, Floods, Bodies, History* (Minneapolis, 1987).

62. Ogburn, *You and Machines*, 3.

63. Barbara Melosh, *Engendering Culture: Manhood and Womanhood in New Deal Public Art and Theater* (Washington, 1991), 92.

64. *Ibid.*, 83.

65. Mosse, *Nationalism and Sexuality: Middle-Class Morality and Sexual Norms in Modern Europe* (New York, 1985), 17. 66. For more on this important point, see Eric Gorham, "The Ambiguous Practices of the Civilian Conservation Corps," *Social History* 17 (May 1992): 229–49. Gorham's essay, like this one, has obviously been influenced by Michel Foucault. See in particular, Foucault, *Discipline and Punishment* (New York, 1980) and *The History of Sexuality* (New York, 1978).

Notes to COMMENTARY
by Louise M. Newman

1. The most interesting discussion of what constitutes a "crisis" in relation to gender can be found in Gail Bederman's excellent book, *Manliness and Civilization: A Cultural History of Gender and Race in the United States, 1880–1917* (Chicago, 1995), 10–12. The historical literature on masculinity is so voluminous

that I can cite but a few of the better-known examples in the Anglo-American field. In addition to Bederman, see Bertram Wyatt-Brown, *Southern Honor: Ethics and Behavior in the Old South* (New York, 1982); Susan Jeffords, *The Remasculinization of American: Gender and the Vietnam War* (Bloomington, Ind., 1989); David Leverenz, *Manhood and the American Renaissance* (Ithaca, N.Y., 1989); Barbara Melosh, *Engendering Culture: Manhood and Womanhood in New Deal Public Art and Theater* (Washington, 1991); Anthony Rotundo, *American Manhood: Transformation in Masculinity from the Revolution to the Modern Era* (New York, 1993); Kenneth A. Lockridge, *On the Sources of Patriarchal Rage* (New York, 1992); Robert L. Griswold, *Fatherhood in America: A History* (New York, 1993); Anthony Fletcher, *Gender, Sex and Subordination in England 1500-1800* (New Haven, 1995); George L. Mosse, *The Image of Man: The Creation of Modern Masculinity* (New York, 1996); Michael S. Kimmel, *Manhood in America: A Cultural History* (New York, 1996), and Kathleen Brown, *Good Wives, Nasty Wenches and Anxious Patriarchs: Gender, Race and Power in Colonial Virginia* (Chapel Hill, 1996).

In addition, there are numerous anthologies and articles on the subject, including those published in the following collections: Elizabeth H. And Joseph H. Pleck, eds. *The American Man* (Englewood Cliffs, N.J., 1980); Harry Brod, ed., *The Making of Masculinities: The New Men's Studies* (Boston, 1987); J. A. Mangan and James Walvin, eds., *Manliness and Morality: Middle-Class Masculinity in Britain and America, 1800–1940* (New York, 1987); Mark C. Carnes and Clyde Griffen, eds., *Meanings for Manhood: Constructions of Masculinity in Victorian America* (Chicago, 1990) and Michael Roper and John Tosh, eds., *Manful Assertions: Masculinities in Britain since 1800* (New York, 1991). If one were to include works from literary and film studies, sociology, anthropology, and other related fields, a complete list would take up many pages.

In addition to the aforementioned, works that proved most useful for the purposes of writing this comment included, Eric Gorham, "The Ambiguous Practices of the Civilian Conservation Corps," *Social History* 17.2 (May 1992): 229–249; Arnaldo Testi, "The Gender of Reform Politics: Theodore Roosevelt and the Culture of Masculinity," *Journal of American History* 81.4 (March 1995): 1509–1533; Josh Tosh, "What Should Historians Do With Masculinity?: Reflections on Nineteenth-Century Britain," *History Workshop Journal* 38 (1994): 181; Ann Lombard, "Playing the Man" (Ph.D. diss. in progress, UCLA); Joanna Bourke, "Masculinity, Men's Bodies and the Great War," *History Today* 45.2 (February 1996): 8.

2. John Tosh, "What Should Historians Do With Masculinity?: Reflections on Nineteenth-Century Britain," *History Workshop Journal* 38 (1994): 181.

3. Bederman, *Manliness*, 7.

4. Bederman, *Manliness*, 11–12.

5. Bederman, *Manliness*, 27.

6. Bederman, *Manliness*, 13.

7. Bederman, *Manliness*, 14.

Notes to REDESIGNING DIXIE WITH AFFIRMATIVE ACTION: RACE, GENDER, AND THE DESEGREGATION OF THE SOUTHERN TEXTILE MILL WORLD
by Nancy MacLean

1. Gerald Reed, Hunt Park Speech, [1963], series IV, Southern Christian Leadership Conference, Records, 1954–1970, microfilm edition, (Bethesda, Md., 1966), reel 23, frame 0525.

2. Quoted in Victoria Byerly, *Hard Times Cotton Mill Girls: Personal Histories of Womanhood and Poverty in the South*, (Ithaca, N.Y., 1986), 160.

3. See Charge of Discrimination, (including affidavits), *Daisy R. Crawford v. Cannon Mills* No. 1, Kannapolis, N.C., filed 5 June 1975, in Cannon Mills Papers, box 79, Special Collections Library, Duke University, Durham, N.C (hereafter, Duke); Cases 11-CA-6108 and 11-CA-6115, Before the National Labor Relations Board, *ibid.*; and *Daisy R. Crawford and Ruth B. Leazer v. Cannon Mills Company*, Civil Action No. C-76–113–5, U.S. District Court, Middle District of North Carolina, Salisbury Division, *ibid.*; *EEOC v. Cannon Mills Company*, Civil Action No. C-65-S-69, *idem, ibid.*; *Southern Patriot*, Dec. 1975, 5.

4. A 1957 NAACP report found that "among the 400,00 textile workers in Virginia, North Carolina, and South Carolina, there is apparently not a single Negro employed as a weaver, spinner or loom fixer." North Carolina Advisory Committee to U.S. Civil Rights Committee, typescript report, "North Carolina: Segregation-Desegregation: Current," 19, in folder 619, Marion C. Wright Papers, Southern Historical Collection, University of North Carolina-Chapel Hill (hereafter, UNC).

5. Ceasar Cone interview, 7 Jan. 1983, transcript, 27–28, 33–34, Southern Oral History Program Collection, (hereafter, SOHP), UNC. One gets a sense of the movement-like qualities of these legal challenges from the reports of group applications and of aid from experienced complainants in filling out charges in, for example, *Lucy Sledge et al. v. J. P. Stevens and Company, Inc.*, No. 1201, U.S. District Court, Eastern District of North Carolina, Wilson Division, decided 22 Dec. 1975; F.M. Southerland to Senator Sam Ervin, 2 Feb. 1967, box 149, Samuel Ervin Papers, UNC.

6. For working-class dimensions of the movement, see, for example, Robin D. G. Kelley, *Race Rebels: Culture, Politics, and the Black Working Class*, (New York, 1994), and the books and articles reviewed in Rick Halpern, "Organized Labor, Black Workers, and the Twentieth Century South: The Emerging Revision," in *Race and Class in the American South Since 1890*, ed. Melvyn Stokes and Rick Halpern, (Oxford, 1994).

7. On South Carolina U.S. Senator Strom Thurmond's successful efforts to prevent the federal government from applying sanctions to three textile mills that refused to open job opportunities to blacks, see *New York Times*, 1 Feb. 1969, 23; *ibid.*, 8 Feb. 1969, 25; *AFL-CIO News*, 12 April 1969, 1, 10.

8. The interpretation here contrasts sharply with what is fast becoming the conventional wisdom in southern and much of American historical writing. Presenting affirmative action as of value only to middle-class African Americans, writers in this school give the impression that the policy was conceived by freewheeling "elitist" federal bureaucrats out to convert the black freedom struggle, as one southern historian portrayed it recently, into a "symbolic" charade. See, respectively, David R. Goldfield, *Black, White and Southern: Race Relations and Southern Culture, 1940 to the Present* (Baton Rouge, 1990), 249; Numan V. Bartley, *The New South, 1945–1980* (Baton Rouge, 1995), 310, 378, 428, 465–66.

9. On the change in the union's attitude toward black workers and racial fairness and the reasons for it, see Summary of Southern TWUA Staff Survey, Dec. 1966, box 315, Textile Workers Union of America, mss. 396, State Historical Society of Wisconsin, Madison (hereafter, TWUA, SHSW); Solomon Barkin to John Chupka, 12 May 1961, box 316, *ibid.*; Thomas McNamara to William Pollock,

21 May 1964, box 614, *ibid.*; Scott Hoyman to William Pollock, 15 May 1961, box 638, *ibid.*

When finally admitted to the mills, blacks in fact became so pro-union that their propensity for organizing was the one thing on which both unions and management could agree. "The consensus opinion" of mill officials, reported an industry journal in 1968, is that "as the percentage of Negro employees increase[s], so does a mill's chances of union organization." Rozelle, "The Mill and the Negro," 66. See also Carolyn Ashbaugh and Dan McCurry, "On the Line at Oneita," in *Working Lives*, 210, 212; Frederickson, "Four Decades of Change," 69–70, 76; Cleghorn, "Giant Step," 142; Hughes, "New Twist for Textiles," 76; Reginald Stuart, "Businesses Said to Have Barred New Plants in Largely Black Communities," *New York Times*, 15 Feb. 1983, A:1; Michael D. Schulman, Rhonda Zingraff, and Linda Reif, "Race, Gender, Class Consciousness and Union Support: An Analysis of Southern Textile Workers," *Sociological Quarterly* 26 (1985): 187–204.

10. Michael Omi and Howard Winant, *Racial Formation in the United States*, (New York, 1994), 34; see also David R. Roediger, *Towards the Abolition of Whiteness: Essays on Race, Politics, and Working Class History* (New York,1994), 131.

11. For an important exception regarding African American oral histories published after this article went into production, but one that offers a valuable complement to it, see Timothy J. Minchin, *Hiring the Black: The Racial Integration of the Southern-Textile Industry, 1960–1980*, (Chapel Hill, 1999). Many leading studies on black workers and organized labor, Rick Halpern has observed in an important review of the literature, "maintain a conspicuous silence on issues of gender, declining to explore the important connections between the sexual division of labor, the specific form of workplace struggles, and the construction of racial identities." Halpern, "Organized Labor," 46. See also David Roediger, "What If Labor Were Not White and Male? Recentering Working-Class History and Reconstructing Debate on the Unions and Race," *International Labor and Working-Class History* 51(Spring 1997): 72–95.

Feminist scholars, meanwhile, have called for more analysis of "difference" not in the abstract, but in relational terms. For one such call to examine gender ideologies "for their racial specificity" and recognize "whiteness, not just blackness, as a racial categorization," see Hazel V. Carby, *Reconstructing Womanhood: The Emergence of the Afro-American Woman Novelist*, (New York, 1987), 18. See also Elsa Barkley Brown, " 'What Has Happened Here': The Politics of Difference in Women's History and Feminist Politics," in *"We Specialize in the Wholly Impossible": A Reader in Black Women's History*, ed. Darlene Clark Hine, et al. (Brooklyn, 1995); Tessie Liu, "Teaching the Differences Among Women from a Historical Perspective: Rethinking Race and Gender as Social Categories," *Unequal Sisters*, ed. Vicki L. Ruiz and Ellen Carol DuBois, (New York, 1994), esp. 574–5; Nancy A. Hewitt, "Beyond the Search for Sisterhood: American Women's History in the 1980s," *Social History* 10 (Oct. 1985): 229–321; Linda Gordon, "On Difference," *Genders*, 10 (Spring 1991): 91–111.

12. Quoted in Byerly, *Hard Times*, 100.

13. Eva B. Hopkins interview, quotes from tape index, SOHP. For moving, first-hand complaints about mill work, see Mildred McEwen interview, transcript, esp. 5–9, Southwest Institute for Research on Women, Oral History Interviews, (hereafter, SIRW), housed at UNC; Mary Robinson interview, transcript, 126, *ibid.*

14. Marc S. Miller, "Labor on the Move: The Future," in *Working Lives: The*

Southern Exposure History of Labor in the South, ed. Marc S. Miller, (New York, 1980), 354; TEAM, "Equal Employment Opportunity in the Textile Industry of South Carolina: Workbook for Community Leaders," [1967], box 28, Boyte Family Papers, Duke.

15. U.S. Equal Employment Opportunities Commission, *Textiles Are Getting a New Look*, (Washington, D.C.: GPO, 1967), 4; Leonard R. Mitchell to Randolph T. Blackwell and Harry G. Boyte, 1 Feb. 1966, series IV, reel 23, frame 0550, SCLC Papers.

16. Celeste King, quoted in Byerly, *Hard Times*, 94; SCLC Press release, "Atlanta SCLC to Launch 'Operation Bread Basket,'" 23 Oct. 1962, series IV, SCLC, reel 23, frame 0713.

17. Vivian W. Henderson, *The Economic Status of Negroes: In the Nation and in the South* (Atlanta, [ca. 1962]), 17; [North Carolina A & T], "Survey Report," 24 Feb. 1961, box 8, United States Commission on Civil Rights, North Carolina Advisory Committee (hereafter, NCAC), Duke.

18. Quoted in Byerly, *Hard Times*, 150. See also, in the same volume, interview with Johnny Mae Fields, 138, and with Amanda King, 195.

19. Richard L. Rowan, *The Negro in the Textile Industry*, The Racial Policies of American Industry Series, Industrial Research Unit Report No. 20 (Philadelphia, 1970), 1, 7, 11, 24; Alice Kidder, et al., "Changes in Minority Participation in the Textile Industry of North and South Carolina, 1966–1969," Report Submitted in compliance with EEOC Contract No. 70–18, (Greensboro, N.C., 1972), 1, 5; Ray Marshall, "Black Employment in the South," in *Women, Minorities, and Employment Discrimination*, ed. Phyllis Wallace and Annette LaMond (Lexington, K.Y., 1977), 71.

20. James J. Heckman and Brook S. Payner, "Determining the Impact of Federal Antidiscrimination Policy on the Economic Status of Blacks: A Study of South Carolina," *American Economic Review* 79 (March 1989): 138–76. For a pathbreaking early historical treatment, see Mary Frederickson, "Four Decades of Change: Black Workers in Southern Textiles, 1941–1981," reprinted in *Workers' Struggles, Past and Present*, ed. James Green (Philadelphia, 1983).

21. For a significant exception, see Alice Kidder, "Federal Compliance Efforts in the Carolina Textile Industry: A Summary Report," *Proceedings of the 25th Annual Meeting of the Industrial Relations Research Association* (Madison, Wisc., 1972). "Community pressure," argued Kidder elsewhere, "and a network of informal contacts between the black community and the textile industry must be given greater credit." See Kidder, et al., "Changes in Minority Participation," esp. x.

22. Mrs. Margie W. Joyce to Asa T. Spaulding, 22 June 1959, folder 616, Wright Papers; Mrs. Johnson to Mr. Smith, 25 Jan. 1960, box 6, NCAC; Helen Clinton to Dr. Rankin, 2 Feb. 1961, box 7, *ibid*.

23. Kelly M. Alexander to North Carolina Advisory Committee, [1960], box 6, NCAC. For other NAACP efforts to get jobs in the mills and elsewhere, see Smith to Cotter, ibid.; Ada Ford Singleton interview, transcript, 2, SOHP; Lewis M Durham interview, transcript, 42, *ibid*.; Daisy Bates interview, transcript, 59, *ibid*. For the heavily working-class base of the NAACP in North Carolina, see the comments of the state secretary of branches, Willie Mae Winfield interview, tape side A, 190 ff, *ibid*.

24. Sarah Herbin to Marion Wright, 4 Aug. 1961, in folder 622, Wright Papers; Herbin to Smith, 5 April 1960, box 6, NCAC; American Friends Service Committee, "Employment Survey in Greensboro, North Carolina: Report to Em-

ployers, Sept. 1958, box 8, *ibid*. See also William F. Chafe, *Civilities and Civil Rights: Greensboro, North Carolina and the Black Struggle for Freedom* (New York, 1980), 45–51.

25. Durham Committee on Negro Affairs to Gov. Sanford, 29 April 1961, box 7, NCAC; also *idem* to Smith, 16 June 1959, *ibid*.; see also Viola Turner interview, transcript, 39–40, SOHP. For CORE's plans to work on job opportunities for blacks at Greensboro mills, see William A. Thomas, Jr. to James McCain, 28 Jan. 1964, reel 19, frame 0760–61, Congress of Racial Equality Papers, 1941–1967 (hereafter, CORE), Microfilm edition, Addendum, (Sanford, S.C., 1982). For a useful overview of movement activities organized by locality, see Capus M. Waynick, John C. Brooks, and Elsie W. Pitts, ed., *North Carolina and the Negro* (Raleigh, N.C., 1964).

26. Martin Luther King, Jr. and Ralph D. Abernathy to "Dear Friend of Freedom," 25 Oct. 1962, series III, reel 1, frame 0207, SCLC Papers; SCLC, press release, 25 March 1963, reel 3, frame 0940, *ibid*. See also John G. Feild to Hobart Taylor, Jr., 14 Nov. 1962, with attachment, box 139, Vice-Presidential Papers, Lyndon Baines Johnson Library, Austin, Texas (hereafter, LBJL).

27. North Carolina Committee on Human Rights Report, 3/15/63. For early white editorials acknowledging the importance of "economic opportunity" for blacks, albeit in a seeming effort to shift attention from schools, see *The Charlotte Observer*, 5 Sept. 1957, and *Winston-Salem Journal*, 10 Sept. 1957, reproduced in box 7, NCAC.

28. For examples of how scholars tend to assume that pressure for affirmative action, federal and otherwise, began after the passage of the Civil Rights Act of 1964, see Roger Penn and Jeffrey Leiter, "Employment Patterns in the British and U.S. Textile Industries: A Comparative Analysis of Recent Gender Changes," in *Hanging By a Thread: Social Change in Southern Textiles*, ed. Jeffrey Leiter, et al., (Ithaca, N.Y., 1991), 153. For the kind of argument on timing presented here and for examples of the pressure on textile management in the early 1960s, see Kidder, "Changes in Minority Participation," 87; also the "Scope" file of material on the President's Committee on Equal Employment Opportunity, box 86, Vice-Presidential Papers, LBJL; North Carolina Advisory Committee, Draft Employment Report, 21 Sept. 1961, box 7, NCAC. See also the detailed, provocative and no doubt consciousness-raising survey distributed to government contractors by the North Carolina State Advisory Committee of the Commission on Civil Rights in 1961, folder 11 Robert Bruce Cooke Papers, UNC; also George Parks interview, transcript, 17, SOHP. For management response to the pressure of order 10925, see Norman Cone, Jr., for Cone Mills Corporation, "To Our Revolution [Mill] Employees," 20 July 1961, box 316, TWUA, mss. 396; David Terry to H.S. Williams, 24 April 1961, box 638, *ibid*. 29. Harry Boyte, Sr., detailed notes on conversation with Sarah Herbin, Associate Director of Merit Employment, AFSC, 23 April 1963, box 28, Boyte Family Papers. In the same conversation, however, Herbin also expressed frustration at the "tragic absence [in Greensboro] of real Negro leadership of the militant and dedicated type." "If such a person were to move here into the Negro community," she thought, "the present leaders. . . would undertake, in her words to 'clobber' " that person. For other evidence of the influence of defense contracts in producing change, see Carl R. Harris to Colonel Virlyn Y. Jones, 24 July 1963, folder 11, Cooke Papers; Donnell K. Wolverton to Carl R. Harris, 23 Aug. 1962, ibid.; and the heavily underlined annotated copy of the text of Executive Order 10925, "Fair Employment Practices: Execu-

tive Order Establishing the President's Committee on Equal Employment Opportunity," Bureau of National Affairs, 1961, in *ibid.*

30. See, for example, interviews with Celeste King and Corine Lytle Cannon, in Byerly, *Hard Times Cotton Mill Girls*, 134, 150. The latter recalled that after the Civil Rights Act Cannon Mills "just flooded the place with black women. . . . Black women from everywhere, I didn't know there were so many black women" (153).

31. Quoted in Reese Cleghorne, "The Mill: A Giant Step Forward for the Southern Negro," *New York Times Magazine*, 9 Nov. 1969, 147; see also the discussion from employers' perspectives of pressures for affirmative action from the Defense Department and the OFCC in Walter N. Rozelle, "The Mill and the Negro: Let's Tell It Like It is," *Textile Industries*, 132.11 (Nov. 1968): 70–71.

32. Among the large defense contractors in North Carolina were Burlington Industries and J.P. Stevens. See Seidenberg to Wright, 12 June 1959, folder 616, Wright Papers. On defense contracts, see also Rowan, *The Negro in the Textile Industry*, 19; Kidder, "Changes in Minority Participation," 78. On the effort to secure import quotas, see

Daily News Record, 6 April 1961, in box 316, TWUA, mss 396, SHSW; David Newton Henderson Papers, box 417, Duke; Samuel James Ervin, Jr., Senate Records, boxes 49, 61, and 71, UNC. Ironically, by 1971 the preservation of minority jobs in industry was being claimed as a reason for such import quotas. See Office of the White House Press Secretary, press release: "Position of U.S. Textile and Apparel Industry," 15 Oct. 1971, box 365, *ibid.*

33. AFSC, "Employment Survey," 2.

34. Charles A. Kothe to S. B. Fuller, 18 Dec. 1963, enclosure, box 13, National Association of Manufacturers, Industrial Relations Department Papers, Hagley Museum and Library, Wilmington, DE; *Fibre and Fabric*, Oct. 1963, in folder 11, Cooke Papers. See also the pre-scripted diatribe against fair employment in the 1940s, entitled ' "The Real Issue of the FEPC': A Fifteen-Minute Radio Script," in box 83, Cannon Mills Papers.

35. NAACP, press release, 17 Sept. 1965, box A 180, Series III, National Association for the Advancement of Colored People Papers, Manuscripts Division, Library of Congress; United States. Equal Employment Opportunity Commission. *Administrative History* (typescript), 139, LBJL.

36. *Textile News*, 16 Jan. 1967, 1; Kidder, "Changes in Minority Participation," 140–41; also Rozelle, "The Mill and the Negro," 67. For analogous developments in the southern steel industry, see Robert J. Norrell, "Caste in Steel: Jim Crow Careers in Birmingham," *Journal of American History* 73 (Dec. 1986): 689–90.

37. EEOC, *Textiles Are Getting a New Look* (Washington, 1967).

38. On TEAM, see TEAM, "Equal Employment Opportunity; Southern Regional Council *Annual Report* (1968), 26, in folder 3668, Willis Duke Weatherford Papers, UNC; Mordecai Johnson to Jean Fairfax, ("a brief history of the Textile Industry Project"), 7 Aug. 1967, Southern Regional Council Papers, Microfilm Edition (Ann Arbor: University Microfilms International, 1984), reel 163, 0313 ff. This collection also contains the reports of TEAM field staffers.

39. See, respectively, F. M. Southerland to Senator Sam Ervin, 2 Feb. 1967, box 149, Ervin Papers; James P. Wilson and Horace Hill to Ervin, 14 April 1967, *ibid.*; W. N. Jefferies to Ervin, 5 May 1967, *ibid.* Ervin, since lionized for his defense of the Constitution in the Watergate hearings, responded to all these

writers, including the anti-Semite who five times dragged in "Jews," with hearty sympathy and "kindest regards."

40. *New York Times*, 19 May 1969, A1.

41. For the watershed and how it was talked about by blacks in mill communities, see Frederickson, "Four Decades," 71.

42. Kidder, et al., "Changes in Minority Participation," vii, 19–20; Rowan, *The Negro in the Textile Industry*, 1, 136..

43. Penn and Leiter, "Employment Patterns," 153; "Findings of Fact" section of Opinion by Hemphill, in *Lewis, et al. v. Bloomsburg Mills*, No. 73–324, U.S. District Court, South Carolina, Greenwood Division, 30 Dec. 1982.

44. For an excellent discussion of this point, see Heckman and Payner, "Determining the Impact," 138–75.

45. *New York Times*, 4 Jan. 1967, A22; Kidder, "Changes in Minority Participation," x–xi, 20, 105, 135. But for indications of significant improvement by the mid-1980s in black representation in skilled craft positions, see Richard L. Rowan and Robert E. Barr, *Employee Relations, Trends and Practices in the Textile Industry*, Major Industrial Research Unit Studies, No. 65 (Philadelphia, 1987), 16–17.

46. See, for example, the 1962 complaint of Moses Mangum against Erwin Mills and subsequent agency and employer action in folder 11, Cooke Papers. For complaints that J.P. Stevens' management paid lip service to affirmative action by promoting a man everyone knew to be incompetent but easily controlled by the company, see Marva Watkins interview, transcript, 16, SIRW; Robinson interview, 31, 137–38, *ibid.*

47. Vivian W. Henderson, *The Economic Status of Negroes: In the Nation and in the South* ([Atlanta], n.d.), 5, also 9, 11. For follow-up, see Southern Regional Council, *The Job Ahead: Manpower Policies in the South* (Atlanta, July 1975), esp. 4.

48. John Gaventa and Barbara Ellen Smith, "The Deindustrialization of the Textile South: A Case Study," in *Hanging By a Thread*, (Ithaca, N.Y., 1991), 181, 184. For job loss in other industries where blacks had made headway, see Norrell, "Caste in Steel," 690; Robin Kelley, "Birmingham's Untouchables: The Black Poor in the Age of Civil Rights," in Kelley, *Race Rebels*, 78, 80, 93.

49. EEOC, *Administrative History*, 133–134; also Donald D. Osburne, "Negro Employment in the Textile Industries of North and South Carolina," EEOC Research Report, 1966–10 (Washington, 1966); Statement of Emory F. Via, Southern Regional Council at the E.E.O.C. Textile Employment Forum, Charlotte, N.C., Jan. 1967, box 316, TWUA, mss 396; U.S. Department of Labor, Bureau of Labor Statistics, *Technology and Manpower in the Textile Industry in the 1970s*, Bulletin No. 1578 (Washington, 1968).

On the danger of automation to black workers and others with limited educations, see, for example, "Report of the Conference on Jobs and Job Training," held at Tougaloo College, Mississippi, 25 Jan. 1964, series II, Student Non-Violent Coordinating Committee Papers, Microfilm edition, reel 57, frame 1212 ff; John G. Feild, "A New Look at Employment," *North Carolina Law Review* 42 (1963): 160–61.

50. Chicago Urban League, "Notes on the Problem of Negro Employment," 20 Aug. 1964, Part IV, reel 10, frame 170, SCLC Papers.

51. Byerly, *Hard Times*, 138, see also 105, 155, 160; Robinson interview, transcript, 32. See also Cleghorne, "The Mill: A Giant Step," 34–35; *New York Times*,

19 May 1969, A42. For a similar testimonial from a Durham tobacco worker, see Charlie Necoda Mack interview, transcript, 55, SOHP.

52. G.W. Warren to Armstrong Rubber Company, 24 March 1967, series IV, box A36, NAACP Papers; F.L. Dwyer to Roy Wilkins, 14 March 1967, *ibid*. For similar terrorism against black workers trying to change conditions in a Laurel, Mississippi plant, see Peter Nemenyi to Regional Director, Equal Employment Opportunity Commission, 14 May 1967, Box 1, Peter Nemenyi Papers, State Historical Society of Wisconsin, Madison; also Allen Black, Jr. to Nemenyi, *ibid.*, 5 June 1967.

53. Quoted in Cleghorn, "The Mill: A Giant Step"; and Henry P. Liefermann, "Trouble in the South's First Industry: The Unions are Coming," *New York Times Magazine*, 5 Aug. 1973, 26. See also Rowan, *The Negro in the Textile Industry*, 132; *New York Times*, 12 Jan. 1969, C17; *ibid.*, 19 May 1969, A1, 42; Scott Hoyman to William Pollack, attached report, 15 May 1961, TWUA, mss 396, box 638; *Southern Patriot*, June 1967, 1–2. For one white worker's story about how "the ice was broken," see Mattie Smith interview, transcript, 6. Whether the difference was industry-based or workplace-specific, a black tobacco worker complained of a segregated and hostile cafeteria in which "nobody sits together" because older whites in particular were "still trying to hold on to that white supremacy." Margaret Holmes Turner interview, tape 2, side 1, SOHP.

54. Byerly, *Hard Times*, 153, 137, 138, 141–42, 155.

55. *Ibid.*, 136, 159–60, also 150–51, 156–58.

56. F. Ray Marshall, *The Negro and Organized Labor*, (New York, 1965), 190–191, 203; Allen Tullos, *Habits of Industry: White Culture and the Transformation of the Carolina Piedmont* (Chapel Hill, 1989), xiv, 13. For other analyses of white mill workers and race, see Jacquelyn Dowd Hall, James LeLoudis, Robert Korstad, Mary Murphy, Lu Ann Jones, and Christopher B. Daly, *Like a Family: The Making of a Southern Cotton Mill World* (Chapel Hill, 1987), esp. 66; Tera W. Hunter, *To 'Joy My Freedom: Southern Black Women's Lives and Labors after the Civil War* (Cambridge, Mass., 1997), 114–120; Bryant Simon, *A Fabric of Defeat: The Politics of South Carolina Millhands, 1910–1948* (Chapel Hill, 1998), esp. 220–239; also Alan Draper, *Conflict of Interest: Organized Labor and the Civil Rights Movement of the South, 1954–1968* (Ithaca, N.Y., 1994), esp. 27, 30. On race-baiting in the seventies, see Leifermann, "The Unions Are Coming," 25.

57. Aubrey Clyde Robinson to Charles S. Johnson and Howard W. Odum, "Remarks on Textile Policies Affecting Negro Employment at Points in Alabama," 13 April 1945, reel 67, 0327–0339; "Conferences on the Textile Labor Situation," *ibid.*, 0339.

58. Caesar Cone interview, transcript, 5–6. For the courts' discussion of hiring practices, see, for example, *Sledge v. J.P. Stevens*. One important early national study, based on extensive interviews with management and black and white employees in twenty firms, found that "few of the white workers would admit that Negroes had special job difficulties because of skin color." "The major fear of the whites," the author concluded, "is that Negro civil rights demonstrations will lead to preferential hiring for Negroes and thus limit job opportunities in the company *for their own friends and relatives*." Louis A. Ferman, *The Negro and Equal Employment Opportunities: A Review of Management Experience in Twenty Companies*, (New York, 1968), vii, my emphasis.

59. Thomas C. Holt, "Marking: Race, Race-Making, and the Writing of History," *American Historical Review* 100 (Feb. 1995): 1–20; see also Cheryl I. Harris,

"Whiteness as Property," *Harvard Law Review* 106 (1993): 1709–91. I have found the perspectives of performance studies scholars good in thinking about what was going on in these workplace encounters. For a helpful introduction to the field, see Marvin Carlson, *Performance: A Critical Introduction* (New York, 1996).

60. Winnie Mae Winfield interview, tape only, side A, at 230 ff., SOHP.

61. H.S. Williams to William Pollock, 2 Jan. 1962, box 316, TWUA, mss 396.

62. Harriet L. Herring to Guy B. Johnson, 29 March 1945, reel 67, 0323–24, SRC. The labor figure in question was Noel Beddow of the USWA. See "Conferences on the Textile Situation," reel 67, esp. 0342, *ibid.*

63. Byerly, *Hard Times*, 156; Ada Mae Wilson interview, transcript, 19, SOHP; see also Carrie Yelton interview, *passim, ibid.*; Emma Whitesell interview, *passim, ibid.*; Jimmy Elgin interview, tape only, side A, *ibid.*; Mary Robinson interview, 104, SIRW. For the historical roots of these patterns, see Nancy MacLean, "The Leo Frank Case Reconsidered: Gender and Sexual Politics in the Making of Reactionary Populism," *Journal of American History* 78 (Dec. 1991): 917–48; Jacquelyn Dowd Hall, "Disorderly Women: Gender and Labor Militancy in the Appalachian South," *Journal of American History* 73 (Sept. 1986): 354–82.

64. For management views of interracial flirtation or dating as "potentially explosive," see Rozelle, "The Mill and the Negro," 61. For an intriguing glimpse of such interracial shopfloor life as described in a case that the Bush-era EEOC alleged involved racial discrimination in discharge for sexual harassment, see *EEOC v. Mount Vernon Mills, Inc.*, U.S. District Court for the Northern Division of Georgia, Rome Division, Opinion by Harold L. Murphy.

65. Quotes from Mary Robinson interview, 1, 36–37, 51, 62, 97–98, SIRW; see also Marva Watkins interview, 11, *ibid.*; and Mildred McEwen interview, *ibid.*; Liefermann, "The Unions Are Coming," 10–11.

66. Manager quoted in *New York Times*, 19 May 1969, 1; Ethel Bowman Shockley interview, 25, SOHP.

67. Anonymous, by stipulation of interviewee, number H-071, transcript, 38, SOHP.

68. Mildred Shoemaker Edmonds interview, transcript, 33, SOHP.

69. Eunice Austin interview, 32, SOHP.

70. Quoted in Cleghorne, "The Mill," 144; see also Hoyman to Pollock, attached report, 15 May 1961, box 638, TWUA; Chafe, *Civilities and Civil Rights*, 79. For employers' claims that "local custom" tied their hands in hiring, see for example, Southern Regional Council, *The Negro and Employment Opportunities in the South: Chattanooga*, (Atlanta, Feb. 1962), 6. I am grateful to Jacquelyn Hall for helping me think through the class dynamics of this situation through a comparison with the fate of school desegregation.

71. As a Catholic, she had been attending an integrated church for decades. Mildred Shoemaker Edmonds interview, 33, 35–36, SOHP. For something of a parallel from the 1930s, see Hall, et al., *Like a Family*, 317–9.

72. Nell Putnam Sigmon interview, 38–39, SOHP.

73. Quoted in Cleghorn, "Giant Step," 142.

74. Lessie Norman interview, tape 1, side , SOHP. Another man spoke in similar terms: "I reckon they had to have a little revolution to get what they wanted," reflected this furniture factory foreman. "All that I ever knew," he said, "were pretty decent kind of people." Frank Gilbert interview, 87–91, SOHP.

75. Anonymous by interviewee's request, number H-017, transcript, 22, SOHP.

76. Quotes from Gwendolyn Cooper Ellis, transcript, 38, SOHP; Eula Durham interview, transcript, 17, *ibid.*; Theotis Williamson interview, 30–31, *ibid.*; Jessie Lee Carter interview, pp. 36–37, *ibid.*; see also Ethel Bowman Shockley, 25, *ibid.*

77. Kidder, "Changes in Minority Participation," 99. 78. Byerly, *Hard Times,* 156.

79. He was describing firefighting, but the words capture the building trades as well. Roxanne Brown, "Black Women Firefighters," *Ebony,* March 1988, in box 57, Southeast Women's Employment Coalition Papers, Duke.

80. On the building trades generally and integration struggles specifically, see respectively, Joshua B. Freeman, "Hardhats: Construction Workers, Manliness, and the 1970 Pro-War Demonstrations," *Journal of Social History* (Summer 1993): 725–745; Roger Waldinger and Thomas Bailey, "The Continuing Significance of Race: Racial Conflict and Racial Discrimination in Construction," *Politics & Society* 19 (1991): 291–323. Generalizations in text also emerge from my own research on race and gender in construction, which will form a chapter of my forthcoming book on affirmative action in employment.

81. Brown, ' "What Has Happened Here,' " 43.

82. Ethel Bowman Shockley interview, 26, SOHP. See also Mary Elizabeth Padgett interview, transcript, 6–7, *ibid.*; Paul and Pauline Griffiths interview, transcript, 52–53, *ibid.*

83. Vesta Roberts Ellis interview, 3–4, Orange Factory Materials.

84. This generalization is made from oral history interviews with black domestics and white employers, who regularly cited the same figures. See, for example, Lottie Adam interview, tape index, SOHP; Ada Mae Wilson interview, 6–7, 22, *ibid.*; Stella Carden interview, transcript, 23, *ibid.* Quotes from Mimi Conway, *Rise, Gonna Rise: A Portrait of Southern Textile Workers* (Garden City, N.Y., 1979), 127; Byerly, *Hard Times,* 99, also, on sleeping arrangements, 147. This is not to suggest that all black domestic workers hated their work. "I enjoyed it," one such worker, the child of sharecroppers, said of her live-in job in Charlotte: "It was so much different from being out on that farm and working all year and didn't get nothing." Minnie Lawrence Dunn interview, tape index, SOHP; see also Conway, *Rise, Gonna Rise,* 48–50; Rowan, *The Negro in the Textile Industry,* 13.

85. Ada Mae Wilson interview, transcript, 22–23, SOHP. Her discussion superbly illustrates a point made by Tera Hunter about domestic service in the New South: "The women who performed the labor, and the women and men who employed them were consummate political actors all." Tera Hunter, "Domination and Resistance: The Politics of Wage Household Labor in New South Atlanta," *Labor History* 34 (1993): 220.

86. Rozelle, "The Negro and the Mill," 62; Report of TEAM Aide Alice Gallman, 25 Aug. 1968, reel 163: 1232, SRC; Hunter, *To "Joy My Freedom,* 120; see also Mordecai C. Johnson to Jean Fairfax, 28 Aug. 1968, *ibid.*: 1238. For a similar case of whites complaining about the opening of manufacturing jobs to blacks because "they realized . . . they'd be losing their 50 cents a day maid services," see Interview with Wilbur Jones by Karen McLendon, 2 Dec. 1976, Athens-Clarke County Heritage Foundation, Oral History Tapes, Special Collections Department, University of Georgia Libraries, Athens.

87. For an analogous pattern among a different population of women, see Kathleen M. Blee, *Women of the Klan: Racism and Gender in the 1920s,* (Berkeley, 1991).

88. Mildred Edmonds Shoemaker interview, transcript, 33–34, SOHP.

89. Gwendolyn Mink, "The Lady and the Tramp: Gender, Race, and the Origins of the American Welfare State," in *Women, the State, and Welfare*, ed. Linda Gordon (Madison, Wisc., 1990), 102, 111.

90. Vesta Finley interview, transcript, 49–60, SOHP. For a similar mix of unusual empathy and willful distancing, see Stella Carden interview, 24, *ibid.*

91. Lessie Newman interview, tape 1, *ibid.*

92. Nell Putnam Sigmon interview, transcript, 38–40, *ibid.*; also Anonymous, interview H-017, transcript, 22, *ibid.*

93. On women and kinship, see Micaela di Leonardo, "the Female World of Cards and Holidays: Women, Families, and the Work of Kinship," in *Rethinking the Family*, ed. Barrie Thorne and Marilyn Yalom, (Boston, 1992), 246–61. The way these women worked to reconstitute newly permeable racial boundaries underscores Nancy Hewitt's reminder that "a strong sense of community can also be a source of exclusion, prejudices, and prohibitions." Hewitt, "Beyond the Search for Sisterhood," 1.

94. See, for example, the collection introduction, "Oral History Studies at Orange Factory," box 1, Orange Factory Materials; Hall, et al., *Like a Family*; Tullos, *Habits of Industry*; and Jacquelyn D. Hall and Della Pollock, "History, Story and Performance: The Making and Remaking of a Southern Cotton Mill World," in *Reconstructing American Literary and Historial Studies*, ed. Gunter H. Lenz, et al., (New York, 1990), esp. 327–330.

95. Stephanie McCurry, "Piedmont Mill Workers and the Politics of History," in *Labour/Le Travail* 29 (Spring 1992): 233–34. See also interviewer's notes, Annie Mae Perkins interview, SOHP.

96. Liu, "Teaching the Differences Among Women," 571, 576.

97. Scott Hoyman interview, transcript, 28, SOHP; see also 50–51 for leads not picked up by interviewers. 98. Marva Watkins interview, 30–31, SIRW. A worker in another industry complained in similar terms. "Regardless of whether they had the ability or not," Alcoa worker Clyde Cook recalled bitterly of the white supervisors in his plant, promotions went along "the color line." "If they had the color of the skin, they was able to be my supervisor." Clyde Cook interview, 5–8; see also Clarence Coe's remarks in Michael Honey, "Black Workers Remember: Industrial Unionism in the Era of Jim Crow," in *Race, Class, and Community in Southern Labor History*, ed. Gary M. Fink and Merl E. Reed, (Tuscaloosa, Ala., 1994), 133, and, more generally, Ferman, *The Negro and Equal Employment Opportunities*, vii.

99. Mary Robinson interview, 104, SIRW.

100. For the earlier history, see Helen Clinton to Dr. Rankin, 2 Feb. 1961, box 7, NCAC; NCAC, Draft Employment Committee Report, *ibid.*

101. Byerly, *Hard Times*, 139, 141; also Annie Adams account in same, 136; Mordecai Johnson to Jean Fairfax, Jan. 2968, reel 163, esp. 0399. For similar complaints in the class action suits, see *Sledge v. J. P. Stevens*, and *Lewis v. J. P. Stevens*.

102. Herbert Hill to Branch Presidents, 27 July 1965, box A180, series III, NAACP.

103. For an example, see *Royzelle Thomas v. West Point-Pepperell, Inc.*, CA No. C80-833A, U.S. District Court, Northern District of Georgia, Atlanta Division, Opinion by J. Shoob.

104. For fear among black workers about filing complaints or becoming active,

see Minutes of TEAM Board Meeting, 8 March 1968, 5, reel 163, SRC; Report of TEAM Aide William Patrick Flack, 22 Aug. 1968, *ibid.*, 0519ff; *ibid.*, 31 Aug. 1968, *ibid.*, 0525; Report of TEAM Aide Juanita Harrison, n.d., *ibid.*, 0873; Mordecai C. Johnson to Jean Fairfax, 28 Aug. 1968, *ibid.*: 1238–39; Mordecai C. Johnson to TEAM's Board, 12 Sept. 1968, *ibid.*: 1249 ff. 105. Bernice Coleman to Dear Sir, 2 Nov. 1971, box 9, TWUA, mss 81–295, SHSW. See also the story of Mrs. Witcher in Report of TEAM Aide William Patrick Flack, 22 Aug. 1968, reel 163, 0519–20.

106. *Sallie Pearl Lewis et al. v. J. P. Stevens & Co., Inc.*, CA No. 72–341, U.S. District Court, District of South Carolina, Greenwood Division; *Lewis et al. v. Bloomsburg Mills, Inc.*, CA No. 73–324, *ibid.*

107. "Unfortunately, most labor historians," as Robin Kelley notes, have proved "unable to see resistance to sexual harassment as a primary struggle to transform everyday conditions at the workplace." Kelley, *Race Rebels*, 27, also 28; see also Brown, " 'What Has Happened Here,' " 46.

108. *EEOC v. Cannon Mills Company*, CA C-65-S-69, Memorandum in Support of Application For Issuance of Order to Show Cause Why Defendant Should Not Be Held in Contempt, box 79 Cannon Mills Papers.

109. This problem in anti-discrimination law is deftly exposed in Kimberle Crenshaw, "Demarginalizing the Intersection of Race and Sex: A Black Feminist Critique of Antidiscrimination Doctrine, Feminist Theory, and Antiracist Politics," in *Feminist Legal Theory: Readings in Law and Gender*, ed. Katherine T. Bartlett and Rosanne Kennedy (Boulder, Col., 1991), 57–80; see also Eileen Boris and Michael Honey, "Gender, Race and the Policies of the Labor Department," *Monthly Labor Review*, (Feb. 1988): 26–36.

110. TWUA, Appeal of the Regional Director's Refusal to Issue a Complaint, 20 July 1975, Cannon Mills Company and TWUA, before the National Labor Relations Board, Cases 11-CA-6108 and 11-CA-6115; *Southern Patriot*, Dec. 1975, 1; Daisy Crawford to editor, *Southern Struggle*, Sept-Oct. 1977, 3.

Contributors

Peter Bardaglio is an associate professor of history at Goucher College. He is the author of *Reconstructing the Household: Families, Sex and the Law in the Nineteenth-Century South* (University of North Carolina Press, 1995).

Kathleen M. Brown is an associate professor of history at the University of Pennsylvania. She is the author of *Good Wives, Nasty Wenches, and Anxious Patriarchs: Gender, Race, and Power in Colonial Virginia* (University of North Carolina Press, 1996).

Laura F. Edwards is an associate professor of history at the University of California at Los Angeles. She is the author of *Gendered Strife and Confusion: The Political Culture of Reconstruction* (University of Illinois Press, 1997).

Jacquelyn Dowd Hall is the director of the Southern Oral History Program and the Julia Cherry Spruill Professor of History at the University of North Carolina at Chapel Hill. She is the author of numerous essays and books, including *Like a Family: The Making of a Southern Cotton Mill World* (University of North Carolina Press, 1987) and *The Revolt Against Chivalry: Jessie Daniel Ames and the Women's Campaign Against Lynching* (Columbia University Press, 1979).

Tera W. Hunter is an associate professor of history at Carnegie-Mellon University and the author of *To 'Joy My Freedom: Black Women's Lives and Labors After the Civil War* (Harvard University Press, 1997).

Winthrop D. Jordan is the William F. Winter Professor of History and professor of Afro-American Studies at the University of Mississippi. He is the author of numerous books and essays, including *Tumult and Silence at Second Creek: An Inquiry into a Civil War Slave Conspiracy* (Louisiana State University Press, 1993) and *White Over Black: American Attitudes Toward the Negro, 1550–1812* (University of North Carolina Press, 1968).

Chana Kai Lee is an associate professor of history at the University of Georgia and the author of *For Freedom's Sake: The Life of Fannie Lou Hamer* (University of Illinois Press, 1999).

Nancy MacLean is an associate professor of history and a fellow at the Institute for Policy Research at Northwestern University. She is the

253

author of *Behind the Mask of Chivalry: The Making of the Second Ku Klux Klan* (Oxford University Press, 1994).

Stephanie McCurry is an associate professor of history at Northwestern University and the author of *Masters of Small Worlds: Yeoman Households, Gender Relations, and the Political Culture of the Antebellum South Carolina Low Country* (Oxford University Press, 1995).

Louise M. Newman is an associate professor of history at the University of Florida and the author of *White Women's Rights: The Racial Origins of Feminism in the United States* (Oxford University Press, 1999).

Bryant Simon is an associate professor of history at the University of Georgia and the author of *A Fabric of Defeat: The Politics of South Carolina Millhands 1910–1948* (University of North Carolina Press, 1998).

Index

255